KU-627-182

PENGUIN BOOKS
NICE RACISM

'Spectacular! With the precision of a social scientist,
Robin DiAngelo dissects and puts under the microscope
seemingly benign "white moves" – including her own – in
ways that make undeniable how each functions to
recalibrate white dominance and comfort again and
again. A critical tool for white progressives wanting
to know better so we can do better'
Debby Irving

'In this illuminating follow-up to *White Fragility*,
Robin DiAngelo integrates sharp insight, personal
vulnerability, and compassionate guidance with the
keen eye of an "insider". Focusing specifically on
the more subtle patterns of white progressives,
her work continues to be invaluable to the
project of ending white supremacy'
Resmaa Menakem

'Makes some worthwhile observations about the
etiquette governing conversations on race and
class . . . DiAngelo can sniff out any kind of
hypocrisy, no matter how trivial'
Clive Davis, *The Times*

'A pointed reminder that good intentions aren't
enough to break the cycle of racism'
Kirkus Reviews

'A fierce critique of the "culture of niceness"
that prevents the hard work of dismantling
racism . . . DiAngelo dismantles unconscious
biases with precision. Readers will feel compelled
to hold themselves more accountable'
Publishers Weekly

ABOUT THE AUTHOR

Robin DiAngelo is an academic, lecturer and author working in the fields of critical discourse analysis and whiteness studies. She is a lecturer at the University of Washington and formerly served as a tenured professor of multicultural education at Westfield State University. DiAngelo has been a consultant and trainer for more than twenty years on issues of racial and social justice.

ROBIN DIANGELO

Nice Racism

How Progressive White People
Perpetuate Racial Harm

PENGUIN BOOKS

PENGUIN BOOKS

UK | USA | Canada | Ireland | Australia
India | New Zealand | South Africa

Penguin Books is part of the Penguin Random House group of companies
whose addresses can be found at global.penguinrandomhouse.com

First published by Allen Lane 2021
Published in Penguin Books 2022
001

Printed and bound in Great Britain by Clays Ltd, Elcograf S.p.A.

The authorized representative in the EEA is Penguin Random House Ireland,
Morrison Chambers, 32 Nassau Street, Dublin D02 YH68

A CIP catalogue record for this book is available from the British Library

ISBN: 978–0–141–99742–1

www.greenpenguin.co.uk

Penguin Random House is committed to a
sustainable future for our business, our readers
and our planet. This book is made from Forest
Stewardship Council® certified paper.

This book is dedicated to Anika Nailah,
a brilliant anti-racist activist, educator, poet,
performance artist, writer, and mentor.
Thank you, my friend. May you be able
to tell they've read the book.

CONTENTS

INTRODUCTION

When Carolyn walked into the orientation session, she inwardly rolled her eyes and let out a sigh. Here we go again, she thought, as she looked out at a veritable sea of well-meaning whiteness. She was attending the orientation to learn more about an organization that described itself as committed to social justice. While the organization was overwhelmingly white, they were working hard to educate themselves on various forms of oppression. This wasn't the first time she was the only Black person in the room, but Carolyn reasoned that at least these white people were committed social progressives. She joined and started attending a weekly subgroup where she was—yet again—the only person of color in the room.

At the end of the sixth week the facilitator, a white male, informed her that the next week they would be studying racism and asked her if she would teach that session. She told him she needed to think about it, and then she called me, in a state of distress.

Carolyn and I have been friends and colleagues for over twenty years. We met when we were both hired as facilitators of a mandated equity training for a government organization. Since that time, we have co-led countless anti-racism sessions and been through many of our own personal challenges navigating a long-term interracial friendship. Her mentorship has had a profound impact on my understanding of systemic racism.

When Carolyn called me that day, she was torn: on the one hand, she wanted to give them this information because they desperately needed it; on the other hand, to be the only Black person in the group and have to explain how racism manifested—both in general and *in the group itself*—was terrifying. She risked being subjected to the patterns of white fragility that are all too common when white people are challenged on race: minimization, defensiveness, anger, invalidation, hurt feelings, guilt. Would she be seen as an aggressor as they positioned themselves as victimized? Would she lose valued relationships? Would this be her last session in the group?

She decided that she would share her experience as a Black person if I came with her and also spoke to them—specifically as a white person—about white patterns of racism. She well understood that white people are generally more receptive to hearing about racism from other white people. My presence would also ensure that she had a trusted ally at her side to support her. I agreed.

As the days passed and she prepared her presentation, she called me many times to vent her fear and anxiety. The request to teach an all-white group about racism took a tremendous toll on Carolyn. In addition to the emotional work she was doing, she spent hours preparing her presentation, trying to make it indisputable so she would not be negated. Being in front of an all-white group also triggered in her a lifetime of racist abuse from white teachers, schools, and society at large. She was up against the relentless messages that as a Black woman, she was unintelligent and had no knowledge of intrinsic value.

Finally, the evening came. The group listened thoughtfully to both of us and then asked questions or made comments. Toward the end of the evening, a member of the group stated, in a tone somewhat critical of the organization, "I am so glad this organization is finally teaching us about racism. I have been waiting for them to do that." This statement was a fish-out-of-water moment for me in which I could see a cross-racial dynamic I hadn't seen before. I had witnessed the tremendous amount of emotional and intellectual work Carolyn had to do in order to make this presentation. Now, watching this group sitting comfortably on their chairs and effortlessly receiving the result of Carolyn's labor, I saw a metaphor for colonialism. The group was in essence saying, "We'll observe you and seek to understand you. In doing so, we'll relax while you work. You'll provide us with the fruits of your labor. We'll receive these fruits and consider them. We'll decide what to keep and what to reject—what we deem worthy of consideration and what we don't. We thank the organization for bringing you to us because we've desired your knowledge. But if you weren't brought before us, we wouldn't (as we have not up until now) expend any effort in seeking it for ourselves." Critical race scholar Sherene Razack, writing about whiteness and the pattern of studying those who are seen as "different," describes this mentality as the "cornerstone of imperialism: the colonized possess a series of knowable characteristics that can be studied, known, and managed accordingly by the colonizers whose own complicity remains masked."[1] Further, this group member positioned not having this knowledge previously as a shortcoming of the organization rather than of himself, so that he also managed to elevate his own moral standing. Still, his credit went to the organization, not to Carolyn. While I assume that none of this was his conscious intention, it was the impact of his comment.

And what role did I play in all of this? While I could clearly see the racial dynamics in the group's behavior, I didn't ask myself at the time what aspects of these dynamics I was in collusion with. Looking back, I realize that while it was exhausting for Carolyn, I found it to be an "interesting" learning experience, one in which I was the "good" white person, there as an ally for my Black friend. I came away from that incident feeling proud of myself and how I had supported Carolyn, and equipped with new insights on how *other white people's* racism worked.

I understand that Carolyn asked me to support her in that particular way, and to decline was not an option I would have considered. But that does not put me outside the racism she was preparing for. And as I write this, I realize that I never checked myself and my own racial arrogance in that situation. What might it have looked like if I had? I could have challenged the judgment I felt as I watched the group interact with Carolyn. I could have shared my insight on the colonialist dynamic I observed in the group, the very people who were there to further their understanding of racism. I could have checked in with Carolyn and actually *asked* if she felt supported by me. But I did not do any of those things. Instead, on our ride home, I assumed *for myself* that she felt supported, and instead of asking, I proceeded to point out everything

I noticed about what the white people in the group were doing. This had the effect of both reinforcing the racism for Carolyn (in case she had missed any nuance of it that I noticed) while positioning me as the "smartest white person in the room"; the white person who "got it." I didn't give her much room to express any pain or disappointment she may have felt about aspects of my own complicity.

Our identities are not separate from the white supremacist society in which we are raised, and our patterns of cross-racial engagement are not merely a function of our unique personalities. Good intentions, so-called open-mindedness, belief in racial justice, and identifying as racially progressive are not sufficient. Wherever we may be on the continuum of seeing and addressing racism, we are not at the end. As a white progressive who has spent years engaged in anti-racist work, I have developed self-awareness, skills, and relationships I would never have had if I had simply followed the path laid out before me by mainstream society. At the same time, I continue to struggle with stubborn and deeply internalized racist patterns. My work is meant to share my learning as well as my failures with other white people so that we might do less racial harm. To that end, when I say "we," "our," and "us," I am referring to white people. I understand that race is a social construct, whose borders and boundaries shift over time. The category "white" is not perfectly discrete. However, for the purposes of this analysis, I use the term "white" to refer to people who are defined and perceived to be white by their societies at large, and in most contexts. In chapter 1, I will explain which white people I mean specifically by the qualifier "progressive."

As a white person who writes about race specifically to my fellow white people, I am not seeking to teach white people about Black people. I am seeking to teach white people about ourselves *in relation to* Black and other people of color. Black people, Indigenous peoples, and people of color may find an insider analysis useful in navigating white social and institutional control and in challenging the gaslighting they so often encounter when trying to talk to us about racism.

I am often asked why white people should listen to a white person on racism. For me, the shift to focusing my work on teaching white people about racism was made when I became aware of the profound injustices of white supremacy and my role in them. I made a commitment personally and professionally to the educational aspect of anti-racism practice. Now, drawing from years of experience, I apply my particular skills as an educator to this commitment. I write books and articles specifically as a white person to white people. My goal is to help us get out of denial about our racism and be less harmful to Black people and other people of color. If I didn't think that was possible, I couldn't continue. We are capable of doing better.

Let me be clear, I have been mentored by and learned greatly from the work of BIPOC people. I am not claiming and would not claim that we should only listen to white people or engage in isolation. I do not believe that white people can think critically about racism, our role in it, and how we can challenge it if we are not in relationship with and if we do not listen to Black people and other people of color. I could not articulate the dynamics of white fragility without that guidance, including years of reading the work of Black writers who came before my time. Particularly influential were W. E. B. Du Bois, Audre Lorde, James Baldwin, and Derrick Bell. I have engaged with the work of BIPOC people in the present, including that of sociologists Patricia Hill Collins and Eduardo Bonilla-Silva; philosopher Charles W. Mills; writers Toni Morrison and bell hooks; psychologist Beverly Daniel Tatum; and ethnic studies professors Linda Tuhiwai Smith, Tracy Lai, Leticia Nieto, Stacey J. Lee, Sherene Razack, and Thandeka, among many others. On a personal level, Black women in particular have been invaluable mentors to me, including Deborah Terry, Darlene Flynn, Anika Nailah, Victoria Santos, Cheryl Harris, and Erin Trent Johnson.

At the same time, as an insider to whiteness, I have a valuable perspective to offer that BIPOC people don't have, and one that is different from and can support that of Black educators. I do not believe that white people can fully understand racism and our role in it if we *only* listen to BIPOC people. We have much of our own personal and collective work to do, and it should not and cannot be the responsibility of people of color to get us to do it. Indeed, I don't think there will be structural transformation without personal transformation. In this sense, personal transformation is an act of anti-racism. White people must understand how race shapes our own lives and how we are conditioned into complicity, regardless of awareness or intention. White people also need an insider perspective—from someone who has "been there" and had that thought, felt that emotion, enacted that behavior, struggled with that feedback, and had that insight—that we can relate to and that can serve as an example. It is also harder to deny a shared experience. Insiders can expose and uniquely challenge us in ways invaluable to our growth. I have also needed mentorship from white activists and scholars. Ruth Frankenberg's work in particular has been deeply impactful, as has that of Michelle Fine, David Roediger, Tim Wise, Lillian Smith, Peggy McIntosh, Teun A. van Dijk, and Joe Feagin.

Finally, I have had to *apply* what I have learned by integrating the range of work that has shaped my thinking with ongoing personal self-reflection, study, research, struggle, mistake making, cross-racial relationship building, risk-taking, feedback, synthesis, and talking to thousands of people about racism. I have not come to my current understanding easily, in a single moment following a single event, or by jumping over much hard personal and cross-racial work. I have been studying, speaking out, co-leading, and writing on whiteness since 1995. My dissertation (2004) was titled "Whiteness in Racial Dialogue: A Discourse Analysis," in which I tracked how white students deflected feedback on racism during a cross-racial dialogue. Following receipt of my PhD, I went into academic teaching. In 2011—*a decade ago*—I wrote the article "White Fragility." I was not paid to write it and receive no royalties from it. Further, it was published in an open-source journal, which means that the article is free and accessible to anyone (non-open-source journals charge high fees for people outside academia to access their articles). A few years later, around 2014, someone quoted from the article on social media and it went viral. I began to receive messages of gratitude and feedback on the value of the article from people worldwide, both BIPOC people and white. The article was so helpful to so many that I decided to turn it into a fuller book and to go through a nonacademic publisher so that it would be more accessible in language and cost. Beacon Press is a nonprofit social justice–oriented publisher (for more details on my financial accountability see my website).

We need many entry points into fighting racism, and mine is to use my learning over decades as a white anti-racism scholar and educator in order to contribute to a more racially just society, one in which white people might cause less pain for Black people and other people of color. This is the particular contribution I bring to the table of anti-racism work. I understand that there are those who do not think white people should be at that table at all, in any public way, but for the reasons already stated, I believe we play a necessary part in building multiracial coalitions.

This is not a zero-sum game wherein we can read only one book and if that book is written by a white person, we have closed ourselves off to books by Black authors. My work is meant to be read in conjunction with and help open readers to the wider world of BIPOC anti-racist thought that so many have been closed to. If white people were already open to the perspectives of BIPOC peoples, we would be in a different place. Many people have strong opinions on how racism should be challenged (even those who are white and living segregated lives and newly introduced to the concepts). But if you have not tried to educate white students, employees, and community members over weeks, months, or even years, you cannot know what it takes to get them to acknowledge the reality of systemic racism. While educating white people on racism and getting them to change attitudes and behaviors is rarely easy, the nature of implicit bias is that white people are more likely to be open to initial challenges to our racial positions, perspectives, and behaviors from a fellow white person. My books are only a few of the numerous books on the topic, and white people can and should read many books on racism, especially those written by Black people and other people of color. But for far too long, because white people tend to see race as "not our problem," we have off-loaded the work of anti-racism onto BIPOC people and exempted ourselves from the conversation. In this way, we protect and uphold white supremacy while falsely maintaining racial innocence. I am offering one of many approaches to the issue, one I believe is important and too often has been missing from the conversation.

I am well aware that I am inside a system I am seeking to challenge, and that my work both upholds and—hopefully—interrupts this system. Writer and activist Audre Lorde wrote, "The master's tools will never dismantle the master's house."[2] She was critiquing feminists of the 1970s and '80s who claimed to represent all women but who focused their concerns on white, middle-class women. Lorde's quote speaks to the dilemma of challenging the system from within. This is one of the major obstacles I face as a white person writing about race. My aim is to use my platform to break with white solidarity, decenter whiteness by exposing its workings, interrupt white denial of racism, and motivate white people to act toward a more racially just society. In large part, whiteness stays centered by being unnamed, the unspoken default against which "otherness" is measured. To decenter whiteness, you must name and expose it, and there is a very specific way that white people can do that. Never the *only way*, but a key and all-too-often missing one.

At the same time, the "master's tools dilemma" recognizes that whiteness is simultaneously being reinforced when white voices are centered and "easier" to hear. As a white person focusing on white people, I struggle with this "both/and" tension but have come to terms with it overall, as none of us is or can be outside the system. One way I work to reconcile the tension is to be "less white." By that I don't mean I want to reclaim my ethnic roots and be more Italian American. For me, to be "less white" is to counter my socialization into whiteness; to be less racially oppressive, less racially ignorant and less arrogant in my ignorance, less defensive and silent and complicit. Racism perverts and distorts reality, and thus white people are generally granted more objectivity and legitimacy when speaking about racism, in spite of our lack of neutrality. To be less white is to use that entry point and work with other white people to interrupt racism. It is unacceptable for me *not* to use the credibility and access granted by whiteness to challenge racism.

I have received and incorporated feedback from many colleagues, mentors, workshop participants, and anti-racist educators over many years. Now, as a very visible white public figure writing and speaking openly and directly about racism, I am overwhelmed with feedback from every side, and that feedback is often contradictory. I cannot and will not get it right by everyone, and I am necessarily limited in full understanding by my racial position. However, I do believe I am in my integrity with Black people and other people of color and with racially conscious white people who have continued to mentor me over many years and with whom I am in close accountability relationships. I hope and recommend that all white people develop similar deep and broad cross-racial networks of support and accountability for lifelong learning so we show up as effective partners and engage constructively in anti-racist efforts.

A NOTE ON LANGUAGE

Language is not neutral. The terms and phrases we use do not simply describe what we observe. In large part, the terms and phrases we use shape how we *perceive* or make meaning of what we observe. This is why the terms used for marginalized groups are constantly being challenged and negotiated. Consider the difference between "illegal alien" and "person entering the country illegally." Or the difference between "China virus" and "COVID-19." Or trace the trajectory of changes over my lifetime of this set of terms: "bum," "tramp," "wino," "hobo," "vagrant," "homeless," "persons without housing." There are significant differences between the images and associations at the start of that list and the end. Those differences impact our perceptions and have real consequences for how people are treated and the resources they receive. Language is political and thus a continual site of struggle over who is deemed worthy of respect and access. Terms can implicitly authorize and normalize forms of domination and control, or interrupt them. Racial terms in particular are in flux, as historic power relations are made visible to the mainstream and awareness of structural inequity is deepened.

As I write this, systemic racism is being directly named and challenged in unprecedented ways, and people will have different levels of understanding. Given the political, contextual, and changing nature of language, none of the language I use will likely be acceptable at all times to all readers. No terms are perfect, and when speaking of racialized people, they all collapse diverse cultures into one. For example, Asian people are the majority of the planet and comprise forty-eight different countries

and cultures. Still, most white people in the United States don't differentiate between these cultures. For the purposes of this limited analysis, I will
address racial dynamics at the macro level, in general terms.

When I am speaking specifically about a racialized group of people,
I will use the current most recognizable term for that group. For example, "Asian," "Latinx," "Indigenous," and "Black." Sometimes I will
use "African American." My choice here will be based on what is being
used in the context I am describing, what flows with what I am writing,
or what is used by the person I am quoting. When I am speaking about
people more broadly, I will sometimes use the term "people of color"
and sometimes use the term "racialized" to make the point that while
we all have an assigned race, mainstream culture consistently marks
race only for those who are not white. The term indicates that this
is a verb—or active process—not a noun or an inherent or biological
state of being. Sometimes I will spell out the name of each group but
most often will use the acronym BIPOC. It stands for Black, Indigenous,
and People of Color. "Black" and "Indigenous" are highlighted to acknowledge the unique historical relationship these two groups have to
the establishment of white supremacy, and that they historically and
currently face the harshest degrees of racism. The acronym is the most
current usage that I am aware of but not necessarily recognized fully in
the mainstream. Further, there's no consensus among people of color
about the term. Some appreciate that it is more inclusive; others see it
as erasure. Sandra Garcia, explaining the acronym in a *New York Times*
piece, noted, "The term has caused confusion, and there isn't universal
agreement about what it means or whom it actually includes, but to
most, the people of color includes Latinos and Asians."[3] I recognize
that the term still collapses a large number of diverse racial groups into
"POC." I will add "peoples" to the end. While that doesn't quite work
grammatically, it feels more humanizing to me.

Whether to capitalize the terms "black" and "white" is also an unsettled political issue. On the one hand, capitalizing "Black" but not
"white" interrupts the historical elevation of white above black. On the
other hand, not capitalizing "white" minimizes its power as a racial category and reinforces white as the default. In explaining the Associated

Press requirement of capitalizing "Black" but not "white," John Dan-iszewski, the AP's vice president for standards, wrote: "We agree that white people's skin color plays into systemic inequalities and injustices, and we want our journalism to robustly explore these problems. . . . But capitalizing the term "white," as is done by white supremacists, risks subtly conveying legitimacy to such beliefs."[4] The *Columbia Journalism Review*, the *Wall Street Journal*, the *New York Times*, *USA Today*, the *Los Angeles Times*, NBC News, and the *Chicago Tribune* are among the organizations that have recently stated they will capitalize "Black" but not white. "White doesn't represent a shared culture and history in the way Black does," the *New York Times* explained.[5] While I argue here that "white" *does* represent a shared history and culture in a racialized sense, I follow these norms and capitalize "Black" but not "white."

I will also be using the term "white supremacy," which elicits a strong reaction for many white people. In popular culture, "white supremacy" connotes people who would wear hoods and explicitly espouse the ide-ology that white people are superior. But this usage is extremely narrow and simplistic and leaves out vast layers of nuance and complexity. I use the broader sociological understanding of the term, which includes the multitude of ways our society elevates white people as the human ideal and norm for humanity and relegates everyone else as a *particular kind* of human, and always a lesser deviation from the white ideal. This relegation is reinforced when we consistently mark the race of anyone who is not white, while not naming our own. I use the terms "racism" and "white supremacy" somewhat interchangeably, but racism can be thought of as the systemic outcome of white supremacist ideology.

Throughout this book I will discuss racism in binary terms: white people and people of color, white people and racialized people, white people and BIPOC people. For the purposes of challenging many prob-lematic dynamics of racism, such as individualism and color blindness, it is important for those of us who are white to suspend our focus on ourselves as unique and/or outside of race and focus instead on our *collective* racial experience. Discussing white people in general terms may be seen as an interruption of the normal dynamics of racism. However, for people of color, being seen as unique individuals outside of race is not a privilege that can be taken for granted. So, while talking about race and racism in general terms may be constructive for white people, it collapses many diverse racial groups into one big category. In so doing, the particular ways that different racial groups experience racism in the larger society are obscured. These differences include specific histories and cultures, how people within a group have learned to adapt to racism in order to survive, how they are represented in the larger society, the role the group has been set up to play in relation to whiteness, how comfortable white people are with the group, the group's perceived adjacency to whiteness, and so on. For example, the experience of a person whose family has been in the US for many generations will be different than a first- or second-generation immigrant. Some people of color have been adopted and raised by white families, and these families often take a "color-blind" approach to raising cross-racially adopted children. These children will have a different experience and sense of identity than those who were raised in families who share their race. Anti-racist practice involves ongoing education on these complexities, as well as flexibility and skill in navigating the many facets and nuances of the racial construct. Unfortunately, those histories and differences are beyond the scope of this book. I encourage my readers to continually educate themselves in these differences well beyond this text. I apologize in advance for the minimization of a broad range of experiences.

When I envision the racial construct upholding white supremacy, I see two anchors fixing it firmly in place. One anchor is white and the other is Black. As I wrote in *White Fragility*, I believe that anti-Blackness is the root of white supremacy. White is not possible without Black; superior is not possible without inferior. As historian Michel Foucault posits, power is a *relation*, not a possession.[6] Racial trauma therapist Resmaa Menakem powerfully writes, "The white body is the supreme standard by which all bodies' humanity shall be measured. If the white body is the standard of humanity, then it stands that the black body is inhuman and the antithesis of humanity. Every hue further away from that standard is deemed less human."[7] In the white mind, Black people are the ultimate racial "Other"—or antithesis of white. Again, this does not mean that other racialized people don't experience racism, or that the dynamics I describe here don't apply. But the dynamics I am describing are made most visible when we view them through the relations between Black and white people. Therefore, many of the examples I use will be based on these interactions.

Like race, gender is a social construct, and essentialist notions of male and female have also been deeply challenged. I am a cisgender woman, which means my gender assignment at birth, my internal gender identity, and my expression of that identity are the same. My gender pronouns are "she" and "her." When I use the terms "man" or "woman," I am referring to people's primary identities. If someone identifies as female or as a woman, as male or as a man, they are included in the terms. I also recognize that there are nonbinary readers who do not identify with either category or not with either one consistently. When I do not need to specify pronouns, I will use "they" and "theirs." For purposes of brevity and flow, I will not be adding a third term. I apologize to those who are marginalized by that omission.

This book is a follow-up to *White Fragility*. I do not set out to establish that systemic racism and white supremacy exist as I did in that book. Nor do I set out to establish that all white people receive, absorb, and are influenced by the racist messages continuously circulating across the society we live in. Rather, I proceed from these premises and assume that my readers do too. In *White Fragility*, I made a claim that white progressives cause the most daily harm to Black, Indigenous, and other racialized people. Here I will explain some of the specific ways we do so. Because many of these ways may be less obvious, they are also more insidious.

CHAPTER 1

WHAT IS A NICE RACIST?

I am trying to establish the outlines of an understanding of
myself in regard to what was fated to be the continuing crisis of
my life, the crisis of racial awareness—the sense of being doomed
by my history to be, if not always a racist, then a man always
limited by the inheritance of racism, condemned to be always
conscious of the necessity not to be a racist, to be always dealing
deliberately with the reflexes of racism that are embedded in my
mind as deeply at least as the language I speak.

—Wendell Berry (1968)[1]

One evening many years ago when I was in college, I went out to dinner with my partner at the time and another couple. My partner, like me, was white. This couple were friends of hers, but I had not met them before. We planned to meet up at the restaurant. When we arrived, the couple were already sitting at the table, and I saw that they were both Black. At this point in my life, I had no Black friends and had rarely spent time with Black people. I was excited and felt an immediate need to let them know I was *not racist*. To that end, I proceeded to spend the evening telling them how racist *my family* was. I shared every racist joke, story, and comment I could remember my family ever making. And yes, I shared these in full, uncensored. "Can you believe they said that?" I would ask. I wanted to establish that I would never say those ridiculous and ignorant things because I knew how racist they were and I was not like the rest of my family.

The couple seemed uncomfortable, but I obliviously plowed ahead, ignoring their signals. I was having a great time regaling them with these anecdotes—the proverbial life of the party! After all, my progressive credentials were impeccable: I was a minority myself—a woman in a committed relationship with another woman. I proudly identified as a feminist. I knew how to talk about patriarchy and heterosexism. I was a cool white progressive, not an ignorant racist. Of course, what I was actually demonstrating was how completely oblivious I was. While I saw myself as a nice person and would have vehemently defended my intentions had anyone challenged me, the impact of my behavior was anything but nice, as I subjected this couple to racism all night long.

Throughout this book, I use the term "white progressive" as a stand-in for a particular strain of whiteness. I am not referring to someone's political affiliation, such as Democrat or Republican, Labor or Tory. I use the term to refer to white people who see themselves as *racially* progressive, well-meaning, *nice*. They might call themselves "woke," or even claim to be "beyond race." White progressives are generally on the left side of the political spectrum but can be moderates, centrists, or "soft" conservatives. Today's white progressives may read The Root and the *New York Times* and listen to NPR or the BBC as they commute to their job at a nonprofit or tech company. They can be any age. They may have a marginalized identity other than race and perhaps were in organizations such as the Peace Corps or Teach for America. They may have travelled extensively, speak several languages, and live in large urban cities or smaller progressive enclaves like Asheville, North Carolina; Northampton, Massachusetts; and Eugene, Oregon. But because they see themselves as progressive in terms of racism, they do not see anti-racism efforts as directed at them; they "already know all this" and are not part of the problem. Thus, they may not involve themselves in anti-racist efforts, but if they do, they can be rather self-righteous as they point out racism in everyone other than themselves. White progressives can be of any socioeconomic class, although middle- and upper-class white progressives tend to off-load racism onto poor and working-class whites (I will address the intersection of class in more depth in chapter 11).

Reverend Martin Luther King Jr., among others, critiqued what he termed "the white moderate" more than fifty years ago. In positioning the moderate in relation to the far end of the spectrum—the Klansman—he could be speaking about today's white progressive in relation to white nationalists. We claim to support racial justice efforts but want to suppress the tensions that accompany achieving that goal. In *Letter from the Birmingham Jail*, written in 1963 while he was imprisoned for protesting racial segregation, King observed that white moderates played a fundamental—albeit implicit—part in the resistance to racial equality:

> I have almost reached the regrettable conclusion that the Negro's great stumbling block in his stride toward freedom is not the White Citizen's Counciler or the Ku Klux Klanner, but the white moderate, who is more devoted to "order" than to justice; who prefers a negative peace which is the absence of tension to a positive peace which is the presence of justice; who constantly says: "I agree with you in the goal you seek, but I cannot agree with your methods of direct action"; who paternalistically believes he can set the timetable for another man's freedom. . . . Shallow understanding from people of good will is more frustrating than absolute misunderstanding from people of ill will. Lukewarm acceptance is much more bewildering than outright rejection.[2]

King speaks to the tendency of white moderates to see a lack of struggle as the indicator of racial justice. He notes that no racial progress has ever been made without conflict. The insistence that the oppressed slow down their efforts, be more patient, and give the oppressor time to change only functions to protect the oppressor's position. Those who benefit from racial inequality are invested in that inequality. The degree of investment may vary along with the ability to see or admit to it, but some investment in systems that benefit us is unavoidable.

As for admonishing the oppressed to "be patient," legal scholar Michelle Alexander points out that 155 years after the end of chattel slavery, "more African American men are in prison or jail, on probation or parole than were enslaved in 1850, before the Civil War began."[3]

Speaking directly to white progressives, writer James Baldwin reminded us, "You want me to make an act of faith risking . . . my life . . . on some idealism which you assure me exists in America which I have never seen."[4] The call to go slow and avoid conflict only serves the status quo of white comfort.

While the de jure (legally inscribed) racism of the civil rights era is somewhat different from the de facto (in practice) racism of today, we see a similar desire to avoid racial conflict in current racial justice efforts. Note, for example, the common guidelines many white organizations use when setting up discussions on race: assume good intentions, respect differences, speak for yourself. Whose interests do these guidelines serve? They serve white expectations for racial comfort: ensuring *niceness* and warding off direct challenges. In so doing, they are not accounting for the ever-present dynamics of power, assuming a universal (white) experience, and policing BIPOC (Black, Indigenous, and people of color) people into not engaging with authenticity lest they face the punitive power of white fragility.

The desire to avoid conflict and keep the content palatable for white people also reveals itself when I'm frequently asked how to "prepare" a predominantly white group prior to a keynote or workshop, and whether the group should be given a "trigger warning." I have lost count of the event organizers wondering aloud if the group is "ready." These concerns are not raised because I engage participants in some kind of confrontational exercise or "walk of shame." They are raised simply because I will be speaking bluntly and directly about what it means to be white in societies that are unequal and separated by race.

Then there are those who see no need to discuss race because they believe they are beyond race. Cultural commentator Jay Smooth points out the irony of believing that *avoiding* the conversation means that we are *beyond* the conversation. Smooth notes, "Most Americans avoid race conversations like the plague. And we often take our ability to avoid it and use it as a measure of our progress and enlightenment, which, I think, is kind of telling in and of itself."[5] I cannot think of any other social issue where it is legitimately suggested that the most effective way to address that issue is to never speak of it. Imagine being urged to not speak of domestic violence, suicide, depression, sexual assault, or child abuse.

Some white progressives do want to talk about racism and voluntarily show up at optional workshops or presentations on racism, but they are more likely to be thinking about the other white people who really should be receiving the message, not their own need to hear it. Their first question is often some form of "How can I tell my family/friend about their racism?" I have begun to respond by asking, "Well, how would I tell you about *your* racism?" My point is that the question assumes it is not the person asking who needs help but always someone else. The asker has arrived and is now ready to go forth and enlighten others. White progressives who are more willing to acknowledge the existence of racism and white advantage will still typically locate it in any white person other than themselves. "Society," "The Administration," or certain political parties are also popular targets—vague categories that cannot easily be addressed and exempt those present in the room.

In workshops, when I discuss common patterns of white people, many participants will want to provide examples involving their coworkers or friends. At the end of the workshop they will say, "I sure wish so-and-so were here—*they* really need this!" Yet it is the white progressive who can cause the most *daily* harm to people of color. While I did not originate the idea that white progressives can be more harmful than explicit racists—as we saw, activists such as King and Baldwin were challenging white progressives as early as the 1950s—I have certainly observed it day in and out, and I stand by this claim in my work. I am often asked about it in interviews by white commentators (Black commentators usually need no explanation), so let me explain.

I am writing this book at a time when white nationalism—the desire for a white ethnostate by and for whites—is on the rise both in the United States and globally. While aspects of white nationalism have existed for decades, Donald Trump's entry in the 2016 presidential race marked a resurgence of the movement. Between 2016 and 2018, there was a major increase in mobilization by far-right groups, making it one of the most active periods of on-the-ground, extremist activity in decades. In 2019, the number of white nationalist groups identified by the Southern Poverty Law Center (SPLC) rose for the second straight year—a 55 percent increase since 2017.[6] In the last three years, the SPLC has also documented 125 rallies, marches, and protests nation-wide, which were organized and attended by far-right extremists. These gatherings are often a mix of groups that include white nationalists, neo-Nazis, Klansmen, right-wing reactionaries, and members of the "alt-right." The more radical of these groups want to accelerate a race war through means of violence. In 2017, the white supremacist and anti-Semitic "Unite the Right" rally in Charlottesville, Virginia, in-volved six hundred extremists and was the largest public rally of white supremacists in more than a decade, according to the Anti-Defamation League (ADL).[7] This marks a violent resurgence of the movement. The ADL also documented 3,566 "extremist propaganda incidents" and events in 2020, compared to 2,704 in the same period of 2019. Almost 80 percent of 2020 cases involved white nationalist ideology.[8] These groups have found the internet a powerful recruitment tool, especially targeting white teen boys. Andrew Anglin, the founder and editor of the neo-Nazi website The Daily Stormer, has openly stated that they target boys as young as eleven, declaring, "My site is mainly designed to tar-get children."[9] Alt-right groups have tripled in Canada since their last election and are on the rise throughout Europe, Australia, South Africa, and New Zealand. This is an absolutely urgent issue of which I am well aware, so why am I focusing on well-meaning white people when those who are *not* well-meaning are growing and emboldened?

I can only imagine how unsettling it might be for a Black person, for example, to interact with someone who openly espouses white suprem-acist ideology. But odds are that on a daily basis, Black people don't interact with those who openly agitate for white nationalism. Yet on a daily basis in the workplace, the classroom, houses of worship, gentri-fying neighborhoods, and community groups, Black people *do* interact with white progressives. We are the ones—with a smile on our faces—who undermine Black people daily in ways both harder to identify and easier to deny. To the degree that we see ourselves as "not racist," we are going to be very defensive about any suggestion to the contrary. We will see no further action needed because we see ourselves as outside of the problem. Complacency certainly prevents us from organizing and acting against the growing white nationalist movement.

Progressive white people are more likely to manifest *aversive racism*, a term coined by psychologist Joel Kovel. Aversive racism is racism that is suppressed from awareness because it conflicts with a consciously held belief in racial equality. It is a subtle but insidious form, because it allows the person to enact racism while maintaining a positive self-image ("I have lots of friends of color"). Writer Tess Martin speaks directly to the particular ways that white progressives respond when our racism is pointed out:

> As a black woman working in mostly progressive spaces, I'm also used to the constant stream of microaggressions and casual racism within our ranks . . . the automatic response whenever I or another person of color dares to point out racist behavior . . . in these so-called progressive spaces. A torrent of defensiveness is unleashed . . . amplified to outrageous levels because, on the whole, progressives believe themselves to be completely "woke." Anything that puts that wokeness in jeopardy is met with brutal defensiveness.
>
> It always arrives in the company of several tried and true excuses for why the behavior or comments weren't problematic at all. These excuses are so common, so often used, so seemingly set in tired, frustrating stone, that you can set a clock by them. . . . And they're always brandished by self-identified allies.[10]

Martin breaks down disclaimers like "I have Black and/or Brown friends," "You don't know my heart," and "Everyone knows I'm not a racist" and lays out why they are absurd and unconvincing. I highly recommend white progressives read her full piece, as well as all of her other excellent blog posts.

Our certitude that we are free of racism prevents us from any further growth and development. For example, in my workshops I ask participants to form groups of three and share their reflections on a series of questions. I give them one minute each, per question. The final question is "What are some of the ways in which your race(s) has shaped your life?"

There are three consistent patterns that emerge in their answers. The first is how uncomfortable this question is for many white people. The second is how difficult it is for so many of us to answer with any depth or criticality. I have seen countless white people unable to fill the sixty seconds, awkwardly waiting out the time. This discomfort and lack of critical awareness is not innocent or benign. The collective impact of our inability has very real consequences for racialized people living and working around us. If I can't tell you what it means to be white, I will not be able to engage with an alternate experience—what it means *not* to be white. Not only will an alternate reality be incomprehensible to me, but I will need to refuse that reality because of what it reflects back and exposes about mine.

Using the term "liberals," James Baldwin spoke to the white progressive inability to comprehend our own whiteness. In response to being invited to the home of the Honorable Elijah Muhammad, whose second in command was Malcolm X, Baldwin said, "In a way, I owe the invitation to the incredible, abysmal, and really cowardly obtuseness of white liberals. Whether in private debate or in public, any attempt I made to explain . . . was met with a blankness that revealed the little connection that the liberals' attitudes have with their perceptions or their lives, or even their knowledge."[11]

Baldwin succinctly traces a line between white progressive obtuseness and the Black frustration that led to the need for more radical strategies ("by any means necessary") of systemic change.

In not thinking critically about our racial positions and how they shape our experiences, we don't develop skills for navigating a sensitive conversation, nor do we develop an emotional capacity to withstand the discomfort of the conversation. This is especially true if my worldview, assumptions, or behaviors are being questioned. The result: white fragility. And Black people know that most of us can't answer the question of our own whiteness, and that we bring that inability to the table. Thus, they are likely to experience more punishment, not less, if they raise race issues. This is one of the great contradictions of white progressives. On the one hand, I would never want to say or do anything racially hurtful. But on the other, don't you dare tell me I have said or done anything racially hurtful!

The third pattern I see when I ask white people how their race has shaped their lives is that many organize their answers around racialized people, and most often a Black person. They tell a story about a childhood friend or something someone said about a Black person, how close they lived to Black people, how their parents felt about Black people, or some other foundational racial incident. Notice that none of the above actually answers the question. But it is revealing in a very important way, for it illustrates how difficult it is for us to see our own lives in racial terms. We can think about race only as it relates to racialized people. If they are not in the picture, there is no race in the picture. Of course, white space is racialized space, and every moment that I spend in white space reinforces in me a particular (and limited) worldview and experience. But the deeper message being reinforced is that we lose nothing of value by living in segregation. In fact, the whiter the space is, the more likely it is to be perceived as "good" and "safe" in the white mind. This is a profound message that we must begin to grapple with, for it shapes every aspect of our cross-racial interactions (or lack thereof).

We can start with the story of our birth and why we could predict our chances for survival based in part on our race. We can reflect on how race has been shaping us from before we took our first breath and will continue to do so until our last. Granted, not all white babies survive their births and not all white people live longer, but there are clear, measurable patterns. Those patterns have meaning and significance for all of our lives. Inequitable racial patterns and institutional policies can and should be interrupted, but that cannot happen if we refuse to acknowledge them. Given that white people control virtually every institution in Western society, the lack of racial awareness that we bring to the institutional table infuses all aspects of society and profoundly impacts those who have few if any seats there. We will not organize to enact systemic change to a system we do not acknowledge.

Do all racialized people necessarily see and acknowledge whiteness and systemic racism? No (think Clarence Thomas, Ted Cruz, Yukong Zhao, and Candace Owens). But they are much more likely to, given that from a very early age they had to know and navigate my racial reality, whereas I can be seen as qualified to do or lead *virtually anything* with no understanding of or interest in theirs.

I am often asked if I think younger white people are less racist. This question rests on the conceptualization of history as an arc of progress. It follows that each generation will be more socially progressive and thus less racist. But the system of racism is highly adaptive. In this political moment, with white nationalist recruitment on the rise, gerrymandering approved by the Supreme Court, the Voting Rights Act of 1965 gutted, and the Confederate flag flown in the US Capitol, it is evident—especially as we're having renewed conversations on racism—that we have not advanced as far as we might think. In 2018, we celebrated the most diverse Congress ever in terms of race and gender, and yet Congress was still 88 percent white, and men were 75 percent of the Senate and 77 percent of the House.

In my work with large tech companies, I often see this lack of critical racial consciousness in white people under thirty, who have no idea how their few Black coworkers experience the workplace. But there are potent examples of even younger white people demonstrating a profound lack of both critical racial consciousness and racial compassion. Take for example the case of a high schooler's invitation to "Tolo," a dance to which the girls ask their dates—typically boys—rather than the traditional norm of boys asking girls (the sexism in these traditions is for another discussion). An incident ended up in the local news when a young woman asked her potential date to the dance by holding a sign that said "If I was black I'd be picking cotton, but instead I'm picking you." When told that her sign was racist, she reacted in shock and professed innocence:

I want you to know that I am genuinely sorry for the hurt feelings, chaos and rage that my tolo poster caused. Unfortunately, the wrong image of myself was portrayed through the words written on the poster.

Those who know my true heart know that I am not racist, and that evil way of thinking is something that makes me sick. I understand that by making that poster it made me out to look like a racist person. Racism is not what lies within my true heart. It was not my intention to upset anyone by what I wrote. . . . From the bottom of my heart, that was not me, that is not how I was raised or what my family believes in.[12]

The student's apology—in which she insists her intention wasn't to hurt anyone and that her "true heart" is not racist—is a classic example of white assertions in the face of racist behaviors (the familiar idea that there is a "true" or "real" person inside of us that is unchanging and *independent of our actions* is in itself worthy of examination). She claims to have been raised not to be racist even as she behaves in racist ways, all the while managing to recast herself as the victim. Yet describing this student's actions as a lack of critical consciousness may be too generous. The joke wouldn't work without some awareness of the differences in position and status. This also speaks to why the claim "I'm not racist," professed by virtually every white person who has ever been caught on camera engaging in public acts of manifest racism, is functionally meaningless.

Most white people have no lasting cross-racial relationships. Thus, the claims that young people today make about how comfortable they are with diversity are based on the most superficial of shared experiences: being a fan of Black musicians or sports figures of color, passing Black people on the streets of large cities, and/or having a coworker of color. The young people I work with in cities such as New York and Oakland don't actually lead integrated lives, despite the racial diversity that may surround them. This diversity is often the temporary result of the process of gentrification. Those who actually have cross-racial friendships tend to have relationships that are conditional. Their friends of color must tolerate constant racist teasing or be dismissed as angry and "not fun" and then abandoned. This dynamic allows younger white people to claim these friendships as proof that they are not racist and insist that their friends of color don't mind their teasing when it is questioned. ("I'm just being ironic.")

So no, I don't think the younger generation is less racist than older ones. Most white people live in racial segregation, at the same time that racist ideology is circulating all around us. While we saw racial progress in Barack Obama's election, we saw the backlash to it in Trump's. In the racial makeup of our current Supreme Court and the recent battles for control of that court, we see that white men still overwhelmingly hold legal authority and institutional control.

While virtually any white progressive you ask will claim to not be racist, consider the following questions for reflection:

- Did you grow up in an integrated neighborhood? If so, do you still live in one? If not and you do now, is it due to gentrification?
- If you did not grow up in an integrated neighborhood, why didn't you?
- If everyone is equal, how did you make sense of living separately?
- Did your parents encourage you to visit the places where Black people lived in order to get to know them and build the relationships that were missing in your environment?
- Did your parents have a significant number of Black friends themselves?
- Did you attend integrated schools? If so, was your school considered to be "good"?
- Did you study systemic racism in your K–12 education? If you graduated from college, did you study systemic racism there?
- Was it integrated throughout your education by your professors, including your Black professors? Or were your professors overwhelmingly white? Did those white professors have to demonstrate that they were able to engage with issues of racism in the curriculum and classroom dynamics before they were considered qualified to teach?
- Did you have to demonstrate that you had a foundational understanding of racism before you could graduate, or teach, manage people, or practice medicine or law?
- If you were not educated about racism, have you sought every— or even any—opportunity to gain that education yourself?

- Do you work in an organization in which Black people are represented at all levels, including the top?
- Does your workplace profess to "value diversity" in their marketing materials and vision statement? If so, is the executive leadership team held accountable to racially equitable outcomes in their policies and practices?
- If you are married and you showed me your wedding album, would I see how integrated your friendship circle is?

Given the way that the majority of white progressives will answer these questions, our confidence that our education is complete, our opinions are valid, and that we are not part of the problem warrants reflection.

In summary, while the rise of white nationalism and explicit acts of racial harm must be addressed, my focus here is on the more subtle forms of racism that I and other white people who do not identify as white nationalists perpetuate. These acts have an accumulative effect that is also damaging. A 2020 Gallup poll on microaggressions—a term used by psychologist Derald Wing Sue to capture the everyday slights, indignities, and allegations that people of color experience in their day-to-day interactions with well-intentioned white people—found that Black Americans disproportionately experience microaggressions compared to those in other racial groups. Gallup concluded, "The flash points that spark national conversations on racism are often instances of violence, but for many Black Americans, their experiences with mistreatment and discrimination are much subtler and are woven into the routines of their normal, daily lives."[13] Who do Black and other Americans of color most likely interact with in their daily lives who are perpetuating these microaggressions? Not likely white nationalists but rather nice white people like myself. And that means we have a critical role and responsibility to address our "nicer" forms of racism.

In this sociopolitical moment, when systemic racism is finally being recognized in the mainstream, many see the interpersonal as a trivial matter, inconsequential and unrelated to structural change; individuals are not institutions. But of course, institutions—legal, governmental, educational, economic—are made of individuals. The people controlling the vast majority of institutions and enacting their policies are white. Given that virtually all white people will profess to believe in racial justice, why is systemic racial *injustice* so enduring? Resistance to anti-racist systemic change is in large part rooted in ongoing white racial indifference, resentment, and perceived threat. As Carol Anderson so meticulously demonstrates in *White Rage*, every inch of Black progress has been met with a white backlash.[14] That backlash manifests on at least four primary levels: institutional, cultural, interpersonal, and individual.

I am interested in the connection between these levels—how the interpersonal dynamics that flow from the individual impact the cultural and institutional. Professor of media Melissa Phruksachart notes, "White feelings structure the everyday realities of BIPOC in ways that engender material consequences, such as the toxic bodily tolls of allostatic load and minority stress."[15] "Allostatic load" refers to the wear and tear on the body, which accumulates as an individual is exposed to chronic stress. When this load is due to chronic racial stress, health researcher Arline Geronimus termed the consequences "racial weathering." Racial weathering is the result of systemic injustice—which is not just policies *but the million daily cuts* inflicted by unaware white people, including progressives. In turn, weathering is related to systemic consequences such as the disproportional impact of COVID-19 on Black people.

While most white people rarely interact with Black people in any sustained way, Black people must interact daily with white people who control many aspects of their lives. I am not among those who claim that ending racism is a simple matter of knowing one another; racism is also perpetrated by people who know those they hurt. I do argue that radical relationality—liberatory action informed by the recognition that *all* living things are interconnected and do not exist independently—is foundational to ending racism. Radical relationality is anathema to white supremacy and the patriarchy it issued from, and can ameliorate the effects of racial weathering while building the coalitions necessary for systemic change. Hence, radical relationships are central to abolitionist organizing, among other forms of liberatory praxis. As Phruksachart asks, "Who benefits when relationality is left off the table? And who is uplifted and healed when relationality is centered?" Organizing for systemic change begins through relationships. Effective politicians certainly understand that they must build relationships in order to move their agendas forward.

Nice racism results in personal complacency toward anti-racist efforts while upholding material consequences. We won't work toward systemic change if we don't even recognize, much less acknowledge, that we play a role, one way or the other. That role either implicitly supports or explicitly challenges systemic racism; policies don't write and enact themselves. Two brief examples may illustrate how the personal and interpersonal connect to the systemic—one historical and one anecdotal.

In 1954, the US Supreme Court ended a key aspect of structural racism in the *Brown v. Board of Education of Topeka* decision, stating that segregated schooling was unconstitutional. The court mandated that schools must desegregate with "all deliberate speed." White resistance in response was swift; integration was not. Twenty-five years later, with little progress, the case was reopened and followed up with several lawsuits. It wasn't until 1998 that the Topeka Unified School District was granted unified status. Legislation is critical, but legislation alone won't end racism. As Heather McGhee states in *The Sum of Us: What Racism Costs Everyone and How We Can Prosper Together*:

> Laws are merely expressions of a society's dominant beliefs. It's the beliefs that must shift in order for outcomes to change. When policies change in advance of the underlying beliefs, we are often surprised to find the problem still with us. America ended the policy of enforced school segregation two generations ago, but with new justifications, the esteem in which many white parents hold Black and brown children hasn't changed much, and today our schools are nearly as segregated as they were before *Brown v. Board of Education*. Beliefs matter.[16]

In 2021, schools are still deeply segregated, and white parents who can afford to send their children to private schools to avoid public education and minimize their children's contact with large numbers of

Black children, do so. While legislation was changed, fears, bias, and resentments were not.

The anecdotal example was shared with me by a white colleague who was called in as part of an interracial team to work with a nationally recognized legal organization committed to social justice activism. The board was composed of twenty-one people: ten were people of color and eleven were white. Of the white people, six were men. Boards are foundational to implementing structural changes in organizations, and this board was exceptional in its racial diversity. A structural policy change was proposed to help keep the board diverse: term limits. This seems like a simple and straightforward policy, and certainly not an uncommon practice. In fact, 72 percent of nonprofit boards have term limits.[17] Yet the majority of white members passionately resisted this policy change. Many meetings and debates ensued. Virtually every white man argued against the change, and no white women spoke up (while the women may have been open to the change but stayed silent in response to feeling intimidated by the hostility from the white men, in practice they maintained white solidarity through their silence). At an impasse, the group brought in facilitators to mediate. The facilitators conducted an exercise to allow the people of color to share the impact of the white resistance. The members of color expressed their deep disappointment about the degree of white fragility and their hurtful surprise at the white members' lack of anti-racist skills and understanding. Still, the majority of white people remained resistant and took the feedback very personally; the facilitators described their efforts as being met with a "wall of white defensiveness."

Months later, they still had not approved this policy change and cross-racial relationships in this progressive activist organization are frayed. The racial equity team has held meeting after meeting and spent hour after hour strategizing on how to either move these board members forward or navigate around them. As of yet, they have made no progress. My colleague shared that this experience gave her another "teeny-tiny glimpse into the daily exhaustion" of racialized people trying to move a racial justice agenda forward in so-called progressive organizations.

Policy change must be taken up *simultaneously* with personal and interpersonal work. Multiracial coalitions are critical but are difficult to sustain when people of color are exhausted by the interpersonal dynamics and efforts are blocked at every turn by white progressives who feel personally threatened.

In discussing white people who define their politics as fiscally conservative but socially liberal, McGhee notes that all poverty in the US could be eliminated by spending just 12 percent more than the cost of the 2017 Republican tax cuts. Resistance to this expenditure is due in part to media's representation of poverty as a Black issue, which distances the white collective from a problem they perceive as belonging to the Other. White people's social liberalism thus more often manifests in "helping" a culture that is seen as deficient. White progressives are more likely to acknowledge systemic oppression as the culprit rather than use biological explanations, but the outcome is a view of Black culture as degraded. Thus, our efforts are often guided by a focus on catching the children before they "fall," while they are still "innocent." This renders our role moot and allows us to feel benevolent and socially progressive, while reproducing anti-Blackness.

McGhee connects individual white emotionality with the structural outcomes when she says that there is:

a moral cost of racism that millions of white people bear and that those of us who've borne every other cost of racism simply don't. It can cause contradictions and justifications, feelings of guilt, shame, projection, resentment, and denial. Ultimately, though, we are all paying for the moral conflict of white Americans. But there isn't an established route for redemption; America hasn't had a truth-and-reconciliation process like other wounded societies have. Instead, it's up to individuals to decide what they need to do in order to be good people in a white supremacist society—and it's not easy.[18]

We can and must change policies that protect and reproduce white supremacy, but we must also address the less formal hostilities of whiteness, including the gaslighting of nice racism, which contributes to weathering and—in the case of organizational inclusion—the gap between recruitment and retention. When we take interpersonal relationships off the table, we also abandon white people who want to engage in anti-racist action, leaving them to deal with the social penalties of breaking with white solidarity while trying to resist the seductive rewards of the status quo without support. I am focused here on illuminating the more subtle or "nicer" aspects of that hostility. It is only *one piece* of the whole, albeit an essential and connecting one.

Ibram X. Kendi tells us that the opposite of *racist* isn't *not racist*; rather, it is *anti-racist*.[19] I understand his point to be that in a society in which racism is the default, to not be actively engaged in disrupting racism—at the minimum—is to collude with the status quo of racism. Historian Howard Zinn, author of *A People's History of the United States*, made a similar point when he said, "You can't be neutral on a moving train." In order to work toward policy change, we need to have critical awareness, continually educate ourselves, build cross-racial skills, develop the ability to respond constructively, and repair racial harm; these are also forms of anti-racism.

CHAPTER 2

WHY IT'S OK TO GENERALIZE ABOUT WHITE PEOPLE

Email: gofuckyourself@racistdumbass.com
Subject: Racism
Message Body:

You should [not] judge people based on
the color of their skin, but by the content
of their character. A wise man once said
that. You are the problem with this country
and need to stop generalizing about white
people. Pathetic. I bet your parents are
disappointed in you.

(email sent to me)

One of the most consistent complaints I have received upon the publication of *White Fragility* is that I am generalizing about white people. While the email quoted above is obviously a cruder version of this complaint (and I assume not written by a progressive), it is merely a variation on a common theme: "How can you claim to know anything about me just because I am white?" This is the ideology of individualism, which can be conceptualized as a set of ideas, words, symbols, and metaphors—a *narrative*—that creates, communicates, reproduces, and reinforces the concept that we are all unique and that our group memberships (such as our race, class, or gender) are not important or relevant to our opportunities. Psychologist Wendy Hollway describes *narratives* as an interrelated "system of statements which cohere around common meanings and values . . . [that] are a product of social factors, of powers and practices, rather than an individual's set of ideas."[1] These narratives are embedded in a matrix of previous statements, stories, and meanings—they connect to, expand, extend, and refer back to narratives already circulating in the culture. If they didn't connect to existing narratives, we couldn't make sense of them. Individualism is a deeply imbedded narrative in Western cultures, and it plays a particularly important role in the maintenance of white supremacy. Thus, speaking about white people as a group who have a shared experience specifically *as white people* is a primary trigger for a white fragility meltdown on a number of levels.

People who raise an objection to generalizing about white people may be confusing speaking about people at the group level with *stereotyping*. Stereotyping occurs when we take a trait demonstrated by one or a few members of a social group and project that trait onto all members of that group. Whether those stereotypes are positive or negative, it is generally understood that stereotypes have hurtful impacts and are unfair. Making statements about well-documented social patterns and outcomes such as "Our institutions were set up to advantage white people" and "White identity is shaped by the ubiquitous messages of white superiority that circulate in the culture at large" is not the same as stereotyping. Systemic racism is well documented throughout society and across history. To say that defensiveness is a common response from white people when Black people try to talk to us about that racism— and that our defensiveness is not conducive to meaningful change—is to state an observation, not to stereotype. One may think that defensiveness is justified, but it is still a predictable pattern that has consequences worthy of exploration.

Let's look to a familiar historical example to illustrate the difference between stereotypes and statements of observable and well-documented patterns: women's suffrage in the United States. Before women were allowed to vote, in 1920, men had an unearned, automatic advantage over women: men could vote on who represented both men and women in government and on laws and policies that impacted their lives, and women could not. This is an undeniable advantage of profound proportions. And not just *some* men had this advantage, but *all* (white) men had this advantage. To point this out is not to stereotype; it is to state a fact. To add that women were denied suffrage for so long because their society viewed them as inferior to men, and that all men (and, of course, women) received the message of female inferiority, is also a fact. This is not true of just a few men and projected onto all men; female inferiority was inscribed in law and disseminated throughout the culture and all its institutions. For example, women could not open a bank account without a husband's or father's permission, had no federal right to own property until 1900, could not be members of clergy or speak from pulpits in most religious denominations, and were severely limited in their ability to attend college. How an individual responded to the belief that women were inferior might have varied, but the message could not have been avoided. Having a role model to counter the messages of female inferiority would have been helpful, but it would not have been enough to completely inoculate one from the myriad ways this message was disseminated throughout the culture.

Eventually, due to the tireless efforts of suffragists and their male supporters, enough minds were changed. After decades of struggle, women were granted the right to vote *by men* (women could not grant that right to themselves). If prior to suffrage men had raised the objection that to say they were advantaged as a group was an unfair generalization ("Not all men!" "I don't see you as a woman!" "Why can't we all just be humans?"), then how could denying women the vote have been challenged? Who does it serve not to name the beneficiaries of unfair policies?

Of course, the message of female inferiority was not eliminated by the Nineteenth Amendment. To pick up the story and show how the message of female inferiority continues in de facto forms today is simply to provide social analysis, not stereotype. For example, the complete text of the Equal Rights Amendment (ERA) is "Equality of rights under the law shall not be denied or abridged by the United States or by any state on account of sex." In 2021, the ERA has still not been federally ratified. And women are still not allowed to be clergy in the two largest mainstream Christian denominations: the Roman Catholic Church and the Southern Baptist Convention, nor among smaller denominations such as Mormonism, Jehovah's Witnesses, and Orthodox Judaism.

Similarly, anti-racist activists work to show how racial inequality continues on in de facto forms, even if de jure forms such as enslavement and Jim Crow have ended. We can't do this without noting the significance of our racial classifications, which means we must speak at the group level. Unfortunately, many white people do not know their country's history, do not understand culture or socialization, and believe that we can be exempt from historical legacies and social conditioning, as demonstrated in the common idea that we have a "true self" within us, untouched by the society that grants the idea its very meaning. This lack of understanding has serious consequences for the ability to understand systemic racism. Returning to the example of women's suffrage and how racism was also at play, only *white* women were granted full access to the right to vote in 1920, by *white* men. We wouldn't have the Voting Rights Act of 1965 if we couldn't mention group-level reality. And these gains cannot be taken for granted; in 2021, the Voting Rights Act has been almost completely dismantled. In order to challenge unequal access between groups of people in a society, we must focus our attention at the group level. It is on readers to take the framework and apply it to their specific case.

White progressives are more likely to acknowledge shared dynamics such as white advantage but may still want to be granted exceptions and be seen as unique. Our own minority status is especially useful to this end, e.g., *I myself am a minority, therefore I don't have any advantage; why aren't we talking about xyz oppression (the one I suffer from)?* Individualism also allows us to position ourselves as morally superior to other white people who "don't get it." While we enjoy attending workshops and anti-racism lectures, when it comes time to ask questions, the first will invariably be "How do I tell so-and-so about their racism?" We rarely ask for insight into seeing our own.

Political scientist Jane Flax notes that there is an irreconcilable tension within US society.[2] The legitimacy of our institutions depends upon the concept that all citizens are equal. At the same time, we each occupy distinct raced (and gendered, classed, etc.) positions that profoundly shape our life chances in ways that are not voluntary or random. In order to manage this tension, we use the narrative of individualism, which posits that there are no intrinsic barriers to individual success and that failure is not a consequence of a systemic structure but of individual character. Individualism claims that success is independent of position, that one succeeds through individual effort alone, and that there are no favored starting positions that provide competitive advantage. We all act independently of one another, and we all have the same possibility of achievement. Starting positions are irrelevant, and emphasizing their relevance actually limits one's ability to stand on one's own. Standing on one's own is both the assumption and goal of individualism; systemic inequality is rendered moot.

Individualism is so deeply held in dominant society that it is virtually immovable without sustained effort. An example of individualism's tenacity occurred during a workplace training I was co-facilitating. This training had two primary components: my presentation (as a white person) on the dynamics of white identity, power, and advantage, and my co-facilitator's presentation (as a Black person) on the dynamics of internalized racial oppression, both individually and between and across groups of color. Included in my presentation was a discussion of the common barriers that prevent white people from seeing racism. One of these barriers is our insistence on seeing ourselves as individuals, outside of social groups. I presented an eight-point list titled "What's Problematic About Individualism?" I prefaced this by emphasizing that I am not denying that we are all individuals *in general*. Rather, I was trying to demonstrate how white insistence on individualism *in discussions of racism in particular* prevents cross-racial understanding and denies the salience of race in our lives.

I had just finished presenting this list and had called for a break, during which two people, a white woman, "Sue," who had been sitting next to a white man, "Bob," approached me and declared, "Bob and I think we should all just see each other as individuals."[3]

Although in my work, moments like this occur frequently, they continue to disorient me on three interconnected levels. First, I had just gone over, in depth, what was problematic about individualism as a means to "end racism." How could Sue and Bob have missed that forty-five-minute presentation? I was left wondering, yet again, what happens cognitively for so many white people in anti-racism education efforts that prevents them from actually hearing what is being presented. Second, if we assume that somehow Sue had missed that part of the presentation (along with Bob), did she really think I had never before heard or considered this most trite and simplistic of suggestions—that if we all just saw ourselves as individuals, racism would go away? And finally, where did she—as a white person presumably living and working in racial segregation, as most of us do—get the confidence to declare the (one-sentence) "answer" to a profoundly complex and perennial dilemma of social life? I did my best to reiterate my previous points, but to no avail. By the afternoon break, Sue and Bob had walked out.

If this were a rare occurrence in anti-racist education, we might be tempted to dismiss it. Unfortunately, their reaction is all too common. So what was Sue and Bob's point? In my experience over the past twenty-five years, in a range of academic, corporate, community, and governmental institutions across the US, Canada, Australia, South Africa, Europe, and the UK, when white people insist on individualism in discussions about racism, they are saying, *My race has not made a difference in my life, so why do we have to talk about race as if it mattered? It is talking about race as if it mattered that makes it matter. I don't see myself as a member of a racial group, so you shouldn't see me that way either. In fact, by saying that my group membership matters, you are generalizing. You can't generalize about me because I am an individual; therefore, unless you know me, you can't profess to know anything about my life. Nor are you aware of all the ways I am an exception within my society. Further, as an individual, I am objective and view others as individuals and not as members of racial groups. For example, if I were hiring, I would hire the best person for the job no matter what their race was.* In essence, Sue and Bob are insisting that racism will disappear when we all proceed as if race doesn't matter. In fact, for Sue and Bob, race *has* disappeared, because they already proceed as if race doesn't matter. It's just misguided people such as myself who refuse to see everyone as individuals and thus are creating problems where none exist, never mind the copious empirical evidence that we are not objective and that who we hire is not a simple matter of who is most qualified. In *Biased: Uncovering the Hidden Prejudice That Shapes What We See, Think, and Do*, Stanford University social psychologist Jennifer Eberhardt pulls together that research to show "we all have ideas about race. Even the most open-minded among us. Those ideas have the power to bias our perception, our attention, our memory, and our actions—all despite our conscious awareness or deliberate intentions. Our ideas about race are shaped by the stereotypes to which we are exposed on a daily basis."[4] Those stereotypes are consistent and we all receive them. The overwhelming whiteness of those at the top is due to so much more than the "cream rising" idea that individualism suggests.

It is important to think critically about the narratives we use because they shape how we think about social problems and what actions we take as a result. There is a question that has never failed me in my efforts to determine whether a narrative and the actions it informs challenge or protect racism. That question isn't whether a particular narrative or behavior is right or wrong. That question is "How does this function?" How does the insistence that we all be seen as unique individuals—specifically in the context of discussions of racism—*function*? What dynamics might the ideology of individualism protect and obscure?

INDIVIDUALISM DENIES THE SIGNIFICANCE OF RACE AND THE ADVANTAGES OF BEING WHITE

You live through that little piece of time that is yours, but that piece of time is not only your own life, it is the summing-up of all the other lives that are simultaneous with yours. It is, in other words, History and what you are is an expression of History.

—Robert Penn Warren[5]

I don't need to hold consciously racist beliefs or intentions in order to benefit from being white, any more than I need to hold consciously ableist beliefs in order to benefit from a society that considers me "able-bodied" and thus "normal" and is set up to accommodate the way I move, see, and communicate. But it goes deeper than just receiving benefits and being able to take them for granted. I have *also* internalized the message of my normalcy and that it is *better* to be white, and better to be "normal" than "disabled." These messages are so ubiquitous that they are impossible not to absorb.

While it is easier to see the unfairness of currents that press against us, it is harder to see currents that move with us and facilitate our efforts. In fact, there is an investment in *not* seeing these currents. For example, I was co-facilitating a session for a group of employees within a large city government. These employees were termed "Field," as opposed to the office workers who were termed "Tower" (because they worked in the downtown skyscraper). The hierarchy was clear in the language: "Field" signified blue-collar workers and "Tower" signified white collar. The group I was working with were pipe fitters, working class and mostly white and male. I cannot say whether they would identify as progressives, although they were clear about the existence of class oppression. My co-facilitator was one of the few racialized people in the room. We showed a video on the history of programs such as the GI Bill and practices like redlining, which benefited white people and contributed to the enduring racial inequality we see today. As soon as the film ended, a white man registered a familiar two-point objection:

- That was the past, so it's not relevant today.
- If someone doesn't like their situation, they can just change it.

Keep in mind that this was a group who had been bitterly complaining about the elitism of the Tower group and the unfair advantage the Tower had because they were salaried (as opposed to working for hourly wages as the pipe fitters did). In addition to being paid more, the Tower workers were able to take long lunch breaks, go to appointments when needed, and (according to the field-workers) "sit on their asses in cushioned chairs" all day.

The pipe fitter who registered his complaint had no problem recognizing the class hierarchy, but he refused to recognize his own racial advantage. In my mind, I imagined the following conversation:

"If the Tower positions are so much better, why don't you just transfer into one?"

"Because you need a college degree!"

"Why don't you have a college degree?"

"My parents couldn't afford to send me to college. I had to get out there and work and help support the family."

"Well, why don't you get one now?"

"I have kids to feed and bills to pay!"

While class oppression was clearly visible to this participant, he resented any suggestion that racial privilege could be attributed to him or any white person, even as he and his coworkers were overwhelmingly white. He stuck to his "individual" bootstraps narrative of open mobility and refused to see whiteness as a shared experience that granted advantage.

Yes, some people "rise above" their initial status, but they are the exception. Most people will remain in the economic class into which they were born. A 2015 report, *Economic Mobility in the United States*, by Stanford researchers Pablo Mitnik and David Grusky, determined that approximately half of all parental income advantages are passed on to children.[6] That means most Americans are likely to remain in the same social class into which they were born. Further, economic advantage increases as you move higher up the income scale. Between the 50th and 90th percentiles, parents pass on roughly *two-thirds* of their advantage to their kids. A child raised by wealthy parents can expect a salary 200 percent larger than that of a child raised by low-income parents. Racial advantage is even more compounded than class advantage because it is at play regardless of a white person's class position.

Our country was founded on the wealth produced from the enslavement of Africans and the genocide and land theft of Indigenous peoples. The 1619 Project—a collection of essays, portraits, oral histories, and curricular materials created by investigative reporter Nikole Hannah-Jones on the four-hundredth anniversary of the beginning of slavery in the US—seeks to reframe the dominant narrative, which places Black enslavement in the distant past, unrelated to our current day. This narrative allows white Americans to insist that African Americans "get over" a system we see as long since dismantled. Hannah-Jones notes that the directive to "get over it" is something that "every black American has heard at some point."[7] She adds, "No one would like to get over slavery more than black people." But enslavement was so foundational to America and its institutions that it cannot be disentangled from the present.

The 1619 Project includes essays addressing the impact of race on a wide range of industries, including sports and healthcare, and provides resources such as lesson plans and speakers. By tracing the effects of slavery into the present, the 1619 Project both challenges the idea that America's birth began in 1776 and shows how the system of slavery undergirds every aspect of society today. The year the first slave ship arrived was deliberately centered to make the point that even before America was a country, slavery was foundational to the establishment of its institutions.

Sociology of law professor Jacqueline Battalora explains that from its founding, the United States established that whiteness—being seen as a white person—would result in access and opportunity *as a matter of law*.[8] For example, the Naturalization Law of 1790 required that an immigrant be white in order to naturalize as a US citizen. This conferred advantage to those immigrants seen as white for more than 150 years. The law of 1790 is one among thousands that constructed a prevailing culture of preference for white people. Out of this culture, multiple dimensions of whiteness took shape by virtue of other statuses, such as gender, class, ethnicity, religion, and region. While greater or lesser access to the privileges of whiteness were mediated by these other statuses, the expectation that white people will be positioned above persons of Latinx, African, Indigenous, Asian, or Pacific Island descent cuts across them all. Given our foundation of whiteness as a matter of law and all that has flowed from that foundation, individualism in the context of race is meaningless.

A critical point Hannah-Jones makes through the 1619 Project is that not only have we never aligned the ideals of a country founded on

Thomas Jefferson's statement that "all men are created equal" with its practices, but any degree of alignment achieved thus far has been from the efforts of African Americans. When Jefferson wrote those powerful words, he owned 130 enslaved human beings. He knew that his words did not apply to one-fifth of the population and perhaps never would (they also did not apply to women). But African Americans heard those words and were determined to make them true. While all colonial powers, such as those of Spain, Portugal, France, and England, need to come to terms with the legacy of slavery, and like the US have yet to do so, the US was the only colonial power founded on the claim of human equality.

The legal exclusion of Black people, in addition to illegal acts of terrorism against them such as lynching, continued all the way through to the 1960s. Black people were denied the Federal Housing Authority (FHA) housing loans in the 1950s that allowed a generation of white people to attain middle-class status through home ownership. Home ownership is critical in the US because it is how the average person builds and passes down wealth, providing the starting point for the next generation. In her acclaimed book *Race for Profit*, professor of African American studies Keeanga-Yamahtta Taylor argues that the transition in the 1960s and '70s from the exclusionary policies of the FHA to inclusionary policies, via the Housing and Urban Development (HUD) Act of 1968, tied HUD and the FHA to real estate brokers, mortgage bankers, and home builders. Taylor explains how, even early in the program, unscrupulous mortgage banks dominated the market. With the federal government guaranteeing loans, these banks sold as many homes as possible to African Americans in poor communities—"the riskier the buyer, the better," because the bank got paid even if borrowers defaulted.[9]

With mortgage banks largely unregulated and incentivized to sell, homes that should have been condemned were pushed on African American buyers. Where redlining and racial profiling had blocked Black Americans from the home ownership that created a booming middle class for white people after World War II, it now made Black Americans targets for exploitative practices within the housing market. Taylor terms these practices "predatory inclusion" and documents how they destroyed whole communities. She argues that there is no affordable housing crisis for Black Americans; the housing market functions as it was always designed to. "Black people had to pay higher interest rates, they had to pay more fees, they were relegated to isolated and neglected housing. Black people's housing wasn't even an asset—it was a debt burden. It will never accrue at the same rate as it has for white people."[10]

The ideology of individualism is dependent on a denial of the past as relevant to the present, allowing us to ignore the results of centuries of systemic racial discrimination. Mainstream accounts of US history can incorporate tales of African American suffering and discrimination, as long as the agents and beneficiaries of that suffering are rendered invisible or reduced to a few "bad apples." This denial is further solidified by relegating the bulk of inequality to the distant past and not tracing the consequences of that past into the present.

Limiting our analysis to the micro or individual level prevents a macro or "big picture" assessment. Individualism keeps our focus on isolated exceptions to the rules and allows us to deny the significance of the rules themselves, who makes the rules, and whom the rules serve. Consider, for example, the ways in which schools are funded through the property-tax base of the surrounding community. Given the reality that, due to systemic and historical racism, youth of color disproportionately live in poor communities and their families rent rather than own, youth of color are penalized by this policy, which ensures that poor communities will have inferior schools. In turn, this practice ensures that middle- and upper-class students, who are more likely to be white, will get a superior education and have less competition in the future workplace. This is a cogent example of both institutional racism and its result: individual white advantage.

Hannah-Jones, in speaking specifically about educational inequality and de facto school segregation, notes, "There's never been a moment in the history of this country where Black people who have been isolated from white people have gotten the same resources. They often don't have the same level of instruction. They often don't have strong principals. They often don't have the same technology."[11] Just as Taylor makes the case that the housing market is designed to exclude African

Americans, Hannah-Jones argues that the educational system was designed to ensure unequal outcomes. While individual actors such as parents, teachers, and school administrators may all claim to be personally against educational inequality, they are still participating in this system. Yet individualism also allows white people to exempt ourselves personally from race-based advantage. In other words, as a white person, if I personally don't agree with receiving advantages, individualism allows me to deny that I receive them, as if a desire that resides in my head can somehow ward off the benefits society automatically grants me.

INDIVIDUALISM LEADS TO UNIVERSALISM

White people are taught to see our perspectives as objective and representative of a shared reality. The belief in objectivity, coupled with positioning white people as outside of race—and thus the norm for humanity—allows us to view ourselves as universal humans who can represent all of human experience. This ideology is termed *universalism*, which functions similarly to individualism but instead of declaring that we all need to see each other as individuals (e.g., "Everyone is different"), we declare that we all need to see each other as human beings (e.g., "Everyone is the same"). The email that opens this chapter manages to invoke both of these narratives in a few short sentences. The writer protests my generalizations, while invoking the color-blind ideology falsely attributed to Martin Luther King Jr. Of course, we are all humans in the same way that we are each unique—I am not critiquing either narrative in general—but when applied to racism, universalism has similar effects as individualism; once again, the significance of race and the advantages of being white are denied. Further, universalism assumes that white people and racialized people have the same reality, the same experiences in the same context (e.g., "I feel comfortable in this majority-white meeting, so you must too"; "Everyone here is so nice to me, so I am sure they are nice to you too"), the same responses from others, and, like individualism, assumes that the same doors are open to all.

White feminism is a relevant example of how individualism can slip into universalism. White feminism refers to the assumption that a subset of white women stand in for all women and can speak for all women, when they actually only speak for their subset of middle-class, white, cisgender women. Therefore, white feminism focuses on issues that exclude women of color and does not recognize, acknowledge, or address the different realities and concerns of women of color. White women who enact white feminism want gender inequality acknowledged and addressed, and in this way differentiate their experience from the experience of men. At the same time, they use the category "women" as if there is one shared collective experience of womanhood, while using their own as a reference point.

A cogent example of universalizing womanhood occurred when I was leading an affinity group for white women. They were asked to brainstorm a list of white advantages. As one group finished sharing their list, which included advantages such as representation in media, not being followed in stores, and being more likely to get loans, they apparently felt the need to put a positive spin on things and added, "But motherhood is universal to all women, regardless of race." I was so taken aback that it took me a moment to collect myself enough to reply, "Motherhood is perhaps one of the *starkest* examples of the differences between white women and Black women—from infant and maternal mortality rates, to empirical evidence of racism in healthcare and education, to having to send your children to schools filled with teachers who fear them and textbooks that ignore them, to terror for your children's lives anytime they interact with the police, to name just a few differences." These women were progressive feminists, attending an equity conference and participating in a white women's affinity group. Yet they left at the break and sent a messenger to let me know they were leaving because they were offended by my response.

WHY COULDN'T SUE AND BOB HEAR ME?

Many white people, such as Sue and Bob, depend on the narrative of individualism to maintain racial equilibrium by positioning themselves outside hierarchical social relations. At stake are very real resources that have concrete effects on people's lives. Also at stake is our very identity—a sense of ourselves as fair, open-minded, and hardworking. Thus white progressives who claim to oppose racism, as Sue and Bob do, must deny the existence of the system that benefits them. Individualism is a very effective form of denial. If we insist that group membership is insignificant, social inequity and its consequences become personally irrelevant. So too does any imperative to change inequity. Insisting that each white person is different from every other white person ("do you have to keep saying 'white'?") enables us to distance ourselves from the actions of other white people. Since we aren't responsible for the actions of other white people, we aren't responsible for challenging their racism. This leaves racialized people to deal with the issue. Yet racialized people are often dismissed in a range of ways: accused of playing the race card, of having a chip on their shoulder, of seeing race in everything, and of being oversensitive or angry. When white people break with racial solidarity and speak up to challenge racism, it is also difficult for us and rife with social risks, yet white people are still seen as more credible, more objective, and the resistance is less painful for us because speaking up doesn't bring up a lifetime of racial invalidation. This gives us a particular entry point in challenging our fellow white people, and we should use that entry point to do so.

There is a final dynamic of whiteness evident in the interaction I had with Sue and Bob I want to raise: the lack of humility in providing me with "the answer" to racism. Because most white people have not been educated to think with complexity about racism, and because it benefits us *not* to do so, we have a very limited understanding of it. We are the least likely to see, comprehend, or be invested in validating racialized people's assertions and being honest about their consequences. And yet, because of white social, economic, and political power within a white-dominant culture, white people are the group in the position to legitimize those assertions (as the majority of teachers, lawyers, judges, policymakers, managers, CEOs, and cultural "authors" via movies and other media). Being in this position engenders a form of racial arrogance, and in this racial arrogance, we have little compunction about debating the knowledge of people who have thought deeply about race, including through lived experience, deep and ongoing critical self-reflection, research, education, risk-taking, and so on. This expertise is often trivialized and countered with simplistic platitudes such as "People should just 'see each other as individuals' or '. . . see each other as humans' or '. . . take personal responsibility.'"

White people's overall lack of racial humility often leads to declarations of disagreement when, in fact, the problem is that we don't *understand*. Yet we feel free to dismiss informed perspectives rather than have the humility to acknowledge that they are unfamiliar, reflect on them further, seek more information, or sustain a dialogue. In other words, *grapple with*—rather than reject out of hand—these challenging perspectives. My co-facilitator and I did not claim that we were the sole authorities on racism in Sue and Bob's workshop, and we did not ask for blind allegiance from participants. But we did ask participants to be willing to engage with the concepts we presented, rather than strive to maintain the perspectives they already held. We also brought years of education and experience on the dynamics of race to the table; Sue and Bob did not.

I offer a bold question to Sue, Bob, and other white people who are so sure their opinions on racism are as informed and complete as they need to be: What informs your disagreement? Having an opinion does not make it informed. While certainly there are people qualified to disagree with our analysis, Sue and Bob were not among them. As Neil deGrasse Tyson tweeted, "A great challenge of life: Knowing enough to think you are right, but not knowing enough to know you are wrong."[12] I repeat: Sue and Bob had no requirement to ultimately accept our analysis or share our beliefs and values, but they were expected to openly and thoughtfully explore them. One of the most transformative qualities we can strive to develop as white people grappling with racism and our role in it is humility about the necessary limits of our understanding.

APPLY THE RULE TO THE EXCEPTION

If we use the line of reasoning that we are all individuals and that social categories such as race, class, and gender don't matter and are just labels that stereotype and limit us (pejoratively dismissed as "identity politics"), then it follows that we all end up in our own "natural" places. Those at the top are merely a collection of individuals who rose on their own individual merits, and those at the bottom are there due to individual deficiencies. Group membership is thereby rendered inoperative, and racial disparities are seen as the result of essential character attributes rather than the result of consistent structural barriers. Via individualism, it is either "just a fluke" that those at the top are a very homogenous collection of individuals, or else white, middle- and upper-class cis men and sometimes cis women are better at everything. White advantage is not a factor because we don't see color anyway—we see each person as a unique individual, and we treat them as such. Thus individualism not only upholds the myth of meritocracy (success is the result of ability and hard work) but also upholds social Darwinism (survival of the fittest) and belief in the overall superiority of those at the top. Again, the ideology of individualism is foundational to white supremacy.

Ibram X. Kendi notes that because the ideology of individualism is only granted to white people, it allows us to see negative behavior by any Black person as proof of what is wrong with Black *people*, while negative behavior by any white person only proves what is wrong with that individual person.[13] This is why generalizing about white people in the context of challenging racism is different from generalizing about Black people. Granting Black people individuality interrupts a racist dynamic within a culture that has denied their individuality. Conversely, suspending individuality for white people is a necessary interruption to our denial of collective advantage.

Let me be clear. I understand that each person is unique and has a story that I do not know if they haven't shared it with me. I cannot know what each person thinks or feels, or what is "in their heart." At the same time, we are members of racial groups that profoundly shape the trajectory of our lives. We are all swimming in the same cultural water, receiving the same cultural messages, interacting with the same institutions and laws, seeing the same advertising and media representations, and so on. We have to be willing to grapple with that collective experience. Of course we respond differently to the collective process, but we are still responding. One may insist that race has absolutely no meaning to them, but it certainly has meaning to the society in which we live. Their race will either be assumed and responded to accordingly, or if ambiguous enough, they will constantly be asked to explain themselves.

There is nothing I have heard to this point in my work that has convinced me that someone can exist outside the social forces of race and be untouched by the racist conditioning, practices, and outcomes infused in the society in which they live. How we respond to that conditioning varies based on many factors, but none of those factors provides immunity. I am asking those of us who are white to grapple with that reality, rather than deny it based on simplistic and unexamined ideas about what racism means. A simple question can be applied to any exception white people offer up as evidence that they are free from racial conditioning: How does being white shape how you experience that exception?

I have found that if there is any way out of owning our inevitable participation in systemic racism, white people will take that way out. So while I acknowledge there may be exceptions to the rule, I ask white readers to practice grappling with the rule: the shared experience of being white. There are consistent, observable patterns that apply to all of us, and we need to be willing to look at these patterns. We receive plenty of reinforcement on what makes us special. We have likely offered up our exceptions countless times when the conversation is on race. Let's try stretching in a new direction. One day, we may treat every person as a unique individual, but it is precisely because that day is *not* here that the insistence on individualism is so pernicious.

CHAPTER 3

THERE IS NO CHOIR

*Being with white progressives is like being a driving
instructor and having someone who does not know how to
drive but thinks that they do get in the car with you. They're
at the wheel, but because of how they see themselves, they
can't hear you, and if they do hear you, they're not really
listening. And that makes them dangerous.*

—Anika Nailah[1]

On a weekly basis, I speak to groups of mostly white people and give
a presentation on whiteness and white fragility. Quite often I am told
beforehand by the white organizers that I am "preaching to the choir."
In other words, trying to persuade people who already know and agree
with the message I am delivering. In this case, the choir in agreement
with my message would presumably be white people who understand
systemic racism, see their role within it, and are actively engaging in
anti-racist practice. And right there I know there is no way I can be
standing in front of the choir. In fact, I do not believe that there is a
white "choir," raising their voices in anti-racist harmony. The very idea
that there *could be* is problematic. As soon as I see myself as a member
of that choir, I am going to be unconcerned about my own complicity, as so many white progressives are. Members of the so-called choir
can and do perpetuate racial harm and are rarely involved in ongoing
self-examination or anti-racist practice. In fact, while the white organizers are telling me I am preaching to the choir, the BIPOC people behind

the scenes are usually pulling me aside to tell me how toxic the culture is for them. Even if the organizers mean that the audience is open to the challenge, I still have not found that to be true. What I *have* found is that time and time again, most often those who consider themselves the choir are receptive to critique only as long as their *own* patterns of racism are not highlighted.

Most members of the "choir" do not have the ability to articulate an anti-racist framework, are all too often silent in the face of explicit racism, and fall apart when directly challenged. Voluntarily or even enthusiastically participating in an anti-racism seminar doesn't mean that one acts in allyship in daily life.

The idea that there is a choir of enlightened, racially aware white people rests on the idea that racism is a simple formula: conscious prejudice + intentional meanness = racism, or *individual malicious intent across race*. A racist, according to this criterion, is a person who doesn't like people based on their race, knows this, and intentionally seeks to harm them. This definition beautifully protects systemic racism by exempting virtually all white people. The vast majority of racist acts perpetuated daily by white progressives are neither conscious nor intentional. Even if these acts were, it is very difficult to prove intent and a rare person who would admit that their motives were less than pure.

The workplace is particularly rife with unconscious racism. These acts include the following:

- Talking over and silencing BIPOC people in meetings
- Ignoring or taking credit for their ideas
- Leaving BIPOC people out of information loops
- Assuming BIPOC people are inherently unqualified "diversity hires" (and all the ways that assumption and resultant resentment is implicitly expressed)
- White solidarity in the face of racism
- Relentless pressure on Black people to keep white people comfortable, including pressure to modify their hairstyles or speech patterns
- Inequities in promotions

- Assigning Black people to train white people who are then promoted above them
- Double standards in what emotions can be expressed and by whom
- White women weaponizing their emotions so that any feelings of racial discomfort around a colleague of color become an HR issue for that colleague
- Over-scrutinization
- Gaslighting
- Off-loading all diversity work to BIPOC people
- Punishing BIPOC people who challenge racism

A reader related a workplace experience that could easily be a composite of many others that have been shared with me. She is a Black woman with both expertise and seniority in her field. I will refer to her as Kendra. A white woman was hired to assist her. They disagreed on a key project decision, and the white director went with the white assistant's advice. It turned out to be the wrong choice—as Kendra had warned it would be. She wrote to me, "The entire situation made me feel devalued because this was the one topic that was my area of expertise." When Kendra shared with her boss the racial impact, she was let go, even though there were no issues with her job performance. "The job I've loved so much is coming to an end because I made one white person uncomfortable," she told me. We can assume the white assistant now holds Kendra's former position. As is usual, we claim to value diversity as long as problematic racial dynamics are not named or challenged.

By every measure across virtually every institution in every society where white people dominate, racial inequality persists. For example, a 2019 psychological study showed not only the vast difference in wealth between white Americans and Black Americans but also how skewed white Americans' perceptions were of that gap. Researchers asked participants to imagine that the average white family in the United States has a hundred dollars.[2] When asked what a comparable Black family has, most Americans guess eighty dollars. The answer is less than ten dollars. Drawing on a nationally representative sample of 1,800 adults, researchers found persuasive evidence that white Americans vastly underestimate economic inequality, especially the racial wealth gap. In particular, respondents thought that the Black-white wealth gap was smaller, by around 80 percentage points in 2016, than its actual size. Most white people, including those in the so-called choir, have no idea how racially unequal society is.

As white people, we are socialized into a white supremacist society in which racial inequality is the bedrock. Most of us grow up in racial segregation and continue to live segregated lives into and throughout adulthood. Just following the life trajectories laid out before us—especially if we grow up in what are considered "good" neighborhoods and attend "good" schools—will virtually guarantee that our lives remain segregated. In myriad ways, we are conditioned to not have authentic cross-racial relationships, to not be particularly interested in having them, and certainly not if building these relationships requires us to go outside of our comfort zones. A Black woman recently shared with me that a white woman living in the wealthy white area of the San Francisco Bay Area told her, "I'd like to have relationships with Black people, but who has the time?"

Even as most white people live our lives in segregation, we remain confident that we hold no racial bias. Yet how would we know? As demonstrated in the study on perceptions of the wealth gap, most of us have *no idea* what Black people's realities are. We have no accountability to Black people, and our self-images are rarely tested. We can position ourselves as the choir because we don't have relationships with people who can or will challenge our self-perception. The ability to be nice to Black people when we do encounter them does not interrupt the lived segregation of our daily lives and the false consciousness that segregation engenders. Nor does niceness provide cover for the inevitably problematic ways we will engage across race, given our limited experience and unchecked biases.

Let's use a checklist adapted from a handout created by professor of education John Raible to measure how likely it is that the white people I stand in front of every day are in fact the choir and can claim most of these skills:

- I demonstrate knowledge and awareness of racism.
- I continually educate myself about racism and the perspectives of BIPOC people.
- I hold awareness of my whiteness in all settings and that awareness guides how I engage.
- I am involved in anti-racist projects and programs.
- I raise issues about racism over and over, both in public and in private.
- I make sure anti-racism is part of the discussion in meetings and project planning.
- I avoid personalizing racial issues as they are raised in conversation.
- I can identify many aspects of racism as they are happening.
- I attend to group dynamics to ensure the inclusion of BIPOC people.
- I support and validate the contributions of BIPOC people.
- I have personal relationships and know the private lives of a range of BIPOC people, including Black people.
- I use my position as a white "insider" to share information with BIPOC people.
- I have developed the skills to strategically intervene in racist dynamics.
- I have demonstrated that I can accept leadership from BIPOC people.
- I debrief with BIPOC people to give and get "reality checks" and affirmations after meetings and interactions.
- I accept—with no explanations or "proof" necessary—a person of color's experience.
- I can be present emotionally when individuals need to express feelings about racism.
- I have demonstrated that I am trustworthy and BIPOC people consistently confide in me and also challenge me on my racist conditioning.
- I have demonstrated that I am open to feedback on my own unaware racist patterns.

- I have the skills to repair racism when I realize I have perpetrated it.
- I recognize my own limitations in doing anti-racist work and
  have set up ways to be accountable to BIPOC people.[3]

When we look at actual risk-taking, skill development, relationship building, and strategic anti-racist practice, it becomes clear that the qualification most often used to establish membership in the choir is simply being nice.

For any white readers thinking that the results of living a segregated life don't apply to you because you do, in fact, have relationships across race—congratulations; you are indeed an exception. One of the most important ways that I have worked to challenge my racial socialization has been to build authentic cross-racial relationships. Yet I still perpetrate harm on occasion in those relationships as a result of the unavoidable reality that I was raised in a white supremacist culture. Of course, I have absorbed the messages of that culture and developed patterns of interacting in the world that are informed by racism. As Ibram X. Kendi notes, I may not be a producer of racist ideas, but I have been a consumer.[4] This changes the question from "Have I been impacted by the racist ideology circulating in the culture?" (a question most white people answer with a reflexive "No!" thereby requiring no further action) to "*How* have I been impacted by the racist ideology circulating in the culture?" And "*How* does this show up in my relationships and interactions?"

We simply cannot move forward in addressing racial inequality if we don't move beyond the idea that racism only operates at the individual, conscious, and intentional level; we must understand racism as a system. Psychologist Beverly Daniel Tatum succinctly defines racism as "a system of advantage based on race."[5] This system encompasses economic, political, social, and cultural structures, and actions and beliefs that institutionalize and perpetuate an unequal distribution of resources between white people and Black, Indigenous, and people of color. In my work, I describe racism as collective racial bias backed by legal authority and institutional control. Only white people's collective bias is backed with this level of power, so I do not use "racism" to describe the bias of BIPOC people. Of course BIPOC people have racial bias, but it is not backed in a way that embeds it into the entire fabric of the society and all of its institutions. I simply refer to their bias as "bias." Systemic racism consistently works to the benefit of white people *overall* and to the disadvantage of BIPOC people *overall*, which is why I reserve language to capture its directional nature. For white readers who feel unsettled by the idea that BIPOC people are not "just as racist as we are," I ask you to reflect on why that is such a sticking point for you. What do you think you lose by acknowledging that the impact of bias is profoundly different based on the institutional weight behind it?

Systemic racism operates 24-7 and 365, and is not interrupted by an individual's self-image, good intentions, or niceness. There are, of course, exceptions to every rule. Ibram X. Kendi notes that Black people can and do have some institutional power and can wield that power to support or challenge racism.[6] However, that institutional power is limited given the foundations of the institutions in which they act. They did not set these institutions up, and their inclusion is conditional. To put it more directly, it has been up to white people all along whether Black people could be included and under what conditions. Any progress made has come from centuries of organizing by Black people and despite violent resistance.

For white readers who will raise the tired objection that the dictionary doesn't define racism as a system, the Merriam-Webster dictionary states (emphasis is mine):

1 : a belief that race is the primary determinant of human traits and capacities and that racial differences produce an inherent superiority of a particular race

2a : *a doctrine or political program based on the assumption of racism and designed to execute its principles*

b : *a political or social system founded on racism*

In fact, 2a and b do define racism as a system. Still, Merriam-Webster includes a usage note stating that dictionaries do not provide the be-all-end-all definition of words: "Dictionaries are often treated as the final arbiter in arguments over a word's meaning, but they are not always well suited for settling disputes. The lexicographer's role is to explain how words are (or have been) actually used . . . and they say nothing about the intrinsic nature of the thing named by a word."[7] Given the simplicity of the dictionary definition in relation to how complex and nuanced racism is, writer Annie Reneau chides, "Honestly, as soon as someone refers to the dictionary when discussing racism, it's clear that person has never delved deeply into trying to understand racism. It's a big old red flag, every time."[8] She goes on to explain, "Whenever someone's words or behavior are called out as racist, a few predictable responses always follow. One is to see the word 'racist' as a vicious personal attack. Two is to vehemently deny that whatever was said or done was racist. And three is to pull out the dictionary definition of racism to prove that the words or behavior weren't racist." In other words, white fragility ensues.

Professor Peter Wade, a sociologist from the University of Manchester, in explaining how much more complex and insidious racism is than traditional dictionary definitions allow, says, "Racism is an ideology and a practice that produces a society in which some people systematically have less access to resources, power, security, and well-being than others. These systemic inequalities reflect hierarchical differences between people originally created by colonialism, which produced patterns of historical inequality that make it difficult for certain people to access opportunities and resources."[9] If we limit racism's scope to individual acts, then we are actively ignoring the insidious ways it operates. We also open the door for each of us to take an exemption.

Explicit forms of racism are not typically perpetrated by white progressives (although when cornered white progressives can and do erupt in straight-up racism, we don't generally do so casually). Our racism avoids the blatant and obvious, such as saying the N-word or telling people to go back to where they came from. We employ more subtle methods: racial insensitivity, ignorance, and arrogance. These have a racist *impact* and contribute to an overall racist experience for BIPOC people, an experience that may be all the more maddening precisely because it is easy to deny and hard to prove. I am constantly asked for examples, so here are a few:

- Confusing one person for another of the same racial group
- Not taking the effort to learn someone's name; always mispronouncing it, calling them something that's easier to pronounce; making a show of saying it, or avoiding the person altogether
- Repeating/rewording/explaining what a BIPOC person just said
- Touching, commenting on, marveling at, and asking questions about a Black person's hair
- Expecting BIPOC people to be interested in and skilled at doing any work related to race
- Using one BIPOC person who didn't mind what you did to invalidate another who did
- Calling a Black person articulate; expressing surprise at their intelligence, credentials, or class status
- Speaking over/interrupting a BIPOC person
- Lecturing BIPOC people on the answer to racism ("People just need to . . .")
- Bringing up an unrelated racial topic while talking to a BIPOC person (and only when talking to a BIPOC person)
- Blackface/cultural appropriation in costumes or roles
- Denying/being defensive/explaining away/seeking absolution when confronted with having enacted racism
- Only naming the race of people who are not white when telling a story
- Slipping into a southern accent or other caricature when talking to or about Black people
- Asking for more evidence or offering an alternate explanation when a BIPOC person shares their lived experience of racism
- Making a point of letting people know that you are married to a BIPOC person or have BIPOC people in your family
- Not being aware that the evidence you use to establish that you are "not racist" is not convincing

- Equating an oppression that you experience with racism
- Changing the channel to another form of oppression whenever race comes up
- Insisting that your equity team address every other possible form of oppression, resulting in racism not getting addressed in depth or at all ("It's really about class")
- Including every possible form of difference in your diversity work—such as personality styles and Myers-Briggs scores—so that everyone in your majority-white organization feels included
- Gossiping about the racism of other white people to BIPOC people to distinguish yourself as the good white person
- Using an experience as the only white person in a group or community to say that you've experienced racism (which you call reverse racism)
- Telling a BIPOC person that you witnessed the racism perpetrated toward them but doing nothing further
- Equating your experience as a white immigrant or the child of white immigrants to the experiences of African Americans ("The Irish were discriminated against just as bad")
- Using your experience with service learning or missionary work in BIPOC communities to present yourself as an expert on how to address the issues experienced by those communities
- Loving and recommending films about racism that feature white saviors
- Deciding for yourself how to support a BIPOC person without asking them what they want or need
- Claiming to have a friendship with a Black colleague who has never been to your home
- Being involved in your workplace equity team without continually working on your own racism
- Attending your first talk or workshop on racism and complaining that the speaker did not provide you with the "answer"
- Asking how to start a diversity consulting business because you attended a talk and found it interesting

- Focusing your diversity work on "increasing your numbers" with no structural changes and equating increased numbers with racial justice
- Blocking racial justice efforts by continually raising a concern that your organization is "not ready" and needs to "go slow" to protect white people's delicate racial sensibilities
- Not understanding why something on this list is problematic, and rather than seeking to educate yourself further, dismiss it as invalid

These behaviors demonstrate white entitlement, ignorance, arrogance, and protectionism. The intentions are irrelevant to the impact, which include minimizing, silencing, dominating, invalidating, excluding, isolating, denigrating, interrogating, objectifying, exoticizing, diminishing, controlling, and undermining. As long as we only focus on the obvious extremes, we will protect the ordinary everyday versions that *we* perpetuate and that make racialized people's daily lives so often exhausting.

Consider a study of racial activist burnout, in which educational researchers Paul Gorski and Noura Erakat noticed a pattern.[10] While both white activists and activists of color experienced burnout, the reasons varied. Of particular relevance, these researchers found that 82 percent of the activists of color they interviewed identified *white racial justice activists* as a major source of their burnout. The activists of color "attributed their burnout to the attitudes and behaviors—the *racism*—of white activists" (italics in original). Yes, even white people involved in racial justice activism—the far end of the progressive spectrum—perpetrate racism. The white racist attitudes and behaviors the study identified included (1) harboring unevolved or racist views, (2) undermining or invalidating the racial justice work of activists of color, (3) being unwilling to step up and take action when needed, (4) exhibiting white fragility, and (5) taking credit for participants' racial justice work and ideas.

Activists of color were forced to expend extra energy teaching these white "allies" about racism. They had to endure pushback from white activists who refused to engage in self-examination, viewing themselves as more racially conscious than they actually were. As one study participant stated, "I got burned from so-called white liberal progressive allies who were on board until it meant that they needed to do self-reflection, until it meant that they needed to learn about themselves and this wasn't about learning about . . . the poor black kid from the Bronx . . ." Another participant made the point that "a lot of white folks want to benefit from [identifying with racial justice]. . . . But they don't want to call [racism] out because they don't want to hurt anyone's feelings. They don't want to press it. It's like, well what about those people who deal with it? I have to deal with it. . . . That's been a huge source of stress and burnout."

Participants also attributed their burnout to white activists asking them to temper their emotions. Responding with strong emotions to injustice is, of course, rational. But the passive-aggressive, conflict-avoiding culture of niceness, along with the ever-looming threat of triggering white fragility, puts enormous pressure on activists of color not to show emotions that make white people uncomfortable. One participant described how, despite pressure from white activists he worked with, he could not temper his emotional response to injustice: "This [victim of racism] could have been me; this could have been my kid." This participant explained how exhausting it was when "well-intentioned, progressive [white] people who think they are lovers of justice" consistently policed his emotional responses to racism. Many activists of color felt that the racism coming from white activists compounded and made more painful, frustrating, and debilitating the racism of white people not necessarily identified as "allies." I repeat, there is no choir.

The sad irony is that the moment we believe we "get it" is not the moment our journey to racial enlightenment comes to an end. "Getting it" should immediately engender humility in recognition of how much we don't—and likely never will—completely know. Deepening our understanding, building our skills, and demonstrating anti-racist practice are ongoing. Awareness should add new dimensions to the continuing journey: humility and accountability. Awareness that does not lead to sustained engagement is not meaningful.

CHAPTER 4

WHAT'S WRONG WITH NICENESS?

The will to be polite, to maintain civility and normalcy, is fearfully strong. I wonder sometimes how much evil is permitted to run unchecked simply because it would be rude to interrupt it.

—Alix E. Harrow, *The Ten Thousand Doors of January*[1]

While the thin veneer of a "post-racial" society during the Obama years has been ripped away in the years of the Trump administration, most white people continue to conceptualize racism as isolated deeds of open cruelty. If racists are intentionally and openly cruel, then it follows that nice people cannot be racist. How often have we heard a white person respond to a charge of racism by gathering friends and colleagues to testify that their friend cannot be racist because "he's a really nice guy" or "she volunteers on the board of a nonprofit serving underprivileged youth" or "they adopted Black children." Characteristics of a culture of niceness include white solidarity, avoiding causing or experiencing social discomfort, focusing on connections and commonalities, privileging concern for the feelings of perpetrators of racism over the victims, helping others to maintain face, and elevating intentions over impact. Intentions are particularly important in a culture of niceness.

Niceness requires that racism only be acknowledged in acts that *intentionally* hurt or discriminate, which means that racism can rarely be acknowledged. Being nice also allows for absolution: if they didn't intend to perpetuate racism, the act cannot and should not count. For example, in response to some of his elementary school staff dressing up like stereotypical Mexicans and other staff dressing as a border wall with "Make America Great Again" written on it, Middleton, Idaho, school superintendent Josh Middleton acknowledged "poor judgement" but insisted there was no "malicious intent."[2] In response, writer Kaitlyn Greenidge tweeted, "Sometimes I think white people use the 'I didn't intend to be racist' to really mean 'I was hoping my racism would have no consequences.'"[3]

This conception of racism and good intentions as mutually exclusive makes it essential that white people quickly and eagerly telegraph their niceness to racialized people. Niceness in this case is conveyed through a light tone of voice, eye contact accompanied by smiling, and conjuring affinity such as a shared enjoyment of a music genre, compliments on hair or style, having travelled to the country the "other" is perceived to have come from, and knowing people from the other's group. Smiling as we encounter racialized people also provides the bonus capital of feeling benevolent. (However, it should be noted that if they are Black and somewhere they aren't expected to be, such as a park, coffee shop, dorm lounge, pool, or neighborhood deemed white, we forgo the thin veneer of niceness and allow the barely suppressed assumption of criminality to guide us.)

To be clear, I am distinguishing niceness from kindness. Kindness is compassionate and includes behaviors that are supportive. Kindness is driven by values that the person demonstrates in action, even—and perhaps especially—when those actions are inconvenient. For example, I am having car trouble and you stop and see if you can help. I appear upset after a work meeting and you check in and listen, asking how you can support me. Kindness, because it is active, can be one aspect of white allyship. Niceness, by contrast, is fleeting, hollow, performative, and requires no further action. Niceness is not the same as authenticity. In fact, niceness often functions as cover for a *lack* of authenticity.

Niceness can protect racism in several ways. First, it is difficult to get under the surface in a culture of niceness. To challenge and break through the facade requires conflict, and conflict is forbidden in a culture of niceness. How can we raise an uncomfortable and often contentious issue such as racism when niceness has been established as the

procedural norm? In this way the unspoken social agreement of niceness creates a kind of protective force field around racial dynamics. If
that force field is broken, white solidarity will rally to protect the status
quo. If it is a white person who creates the breach, they become the
outsider—deemed too shrill or combative. If a person of color dares to
speak out, their outsider status is reinforced, along with the narrative
that they are angry, aggressive, and threatening.

Second, the continual pull toward niceness makes it difficult to
address the strong emotions anti-racist work often brings up, such as
grief, pain, and anger. Left unaddressed, these emotions prevent us from
moving forward. I recently co-led a three-day workshop for a group
of wealthy white women. They were so nice! There was lots of head
nodding, smiling, politeness, and respectful listening. The women were
not debating or appearing to resist the content. Yet niceness in this context actually functioned as a passive-aggressive way to conceal difficult
feelings such as anger or numbness. All of this niceness may have been
more comfortable for the participants, but it also prevented them from
an honest accounting and exploration of racism, which was ostensibly
what they had signed up for. By the end of the second day, those tensions
finally erupted, allowing us to get real and address what the group was
holding. Several women were upset that they had not been called on
when they raised their hands and felt silenced. Another was angry that
we did not validate her claim that she grew up in Canada and so was
different from the rest of the group. And while the resentment brewing
under the facade of niceness was not openly expressed until the second
day (and regardless of how petty the basis of that withholding was), it
was still present and impacting their ability to take in and engage with
the content. In this way, niceness functioned as a shield, protecting the
group from the honesty and vulnerability needed for growth and change.

Writer and anti-racism educator Debby Irving, in her poignant mem-
oir *Waking Up White*, describes the cost of her socialization into upper-
class culture:

> Like so many of the behaviors I adopted in childhood, silence and avoid-
> ance became subconscious habits. My parents didn't silence me because

they didn't care about my ideas. They silenced me because their own childhood socializations ingrained in them a subconscious habit of steering away from conflict and authenticity and toward the more socially acceptable culture of niceness. They were passing on to me a survival skill, one that bought a place in the high-class world of comfort and gentility, even if this meant diminishing one's capacity to plug into the circuitry of feelings, cutting oneself off from one's own heart and soul.[4]

In strategizing on how to break the facade of niceness with a group of owning-class white women, we asked ourselves what that room might have felt like for a Black woman. I imagine that for her, that room would not have been experienced as a safe space; inauthenticity does not feel supportive. In addition to enduring the inauthenticity, certainly any challenge she raised or strong emotion she expressed risked her being labeled as angry and blamed for a threatening breach of the social contract. Irving speaks to this risk when she asks, "Whom exactly does the culture of niceness serve? I suppose it serves the people for whom life is going well, the people in power. But where does this leave less empowered individuals and populations with legitimate complaints? Speaking truth to power too often results in feelings of judgment and anger at the complainer."[5]

In the same way that silence from a position of power is a power move, niceness from a position of power can also be a power move. Both leave the marginalized to wonder what is really going on. What is this white person thinking? What are they feeling? What are they going to do as soon as they leave this situation? Racialized people are well aware the visible reality is not the only one operating. Given the history of harm, the safe assumption is that nice white people are not going to step up and offer support. Both silence and niceness (and they are often one and the same) protect the racist status quo. It is a tragic irony that the very behaviors so many white people cite as evidence that we couldn't possibly be racist convey the exact opposite to Black people. We might ask ourselves why we think the best response to racial inequality is niceness.

I have heard Black people talk about the awkwardness of white people "over-smiling." A friend described going to Whole Foods and feeling exhausted by the pressure to validate all of the over-solicitous white people making a point of smiling at her when she just wanted to get her errands done and get home. She understood that the act was meant to convey acceptance and approval, but what it actually conveyed to her was a way for white people to maintain moral integrity in the face of racial anxiety. Over-smiling allows white people to mask an anti-Blackness that is foundational to our very existence as white. Our fleeting benevolence has no relation to how Black people are actually undermined in white spaces. Some Black friends have told me that they prefer open hostility to niceness. They understand open hostility and can protect themselves as needed. But the deception of niceness adds a confusing layer that makes it difficult to decipher trustworthy allyship from disingenuous white liberalism. Niceness masks controversy and suppresses difference. Gaslighting ensues.

Professor of educational leadership Angelina Castagno, in *The Price of Nice: How Good Intentions Maintain Educational Inequity*, writes that niceness functions not only to protect white educators from having to do the hard work of challenging educational inequity but also as a "disciplining agent" for those who attempt or even consider engaging in that challenge. Niceness is assumed to be a basic trait that is universally applauded. Castagno notes that it is precisely this commonsense status that allows it to go uninterrogated.[6]

I asked social justice consultant and author Anika Nailah, a Black and Indigenous woman who identifies as a "woman of the Global Majority," about her thoughts on white niceness. She brought Castagno's observations to life in her reply, explaining that "white nice" functions as a kind of shield against being touched or moved in the face of racism, a shield that actually made it more dangerous for her, "especially if you have direct power over any aspect of my life."[7] Anika shared her lived experience and broke down the impact of white niceness from two directions: when it is expected *of* her and when it comes *at* her. She shared the following lists with me.

When you want *me* to be "nice" as a Black person, you mean:

- Don't talk about race
- Don't cause conflict
- Don't say anything that might upset me or other white people I care about
- Don't be direct
- Don't tell me what you really think
- Tell me I'm a good person
- Smile, be friendly
- Don't cause me to feel anything
- Don't pressure me to take action or own something I did
- Don't defend yourself against my racism lest you be seen as a bitter, angry person
- Don't name my racism

When *you're* being "nice" as a white person, you:

- Believe that means you can't possibly be racist
- Set me up as the mean Black person if I call you on your racism
- Smile as a shield against genuine vulnerability
- Assume that your whiteness/white space is comfortable for me
- Are just being "professional" and following "the rules" because "nice" people don't make waves
- Think it's not fair that I'm not being "nice" back (you've been magnanimous to include me; why am I not granting you the benefit of the doubt that you are not racist?)
- Justify not interrupting racism because you didn't want to hurt another white person's feelings (at the expense of my feelings)
- Leave me to take risks and be vulnerable
- Will objectively watch from a "nice" distance to "learn what you and your people are feeling"

Anika sees white niceness in the face of racism as a form of the plantation relationship. During the enslavement of Africans, white people didn't have to be nice. Black people of course did, but no pretense of niceness was needed on the part of white people. Today that pretense is necessary to some degree, especially in order to qualify as a white progressive. But that doesn't mean that anti-Blackness isn't simmering just below the surface, and Black people are still required to be nice or risk punishment. Consider the case of a white woman calling the police when a group of Black Airbnb guests did not behave nicely toward her. As they checked out and left the home, dragging luggage to their car, they were met by seven police cars and told to put their hands in the air. They tried to explain to the officers that they were renting an Airbnb, but the officers didn't believe them and detained them for up to forty-five minutes. Attorneys for the guests said a neighbor called authorities because they didn't return her wave or smile at her. As this story illustrates, the white smile is not without strings; it comes with an entitled expectation that there will be acknowledgment and gratitude for the white "nod of approval."

I am all for niceness in general. I don't enjoy mean people, and I am not advocating for white people to be unfriendly. But niceness is not *anti-racism*. Niceness does not indicate a lack of racism and is not the solution to racism. Nor does a culture of niceness indicate that racism is not present in the environment. The critique here is directed at white progressives who think that niceness means that they hold no racism and that it conveys that same meaning to others. Given that niceness is not a neutral, objective term, we might also reflect on what qualifies as *not* nice in the context of challenging racism.

CHAPTER 5

THE MOVES OF
WHITE PROGRESSIVES

*I don't think there is anybody here who's fully
anti-racist. Part of being anti-racist is recognizing
the ways in which we are steeped in racism, and
that it imbues our thoughts and our judgments in
really surprising and surreptitious ways. We have
to constantly be on guard against it.*

—Ian Haney López[1]

At the start of a community seminar on systemic racism, my co-facilitator
and I went around the room and asked each person to share their name
and racial identity. I began by saying, "I am Robin and I am white."
About halfway through we came to a white man who said, "I am David, and I was white but I am now a person of color." My co-facilitator
and I paused and asked for clarification. "Which racial group do you
identify with?" He replied that he is a member of an Indigenous tribe.
We continued to press him. He explained that he recently returned from
a few months living with this tribe, and they accepted him as a member
of their community and consider him a member of their family. His
final statement was, "If they were here, they would want me to identify
as one of them and they would be hurt if I didn't." Taken aback but
also concerned about derailing the workshop in the first fifteen minutes,
we moved on. At various points and in a range of ways we returned
to challenge David's refusal to identify as white and his use of a group

of Indigenous people—who were not present and could not speak for themselves—to legitimize his refusal. David held fast to his opening claim, which had a powerful impact on the seminar and which continued to direct our efforts and distract the group.

David's narrative—like all narratives—is a form of *discourse*: the use of language and non-language (ideology, beliefs, expressions of thought and feeling, behaviors, body movements, tones, etc.) to produce and interpret meaning. *Discourse analysis* is the study of discourse, how language is used to make meaning and communicate ideologies in social contexts. Professor of literary studies James Paul Gee explains, "Meaning is not general and abstract, not something that resides in dictionaries, or even in general symbolic representations inside people's heads. Rather, it is situated in specific social and cultural practices, and it is continually transformed in those practices."[2] Discourse analysis is a method for identifying how language positions speakers in relation to social others in recognition that language is *sociopolitical*, not simply a neutral transmitter of a person's core ideas or self.

Discourse analysis is a useful tool in explicating whiteness because it allows for a nuanced examination of the framing we use to negotiate racial positions. The crucial feature of a discourse analysis is that this framing is viewed as meaningful by virtue of its articulation and impact within a specific social context and set of relationships, rather than by what consciously motivates or is intended. Thus discourse analysis can identify the dynamics of racism that otherwise would be difficult to establish or would be formally denied.

My academic training and much of my scholarship is in discourse analysis, and I am attentive to social "moves," the discursive strategies used to support or challenge current power relations (examples of moves are eye-rolling, silence, interrupting a speaker, debate, withdrawal, or invoking dominant ideologies such as meritocracy and individualism). Moves are sociopolitical in the sense that they impact the social conditions of the environment we are in. In the context of discussions on race, a move is the particular choice each of us makes about how and when to engage. We make moves that either maintain or challenge the racist status quo. There are no neutral moves—inaction is a choice that has consequences and, thus, is a form of action. Our racial moves don't have to be conscious and intentional in order to generate meaning and have impact—in fact, they seldom are—although they should be. We need to continually pay attention to our social positions and how we can leverage them strategically to achieve anti-racist goals. For example, a white man doing most of the talking has a different impact on group dynamics than an Asian American woman doing most of the talking. The former reinforces traditional power positioning and the latter interrupts it. Racial moves, both our own and those made by the people around us, are rich with information about how whiteness is at play and can guide us toward strategies to interrupt it.

In most professional group discussions—regardless of topic or context—speaking time is limited simply due to the reality that there is a certain amount of time allotted and a certain number of people, so unless it is a small group and a significant amount of time, not everyone who wants to contribute can, and certainly not every time they want to. The reality of limited time is especially relevant when the topic is race, because these conversations require facilitators to be especially conscious of power dynamics and attentive to social patterns, such as who is taking up airtime and whose voices have been left out. This is why facilitators of racial discussions will often use guidelines such as "No one can speak more than twice until everyone has spoken at least once." Given the limited resource of time, those of us who are white should be asking ourselves, "Given that space for contribution is limited, do I really need to weigh in? If so, what is the strategy behind what I am choosing to add?"

The following are common white moves that perpetuate and protect daily forms of racial harm. Some do so more subtly, by being irritating and exhausting and thereby contributing to racial weathering. Others more directly support and protect the racist status quo.

CREDENTIALING

Credentialing is a term I use to describe the ways in which white progressives attempt to prove that they are not racist. Credentialing surfaces whenever race enters the conversation and white people feel the need to establish their goodness. It functions as a kind of certificate of completion that preempts any further discussion, akin to going to a professional's office and seeing degrees and awards posted on the wall to assure you that you are in good hands. Prompts for credentialing can range from merely engaging with a Black person to being directly charged with racism. I inevitably encounter it in the context of presenting my work, but any time the topic of race surfaces, credentialing can be anticipated. Because I am white, the topic of race has to come up before I see credentialing, but Black colleagues have shared that their mere presence will trigger it.

For example, when on a plane and chatting with my seatmate, as soon as my line of work enters the conversation, I can expect credentialing from a white progressive (I am more likely to get anger and even mild ranting from white people who would not identify as progressive). Familiar forms of credentialing include claims such as "I was taught to see everyone the same"; "I don't see color"; "I work in a very diverse environment"; "My best friend or partner is Black"; "I speak several languages"; "I have travelled extensively"; "I am a minority myself"; "My parents taught me x"; "I was in the Peace Corps"; "I grew up in an activist community"; "I was the only white person in my school"; "I was on a mission in Africa"; "I adopted children of color"; "My parents were foreign ambassadors"; and so on. Credentialing is important to examine because it reveals the underlying framework of racial meaning. While credentialing is intended to establish that we are *not* racist, it simultaneously conveys its opposite: what we think would indicate that we *were* racist.

We can see two broad categories of credentialing in the list above: color-deny and color-celebrate. As I described in *White Fragility*, the color-deny theme absurdly posits that one does not even notice race and therefore it holds no meaning and informs no response. The person is thus objective on the matter and cannot be racist. "I was taught to treat everyone the same" is an example of color-deny credentialing. The color-celebrate theme posits that the person welcomes, enjoys, and even seeks out racial difference. The person is thus comfortable with racial difference and cannot be racist. "My best friend is Black" is an example of color-celebrate credentialing.

Let's look more closely at the logic of these two types of credentialing. If *no one* notices race, then my not noticing is not worth mentioning. But if not noticing race means I am not racist, then those who do notice race and see meaning in racial difference will be the racists ("It's focusing on race that divides us"). Color-deny credentialing reveals an underlying belief that it is racist to acknowledge that we live in a racially unequal society (and apparently it is especially racist if this acknowledgment is made in order to challenge that inequality). Color-deny credentialing also grants the claimant racial objectivity: if I do not see race, then it has nothing to do with my response; therefore, I am not racist, end of discussion.

Color-celebrate credentialing relies on proximity to racialized people for its validity. Living in large urban cities or world travel is enough to certify a white person's lack of racism. Via color-celebrate credentialing, people who live in small towns or who have not been exposed to racial difference will be considered racist (apparently racists are unsophisticated rubes who cannot tolerate even the sight of racialized people). Sometimes color-celebrate credentialing includes a blasé and weary "I've been around diversity for years and am so beyond this" undertone. Of course, living in proximity does not mean one actually has an integrated friendship circle, but according to this logic, if one can work in a diverse environment, play on a diverse sports team, or smile as they walk past racialized people on crowded city streets, they cannot be racist.

Anthropologists Signithia Fordham and John Ogbu describe a "fictive kinship" between African Americans, a kinship that is not consanguineal (by blood) or affinal (by marriage) but is derived from the assumption of a shared sociopolitical experience, a nod-of-the-head moment of seeing one another in the context of racist structures. Fictive kinship functions as a form of collective identity, a moment of unity in the face of white racial hostility and isolation.[3] The kinship with African Americans that white people attempt to create from proximity might be termed false or fabricated kinship. This fabricated kinship is not based on a shared experience or even a shared sense of goodwill and connection. It is centered on and serves highly problematic white needs: the need to feel benevolence by granting the Other a condescending nod of acceptance and approval and the desire to attain "not racist" social capital, no matter how fleeting or trivial the encounter. "I accept you because I am in charge and I am not racist."

A relevant example of the convergence of several white progressive moves came from a woman who wrote to me after I delivered a keynote. She explained, "I work at a firm that prides itself on being progressive and 'woke.' Unfortunately, this is not necessarily reflected in the racial make-up of the firm." Following my presentation, her work group met to discuss the content. She shared:

> Upon starting this conversation, the first thing that my white supervisor said was "that was a great presentation; I just wish they had the more advanced version of that. It was too beginner for me." The phrase caught me abruptly by surprise as I, being Latinx and a woman of color myself, would have never even thought of the presentation as an introduction to racism but rather a more detailed deep dive into it.

The supervisor continued to say that she has lived in places and communities that are very diverse, i.e., New Jersey, New York, San Francisco, and that she's always been surrounded by people of color.

The writer expressed her frustration that her supervisor was making a move I had just described in my talk: proximity as evidence that one is beyond the discussion. She tried a few times to counter her supervisor's claims, but to no avail. In addition to the supervisor's credentialing, note her additional move of being beyond the discussion, *even as she is enacting* the very basic problematic behavior that was named in a talk she just heard. Also worthy of note, not one other white member of the group spoke up in support of their coworker of color.

I urge my readers to notice how often proximity is used as evidence of a white person's lack of racism, and how ridiculous yet unquestioned is the underlying belief that a racist cannot tolerate proximity to Black people. In an interview I did for a Boston-based radio show—whose host was a white progressive and represents a mainstream progressive organization—I was asked if I really thought that racism was an issue, given that we were in Boston. The idea that an entire city can be assumed to be "not racist" is in itself absurd. But this rhetorical question was referencing *Boston* of all places, with its history of violent riots against school desegregation and submitted in the context of a 2017 national survey commissioned by the *Boston Globe* that found that among eight major cities, Black people ranked Boston as least welcoming.[4] Actor and comedian Michael Che described Boston as the most racist city he has ever visited.[5] Only 1 percent of corporate board members in publicly traded firms in Massachusetts are Black. Black enrollment in Boston's many universities has not appreciably increased in three decades. Boston neighborhoods are among the most segregated in the US. A Black resident interviewed for the *Globe*'s seven-part exposé of racism in Boston stated, "To be a black person in Boston, is [often] to be the only one. You're aware of the racism. You're aware of the subtleties. It's like the air we breathe, if you're black."[6] Yet being a resident of Boston was used by a white journalist as evidence of progressive anti-racist credentials, demonstrating just how out-of-touch white progressives can be with historical and current realities. Pause and consider how this lack of awareness might inform our response when Black people raise race issues.

People with racist attitudes can tolerate proximity to Black people and have for centuries. Certainly, people who held (and raped) enslaved Africans could tolerate proximity, as could people who fought to maintain enforced segregation in the Jim Crow South and had Black servants in their homes. To take a current example from patriarchy, film producer Harvey Weinstein is a misogynist sexual predator, yet he didn't prey upon every woman he encountered. We can assume he had numerous family and business relationships with women whom he did not assault. Yet it strains credibility to believe that these women did not experience his misogyny in myriad other ways. While he may not have assaulted all women he had proximity to, I imagine that his general misogynist orientation could still be felt by women he wasn't explicitly assaulting.

Racial bias does not prevent us from interacting calmly and respectfully with racialized people when decorum demands it, especially when so much of racial bias is implicit rather than consciously held. But even avowed white nationalists can and do tolerate proximity to

Black people. Still, implicit forms of bias do surface, often in ways that are unnoticed by the perpetrator. The research on implicit bias is clear; we notice and ascribe meaning and value to racial difference and act accordingly.[7]

Both types of credentialing have the same result: they exempt the person from any further engagement or involvement, take any discussion of racism off the table, and protect the racially unequal status quo.

An interaction between US senator Mark Meadows (Republican-North Carolina) and then senator Joe Biden (Democrat-Delaware) provides an example of color-celebrate credentialing, from both sides of the political spectrum. In response to charges that President Trump is racist, Mark Meadows had Lynne Patton, who is Black, silently stand behind him as evidence of both Trump's and his own ability to tolerate proximity. Ms. Patton, who was the only visible Black person in the group, was a Trump appointee who oversaw New York and New Jersey for the Department of Housing and Urban Development. The reasoning behind this staging was presumably that a racist couldn't work with or would not appoint a Black person. Congresswoman Rashida Tlaib (Democrat-Michigan) challenged Meadows by stating, "The fact that someone would actually use a prop, a Black woman, in this chamber in this committee, is alone racist in itself."[8] In the white-fragility meltdown that ensued, an outraged Meadows, positioning himself as the victim, declared that his "nieces and nephews are people of color" and invoked his relationship with committee chair Elijah Cummings as further proof of his lack of racism. "It's racist to suggest that I asked her to come in for that reason!" he exclaimed, demanding that Tlaib's statement be struck from the record.

In another example of using proximity as evidence of a lack of racism, then vice president Joe Biden recalled how he'd worked productively alongside two segregationist senators, including the virulently racist Senator James Eastland (Democrat-Mississippi). "At least there was some civility. We got things done. We didn't agree on much of anything," Biden said.[9] "Today, you look at the other side and you're the enemy." Mr. Biden then recalled his time serving in the Senate. "I was in a caucus with James O. Eastland. He never called me boy, he always called me son." In response, Senator Cory Booker released a statement saying Biden's "relationships with proud segregationists are not the model for how we make America a safer and more inclusive place for Black people, and for everyone." He added that he was disappointed that Biden "hasn't issued an immediate apology." Biden's response included invoking his past work on civil rights: "I've been involved in civil rights my whole career" and the classic "There's not a racist bone in my body." Biden insisted that it was Booker who owed *him* an apology for suggesting his comments were racist.

Notice that while Biden and Meadows are on different ends of the political spectrum, their responses to charges of racism were similar. They have been in a political environment for decades that has been dominated by white men. And while it still is dominated by white men, there has been some change; they are now working with younger women of color such as Alexandria Ocasio-Cortez (Democrat-New York), Ayanna Pressley (Democrat-Massachusetts), and Rashida Tlaib who are speaking up and challenging the white-male status quo. The presence of these women of color provides an opportunity for men like Biden and Meadows to expand their understanding of the perspectives and experiences of BIPOC people and evolve in changing times. Yet rather than engaging with curiosity, openness and humility, they dig in deeper, protecting their limited understanding, refusing to listen or learn. They may be nice people—and in Biden's case self-identified as progressive— but neither demonstrated any skill in navigating cross-racial dynamics, and both caused racial harm. In those terms, Biden's identity as the progressive one was functionally meaningless.

OBJECTIFYING

Objectifying refers to the white tendency to overemphasize the race of BIPOC people. It is a form of "color-celebrate" credentialing that amplifies racial difference. A white person may constantly ask a person of color questions related to race, make racial jokes or comments they don't normally make with white people, enact exaggerated and stereotypical mannerisms they associate with BIPOC people, ask personal questions about their racial experiences, ask them to speak on behalf of their group, and generally bring up race in ways they don't with other white people. They may also emphasize how beautiful or "exotic" the person is and make comments about their hair, skin, or size.

Objectification happens in personal relationships but also in organizations, wherein racialized people are made highly visible. They may be continually asked to appear in photos in order to make the organization appear more diverse than it is, or they may be invited to sit on every committee so that the committee "has diversity," or they may be asked to handle anything in the organization related to diversity work. This places a great burden on the person while reinforcing many problematic dynamics, such as the continual reduction of BIPOC people to their race, the perception that BIPOC people represent their race (but white people do not), and the idea that racial or multicultural issues are the domain of BIPOC people but "normal" issues are the domain of white people.

When racialized people do sit on committees, they are in the awkward position of having to represent the "racial perspective," while white people are not often asked to represent the "white perspective." The result is that white people are granted individuality, while racialized people are not. Further, while there is great diversity within and between racialized groups and representing them all is impossible, white people are often satisfied with just one "representative." Yet all too often, the perspectives of that representative are not heard or validated, especially if they are unfamiliar or threatening to the status quo. And rarely do the white people attend to the racial dynamics inevitably playing out in the group or ask how the experience is going for the "diversity" person.

To illustrate, imagine a typical white-dominated organization. There are a few racialized people scattered throughout, but they are mostly concentrated at the lower levels of the workplace hierarchy. A work committee is formed, consisting of ten white people. A woman of color is invited to the committee in order to make it more "diverse." That is problematic enough, but the dynamics present in the group will likely be even more problematic. Given the social and institutional patterns of white dominance, what might that group feel like to her? Will she risk giving her perspective if it is contrary to everyone else's? If she does speak up, will she be heard? Will she be allowed to name the patterns she sees without risking her job? If she challenges these patterns will she be seen as angry, combative, or "always playing the race card"? All too often, her perspective will only be welcome if it doesn't challenge the status quo in any significant way.

Our work does not end once we have invited a person of color to join our group. The white members need anti-racist skills and perspectives. All too often, we equate token diversity with "mission accomplished." We may claim awareness but rarely demonstrate actual intervention or commitment. Without these skills and commitments, racialized people in organizations have to deal with a significant level of unconscious white racism.

OUT-WOKING

The white progressive credentialing discussed thus far is a garden-variety type of evidence meant to establish that a person is not racist. But there is another level of white progressive credentialing that is more common with those who are actively involved in anti-racist efforts. I call this the "out-woking" move. "Rose," a friend of mine who is white and has a long-term commitment to anti-racist activism, shared a particularly painful out-woking experience. Another white person involved in the same activism identified something racist Rose had done. Rather than speak to Rose about it, this person sent Rose an email cc'd to others in their group. Spelling out the racism she saw, she publicly ended her relationship with Rose, signing off with, "I don't want anything further to do with you." Rose explained, "Over the last couple of years I've watched progressive white women going after other progressive white women to expose and shame them for their racism. The ethos seems to be, 'If I can call out and publicly shame you for what you've said or done or got wrong, then I am more enlightened, more "woke," less racist than you.'" This vilification and abandonment does little for supporting one another's growth and is not what is meant by holding one another accountable.

Less extreme versions of the out-woking that Rose experienced often surface among white people who voluntarily engage in anti-racist seminars. For example, a white participant raises their hand and announces that they are not being challenged or learning anything new. This move is not made in service of improving the workshop, nor is it adding anything that could be insightful to others; it is made to position the claimant as *beyond* the workshop. To be fair, I have been to countless workshops and observed a range of competency in facilitators, pedagogy, and analysis. Not learning anything new may be attributed in part to the limitations of a leader. But even a workshop that is poorly facilitated offers rich opportunities for learning. There's so much to gain from paying attention to the dynamics at play—who speaks and who doesn't; what is or isn't being said and how that impacts the direction of the conversation; how various narratives are functioning.

Participants can reach for deeper self-awareness and reflect on why they are responding the way that they are and what their reaction says about their own process. If nothing else, participants can learn how they might want to do things differently. If they sincerely think the session is being poorly facilitated in a way that feedback could help improve, they can speak to the facilitators privately. Making a public declaration that the workshop is inadequate only undermines the facilitator's ability to continue leading with confidence. Alternatively, they can make a public contribution intended to deepen rather than dismiss.

If I am feeling frustrated with how new to the content other participants are, I can practice patience with those who may not be as far along. If, for example, in our small-group discussions people keep defaulting to their own forms of oppression, when we come back to the large group I can raise my hand and say, "I am noticing that many of us are struggling with how to reconcile our racial advantages with the reality that we also experience oppression in other aspects of our lives. Can you give us some help with that?" Or if we are in the large group and facilitators are not being very effective at explaining a key point or are getting hooked into a debate, I can offer something like "That is something that I have really struggled with too. I have come to terms with that tension by reminding myself . . ." or some similar way to bring in my experience and insight without placing myself above other learners.

"I am not gaining anything from this" is a move of arrogance that not only puts the person above the facilitators but also above participants who *are* getting value from the session. If the facilitators are BIPOC people or an interracial team, a white participant claiming to not be gaining anything of value is an especially undermining power move. Imagine the impact if BIPOC people have made themselves vulnerable by sharing the hurtful slights and indignities of racism, only to have a white person announce that they are gaining nothing of value! The lack of awareness or concern about that impact in itself puts the lie to the implication that the person is "beyond" the discussion.

This move was made recently during a webinar for white people that I participated in. About midway through, a white woman submitted the following via the chat window: "This webinar is 101. Some of us have been doing this work for years and want something more advanced." Of all that one could contribute to the group, why choose this? If she was really so advanced as to be beyond the workshop, why not model a way of engaging that could be useful to less experienced participants? This move demonstrates an inability to think strategically about our own role in anti-racist endeavors, a lack of practice articulating what we think we know, and an unhelpful distancing from others in the struggle. I have attended countless anti-racist workshops precisely because my learning will never be finished and there are always deeper layers to uncover. The statement itself reveals how little the person actually understands and a profound lack of humility in the face of that limited understanding.

Another classic example of out-woking occurred during a webinar on the impact of COVID-19 on the Black community and other communities of color. This webinar was organized by a renowned scholar who is a Black woman and featured a prestigious panel of speakers, all but one of whom were BIPOC people. The webinar was timely, free, and accessible, and provided a rare opportunity to hear the perspectives of brilliant thought leaders and activists of color on an issue that was largely being ignored in the mainstream: the specific catastrophic impact of this pandemic on BIPOC people. While the virus does not discriminate, the societies in which it spreads certainly do; systemic racism has compounded the devastation COVID-19 wreaks for BIPOC people, who are vastly overrepresented in death rates.

During the presentation, the chat thread was visible and moving quickly as viewers engaged in conversation with each other, asking questions, sharing resources, and adding their thoughts to what the speakers were saying.

A particular critique that the panelists made was of the "unsung hero" narrative that has surfaced during the pandemic. This narrative allows us to thank those we are calling essential workers for their selfless willingness to risk their lives in order to serve the rest of us. In reality, the vast majority of "essential" workers have no choice at all if they want to eat and make their rent. They tend to be the lowest-paid of workers, engaged in the most menial of labor, with the least job security or benefits: food service, transportation, warehouse and delivery, agriculture, meatpacking, hospital workers, and childcare, among others. They are overwhelmingly BIPOC people. Positioning their necessity to work under conditions that risk their lives as a brave choice obscures structural and economic inequality.

As one panelist of color was making the powerful point that domestic, agricultural, and service workers are essential and *also disposable*, one chat entry caught my eye. Someone I will refer to as Liam wrote in the chat box, "I would like to hear the Indigenous perspective." This was immediately followed by several people thanking Liam for their "great point!" While Liam could be seen as advocating for an oft underrepresented community, this is such a classic white progressive move that it bears further examination. But before proceeding to analyze how a move functions racially, we need to remember that the impact of a move is different based on the racial position of the person making that move.

Let's assume that Liam is white and break down what happens when white people make this particular move. First, for a white person to interject with what *they* are interested in hearing—*while a woman of color is speaking*—is both silencing and entitled. This move says,

"What you are saying is not of interest or value to me. Rather than appreciate this rare opportunity to hear a woman of color advocate for her community, I am going to insert myself into the middle of your talk and let it be known that I want to hear something different. I am entitled to do so because my interests are more important than what you have to say. What's more, I don't need to wait until you are finished speaking or wait until the webinar is over. I don't even need to think about the impact of my actions on you as a woman of color."

This panel was organized by a Black woman, and Liam knew who would be speaking on it before they registered. The webinar was free to attend, so they did not have to pay for the time of anyone on the panel. A woman of color was identifying the impact of racism on her specific community, and as she was speaking, a white person interjected that they wanted to hear about the impact on a different community. How could this comment not land on the panelist as something dismissive and disrespectful?

As a perfect finale, the perspective Liam wanted to hear was the perspective of Indigenous people, a particularly romanticized group for many white progressives (I will address this romanticization in more depth in chapter 6). To offer up the critique that Indigenous people were left out is a guarantee of white progressive social capital, which Liam immediately received from others commenting in the chat box. I was left wondering if Liam really wanted to hear the Indigenous perspective, or if they were merely performing some woke virtue signaling.

Let me be clear: one of the ways that racism manifests specifically toward Indigenous peoples is invisibility. The problem isn't that Liam raised this issue. The problem was how and when the issue was raised *and how it functioned* in that context.

RUSHING TO PROVE THAT WE ARE NOT RACIST

A white colleague who does racial equity consulting shared a conversation she had with members of a majority-white organization. The members told her they wanted to add to their mission statement that theirs was an "anti-racist" organization. My colleague asked them to describe the racism in their organization that they wanted to address with their anti-racist mission. Her question was met with what she described as "crickets." She added, "They wanted to present themselves as addressing an issue they couldn't even name."

The story I shared in chapter 1, of regaling my dinner companions with endless stories of my family's racism, is another classic example of this move, in which white people urgently seek to establish that they are good people and not racist. At that dinner, as a well-intentioned white progressive, I thought this was what I was doing. Sadly, what I was actually doing was subjecting this couple to racism all night long. I was acting from racial anxiety, an anxiety I would not have felt if the couple were white, and steering the conversation to places I would not have otherwise gone. I had a sense that something was wrong, but this incident took place years before I had any racial analysis, so I ignored the feeling.

I realize now that I had engaged in several problematic cross-racial dynamics. First, I had objectified the couple by immediately turning the conversation to race. I would never have done this if they were not Black, and that fact could not have been lost on them. But worse, in sharing racist things that other white people had said, I was forcing the couple to hear these racist comments. It didn't make any difference where the comments originated. They were awful, and I had repeated them to this couple. That did not make me look "not racist" but rather racially clueless at best, and cruel at worst. Imagine what a depressing evening that was for them. No matter my conscious intentions or self-image as a progressive, I inflicted racial harm that night; I enacted racism.

I have seen this dynamic play out in other, perhaps less obvious ways: A white person meeting a person of color at a party and taking out their family pictures in order to show the person, who is essentially a stranger, that they have children of color. Or telling a Latinx person that they had a Latina housekeeper and she was just like a member of the family. These behaviors objectify racialized people, make their race hyper-visible, and put them on the spot. If they don't respond graciously, they risk being dismissed as oversensitive. An irony is that these actions all take place within a culture that professes color blindness.

Psychologist Beverly Daniel Tatum shares that in order for her as a Black woman to have a true cross-racial friendship, the white person needs to have done some work on their own racial identity. While recognizing that these relationships are not easily forged, Tatum says, "our capacity to form them is shaped by our own developmental process and willingness to engage with the historical and contemporary meaning of race in our society."[10] My behavior at the dinner with the other couple who were Black illustrates my limited racial development and its impact. At that dinner, this couple had several choices in how to respond. For example, they could have granted me the benefit of the doubt (deserved or not) that I meant well, endured my behavior, and remained open to me. They could have not granted me the benefit of the doubt, endured my behavior, and decided to avoid any further interactions with me. They also could have decided not to endure my behavior and challenged me. Any one of these choices required an emotional and psychic burden and would have taken a toll that would likely continue after the encounter. While the first two would get them through the dinner with the least conflict, those choices may very well have caused them more internal conflict in the days to follow. Why is it always on racialized people to either silently endure or call out the racism and risk the white fragility meltdown that will suck up even more time and energy? Given how clueless I clearly was, they might have guessed (correctly) that I would not respond well to being told I was perpetuating racism. They were in a "damned if you do and damned if you don't" situation. Let's also note that my white partner—while not participating directly in my behavior—did nothing to intervene. While the other couple had a relationship with my partner prior to this meeting, her allyship was absent that night, adding another layer of potential hurt and disappointment to their evening.

My white narcissism was also informing my behavior at that dinner. I sensed that something was off by the reserve I felt from this couple, but my need for "not racist" validation overrode attending to those signals. White anti-racist educator Christine Saxman calls those signals the "integrity twitch."[11] I felt the twitch but was not able to resist centering myself. And if I am to be truly honest, I must admit that on some level I enjoyed repeating those stories, laughing at the funny images and stereotypes, and believing I was getting away with it under cover of "knowing" they were racist; I was enjoying racism.

Yet for all the layers of racism at play during that dinner and the oblivious white superiority I displayed, inculcated from a lifetime of never being on the receiving end of racism, my desire to connect with this couple was genuine. Racism is taught from an early age—we are not born knowing that it is "better" to be white and are not given the initial choice to live segregated lives. Many white people have shared with me the experience of having had a Black friend when they were children but then losing those friends when they got older—perhaps because they moved away or because they had reached dating age and the potential of a sexual liaison was too threatening for their parents. These people often express some grief about the loss of their cross-racial friendships. There are many contradictions within racism, and one is that we can feel superior to Black people while also "missing them" and desiring deeply to be connected.

Still, rushing to prove ourselves is not useful and rarely leads to connection—quite the opposite. It is best to relax, earn trust, slowly build authentic relationships—and, of course, continuously engage in the process of anti-racist self-awareness and skill building.

DOWNPLAYING OUR ADVANTAGES

A colleague of mine—a white woman who does similar anti-racism work—shared a powerful analogy she heard in a session she was co-facilitating. They had just completed an exercise that required white people to brainstorm a list of privileges they were able to take for granted that could not be taken for granted by racialized people. When asked to read this list aloud in front of the entire group, the white participants became extremely uncomfortable, taking great effort to preface the list with disclaimers about how terrible they felt about having these privileges, how much they didn't really want them, and so on.

When the group was finished presenting their list, a Black man raised his hand and said, "You know what it's like being around white people? It's like you're sitting at this elaborate banquet table with all of this amazing food and you're acting like you're not sitting there and the food isn't any good. *We know* you are sitting there. *We see* you. We know what you have. Why can't you just be honest about enjoying the food? We don't want you to not enjoy the food. What we want is a place at the table!"

As he spoke my colleague pictured the white progressive collective, sitting at this table, shoveling food into our mouths with our heads down, hiding our faces in the hopes that we can't be seen, mumbling assurances to those standing behind us—without a place at the table— that the food isn't really that good and that we are sorry for eating it in front of them. And in that moment she realized how problematic and unhelpful our guilt was, how disingenuous it appeared to Black people. She also realized that while the white participants saw themselves as different from one another (and had been pointing out their differences throughout the session via various forms of credentialing), they were all still sitting at the table. Some might have been served before others, some might be speaking and reaching over others, some might have allergies to the various dishes. Still, they were all at the table, and that table was *whiteness*.

The intersection of race and class provides a common opportunity for upper-class white progressives to downplay their compounded advantage. While they can't deny the implications of their whiteness in the context of anti-racism work, they can minimize their class privilege by highlighting other aspects of oppressed identity, such as gender or sexuality, and minimizing their racial and economic status. I don't think I have ever met an upper-class person who was the richest person in their social circle. I haven't even met one who was in the middle. Sure they went to boarding schools and Ivy League colleges, from which they graduated with no student debt, but they didn't live in the *nicest* house in their neighborhoods; they were consistently the poorest of the rich in their circles. And perhaps they were, and that little taste of being less-than is what motivated them to engage with anti-racist work. But as someone who grew up in actual poverty, I can tell you that this move does not obscure or dilute their class privilege in my eyes. It comes across as disingenuous and not helpful to the cause, functioning to off-load some race and class guilt and prevent acknowledgment of unearned advantage by providing "victim" social capital. We can't proceed with any kind of authenticity in anti-racist work if we continually position ourselves in the victim role.

ASSUMING BIPOC PEOPLE HAVE THE SAME EXPERIENCES WE DO

Because white people are not socialized to see ourselves in racial terms, we often assume that our experiences and perspectives are the same as BIPOC people's. In other words, because I believe that my race does not inform how I experience the world, I don't see how theirs could either. If I feel comfortable in my overwhelmingly white workplace, so will they; if I have only had positive experiences with the police, so have they. Living segregated lives within a culture that centralizes the white perspective (in history, media, literature, role models, etc.) leads to these faulty assumptions. On the infrequent occasion that we do have the opportunity to hear the perspectives of BIPOC people, we often don't listen or, not understanding their experiences, we minimize and discount them.

For example, the first time I attended a conference on white privilege, I was thrilled. I thought the conference was wonderful—I found it affirming to be among people who cared about the same issues that I did. I met new colleagues, made many important connections, and had many new insights. During a break, I rushed over to gush about the conference to a group of Asian American and Black friends who were also attending. I went on about how exciting the experience was, assuming that they would share my enthusiasm. But they did not find the conference exciting and energizing as I did. Being confronted head-on with data on the reality of racial inequality in workshop after workshop was painful and exhausting. Further, they were experiencing many microaggressions from the white participants—just because the conference was about challenging racism didn't mean that racism wasn't being enacted.

Of course, the racial slights my friends were experiencing were not apparent to me (indeed, I had just expressed an invalidating assumption of my own). For me, the conference was more of a stimulating intellectual experience; for them, it was much more emotionally demanding. Not having the history of harm from racism, I could "enjoy" the conference in a way that they could not. They were supporters of this conference and found it valuable, yet we had very different experiences of it based on our racial positions. Now when I attend conferences, I try to be much more attentive to that fact, and instead of making universal declarations with which I assume BIPOC colleagues will agree, I speak for myself and ask them for their perspective, e.g., "I am getting so much from this conference. How is it going for you?"

LECTURING BIPOC PEOPLE ON THE ANSWER TO RACISM

One of the goals of anti-racist efforts is to bridge the racial divide and come together in more liberatory ways. Unfortunately, many white progressives do not currently have the skills or awareness to do so without causing further harm. A pointed example occurred on a trip to South Africa, where I presented my work on white fragility at the Apartheid Museum in Johannesburg. My talk was followed by a panel of speakers who helped place my remarks in the South African context. The audience was multiracial and included many white people whom I assumed to be progressives; they had come voluntarily and made no hateful comments. Nonetheless, deep racial harm was done.

Once the floor was opened to questions, the first person to take the mic was a white woman, who jumped up and began credentialing herself as she marched across the room: "I wrote a paper on racism when I was six years old." "I dated an Indian man." "I worked for the Nelson Mandela Foundation." "I built housing in Townships," etc. Several people, including the moderator, asked her to please sit down and get to her question, but she ignored them, striding around the room, microphone in hand, taking up both physical and psychological space and frustrating everyone, oblivious to the very direct social cues around her. She eventually got to her point, declaring triumphantly, "We just need to see what is in one another's hearts!"

When the white woman finally sat down, a Black woman stood up and expressed very deep pain and anger about the devastating racial inequality in South Africa. This should have been a sobering moment for white people to bear witness to a level of anger that is rarely safely expressed in mixed space. White people could have responded by demonstrating humility, holding back, and listening. Or they could have validated her experience by sharing the insights gained by her powerful testimony. Unfortunately, none of those things happened. The next person to speak was a white man who stood up, faced the woman, and proceeded to lecture her at length on the "answer" to racism ("personal responsibility"). He was followed by another white man who gave his version of this lecture, also pontificating at length ("personal relationships"). A white woman delivered the final lecture of the evening ("let's not point fingers"). None of these white people had questions for the speakers or demonstrated that they had heard—much less understood—a single point made in my talk, by the other panelists, or by Black audience members.

Several Black people later shared with the organizers how wounding this portion of the evening was, as several destructive white progressive patterns were displayed: unconvincing credentialing, racial ignorance coupled with a lack of racial humility, a lack of racial curiosity, the inability (or refusal) to read racial cues, the inability to hold racial discomfort, the entitlement to take up space, and seeing ourselves as the smartest people in the room. Speaking to white people's all too often uninformed opinions about race, Anika Nailah notes: "White people are really hard to manage, really hard. They're very pushy. They're very judgmental. They're very self-centered. . . . This is the way they've been conditioned to be, that's what racism does. Nine times out of ten, there's hardly anyone who's done the work, yet they feel qualified to tell people who have how they're doing it wrong." We do not have the answer to racism, and we need to stop lecturing Black people as if we do.

Another example of the racial arrogance of white progressives surfaced in a recent interview for a European newspaper. The journalist conducting the interview shared that he is multiracial. He has a circle of white friends whom he has known for decades and who "definitely" identify as progressives. Yet across all those years, he has tried repeatedly to talk to them about the racism he experiences, and they refuse to listen. They insist that they don't see anyone as different, that we are all human and have a human experience, that we shouldn't talk about race as if it mattered, and so on. When he shared with one of these friends that he was going to be interviewing me about my book *White Fragility* and that he was excited, this friend replied, "I don't like that term. I think that divides people." Here is a person of color who has just shared that he is looking forward to talking to a white person whose work on race he appreciates. His white friends have an exceptional opportunity to understand the perspective of a person of color whom they claim to love. And yet they refuse. Confident that they know all they need to know on the matter and having had the last word, the subject is closed. Their confidence exists in spite of the fact that they have very few racialized friends, have not had any education on racism, have not engaged in dialogues on race, and are living in a moment when a global Black Lives Matter movement has swept Europe, where they reside.

"How can I get them to hear me?" he implored. I could only sigh. These friends likely cite this journalist of color as their evidence that they are not racist whenever the topic comes up, even as they have silenced him on race for years. This is the maddening daily invalidation of people of color by so-called open-minded white people.

PRETENDING OUR PREFERENCE FOR SEGREGATION IS ACCIDENTAL

There is a common exercise in anti-racist work in which participants meet in affinity groups (also known as "caucusing") based on their shared racial identity: white people meet together, Black people meet together, Asian heritage people meet together, multiracial people meet together, and so on. These groups provide an opportunity to address issues that are specific to that group, and participants can do so without the pressure of being heard by members of other groups. For example, white people can talk about dynamics such as internalized superiority, implicit bias, guilt, confusion, resentment, and so on without causing hurt to racialized people. And racialized people can talk about very sensitive issues and express emotions related to their marginalization without risking retaliation from white people in the room. Racial affinity groups also relieve racialized people from being subjected to all of the harmful behaviors illustrated in the previous example of the talk in South Africa.

In my experience, racialized people usually appreciate racial caucusing because it gives them a break from the white patterns that inevitably surface in mixed groups. Kad Smith, project director of the social justice advocacy group Compass Point, in reflecting on his experience organizing a person of color caucus group in the workplace, shares:

> To be frank, a great many people of color are tired of having to educate white folks on how racism manifests on the interpersonal and institutional levels. We are fatigued from constantly having to "provide examples" of how racism shows up in our organizations and workplaces. We are exhausted from having to hold white folks' hands through their own exploration of what whiteness means in a white supremacist system. We needed a space for people of color to convene outside of the gaze of our white colleagues.[12]

While the ultimate goal of anti-racist work is to bridge racial divides, many white people do not have the skills to engage in cross-racial work without causing further harm. As the examples throughout this book illustrate, well-intentioned white progressives say and do many ignorant and hurtful things in these conversations. Using affinity groups, strong white facilitators can work with white people to identify and address these behaviors before coming back together in mixed-race conversations so that mixed-race dialogues might be more constructive and less harmful. They are simply one tool among many others.

I have been leading white affinity groups for years, and there is a consistent pattern that emerges as soon as it is announced that we will be separating by racial group for a brief period of time (typically sixty to ninety minutes): *white people panic.* In fact, white people freak out so badly that affinity group work is considered an "advanced" method, only done when a group is "ready" (white fragility, anyone?). Now, most white people live their lives in racial segregation. Our schools, our neighborhoods, our friendship circles, the leadership teams in our workplaces are all overwhelmingly white. We might have an acquaintance or two who is not—a coworker we go to lunch with on occasion, that roommate we had in college, someone who plays on or coaches our sports teams. But authentic, sustained, long-term relationships across race? And with Black people in particular? Rarely. I ask white people who are married to show me their wedding albums, a more honest indicator of who our friends are.

The Reverend angel Kyodo williams, addressing white urgency to keep racialized people in the room during anti-racism work, admonishes:

> People who have always been entitled to space and to place have no idea what it's like to have never been entitled to space. I'm entitled to gather to determine the way and the path to my freedom. You will let me do that and not obstruct it. You will not put your needs and your desire for some kind of picture above my necessity. Doing so obstructs my ability to understand what it is to first be with myself. To be with people that I have not been allowed to be with just as I am. Put aside your urgency—we've been separated for four hundred years, kept from one another—for this to just be over.[13]

So let's look for a moment at the forms of separation by race we don't panic or feel urgency about.

White progressives who can afford to send their children to private schools do enjoy the small amount of racial diversity these schools typically have (and make a point of in their advertising materials), because it provides a "valuable experience" for their white children. But that diversity must be from the right groups and in the right numbers. A little "diversity" is hip today, but "too much" and we lose status. In this way, "diversity" becomes a kind of consumer product that can be purchased and controlled. The children of elite international workers in the tech industry, for example, are nice to have at our private Montessori schools, but we definitely do not want our children exposed to African American or Latinx children at the local public school; these schools are not quite so appealing.

In a study of school choice, educational researchers Heather Johnson and Thomas Shapiro found that the school and neighborhood de-

cisions of average white parents were based on avoiding racial diversity
and served to secure education and economic advantage for their children: "Ultimately, no matter how conflicted they are, the end result is
the same," they write. "White families choose to live in, and are re-
warded for living in, White neighborhoods. . . . The social structure
rewards White families for perpetuating segregation through their racialized decisions."[14]

In a study of white parents who identified as *anti-racist*, the majority stated that they chose a school *for* its racial diversity.[15] However, most of their children who attended more diverse schools were in
programs within the school that were whiter and included many more
middle-to-upper-income families.

The "school within a school" phenomenon is well known; honors
programs are often completely different from mainstream school programs, which are typically under-resourced and taught by inexperienced
teachers, amounting to de facto segregation.[16] Some of these anti-racist-
identified parents recognized that institutional racism and tracking
(grouping children according to their perceived ability) was in place in
their school and expressed concern about programs being skewed along
race and class lines. They struggled with the decision about whether to
enroll their child in the non-honors program that was majority children
of color. However, virtually all of them chose to place their child in the
program that was considered "better" academically (and also whiter).
Most did not think it was possible for the non-honors program to be of
quality. Yet it was unclear what they based this assessment on, although
coded racism is inherent in white discourses about schools as "good" or
"bad," and these assessments are largely based on the degree of Black
enrollment. Some of these parents discussed the honors programs as a
"better fit" for their children, which begs the question of what constitutes "fit" in this context.

We are all constantly exposed to messages that Black people should
be feared. It's hard to deny that the vast majority of white parents, regardless of political orientation, do not want their children being around "too
many" Black children and are especially anxious about their children
being in the minority around Black children. One anti-racist-identified

parent clearly described the contradictions between her own values and behaviors around school choice:

> We live in a really diverse neighborhood, more diverse when we moved in than it is now, but . . . our neighborhood middle school, it just really felt . . . like a prison or something. . . . You're welcomed by signs on the window that say things like, "3 Tardies = Suspension and 3 Suspensions = Expulsion." I want my kids to be excited about learning, not feeling like it's punishment. So . . . it was clear that it was not what I want my kids to be exposed to and so I visit a bunch of other middle schools around the city ... *the best* was actually in ... [a white neighborhood] and so lo and behold, it's not a very diverse middle school. . . . You know that mama bear kicks in. And for me, as a parent who was trying to be cognizantly antiracist, it becomes really complicated, where it feels like there's a choice between sort of a "good" education vs. a "sucky" education that's more diverse.[17]

Rationales such as this are consistent with aversive racism, allowing white parents with a progressive—even anti-racist—identity to enact racist practices while still maintaining that identity. On the one hand, these parents have broken with white solidarity in that they generally teach their children about racism, talk about white privilege, and, in some cases, are highly involved in racial justice movement work. On the other hand, they want to ensure privilege for their children, and their anti-racism work—where it occurs—does not challenge their own children's racial advantage.

Nikole Hannah-Jones points out that white parents—rather than work for structural change that could improve public schools and benefit all children—leave other people's children in situations they would find intolerable for their own. She says:

> It is important to understand that the inequality we see, school segregation, is both structural, it is systemic, but it's also upheld by individual choices. As long as individual parents continue to make choices that only benefit their own children . . . we're not going to see a change. . . .

We can't say, "This school is not good enough for my child" and then sustain that system. I think that that's just morally wrong. If it's not good enough for my child, then why are we putting any children in those schools?[18]

If we are being honest, white parents might admit that we are actually invested in school inequality. If schools were equal, my child would have to compete with your child and could not have the best of everything. We might ask ourselves why we think *our* children deserve the best of everything in an unequal society, and what that says about how we see ourselves and what we believe *we* deserve. We might also ask how a segregated life would be best for our children.

Note that every year in the month of February, when we celebrate Black History, we acknowledge the tragedy of imposed segregation on Blacks in the Jim Crow South. Yet white people live the most segregated lives of any racial group. A 2014 survey conducted by the Public Religion Research Institute and reported by the *Washington Post* found that 75 percent of white people have no Black friends and that this segregation is based on decades of policies and practices white people put in place, such as denying African Americans access to the GI Bill, redlining, white flight, subprime mortgages, and underfunding public schools.[19] Also note how we talk about white segregation in glowing terms; a "good" or "safe" neighborhood or school is assumed to be primarily white. I think this is actually one of the most powerful messages of white supremacy: there is no inherent loss in leading a segregated life. Most white people will go from cradle to grave with few if any authentic sustained cross-racial relationships with Black people and not see that anything of value is missing. Reflect for a moment on the profundity of that message.

Yet segregation cannot be seen as intentional or we lose plausible deniability that it is our preference. It's "just a fluke" that we grew up in a white neighborhood and attended mostly white schools, and today we just happen to live in similar neighborhoods and send our children to similar schools. But the moment I say, "We are now going to intentionally separate by race in order to work on challenging racism," white people freak out. A contrived, sixty-to-ninety-minute separation is just too much. "Why are you dividing us?! I don't feel right about that! We need to hear what they are saying and learn from them! This is inappropriate!" The shock of being exposed as white people triggers a kind of existential panic. The irony is that BIPOC people clearly see us as white people; we are the ones in denial. I think this exercise interrupts individualism, universalism, and color blindness, and it is likely the only time we have been so explicitly seen and named as white people, rather than as *just individuals* or *just people*. In other words, separating by race exposes us as *white*.

FEELING UNFAIRLY ACCUSED

Don't spend so much energy fighting this idea that you could possibly be racist. That's a total waste of time. It's like a bunch of white people lined up, hiding behind this real skinny pole. And we see you. We already know you're racist, so, get over yourselves.

—ANIKA NAILAH

For most white people, the worst thing to be called is "racist." We become downright irrational in the face of this charge, claiming to have been falsely accused of something akin to murder. This hysteria or white fragility is the result of the internalization of racial superiority coupled with the need to deny it, our investment in a system that serves us, and our attachment to ideologies such as meritocracy and individualism. We see this indignation in a disingenuous question white progressives often ask when given feedback that something they have said is racially problematic: "Well, what am I *supposed* to say?" I see the question as disingenuous because it is so consistently asked with an attitude of resentment. The emphasis on the word "supposed" is used to make the point that there is some set of rules out there that racialized people will not share, and since these rules cannot be known by white people, they are inherently unfair. If we are genuinely interested in increasing our awareness and minimizing the harm we cause, and that interest is greater than the interest in maintaining face and protecting ourselves from any inconvenient need for further education, then this is not the question we should be asking. Nor is resentment the reaction we should be expressing. Let's drop the snark in "supposed to" and ask questions driven by humility and sincere curiosity, and then listen to and reflect on the answers we receive.

An experience I have written about previously may illustrate this inability for many white people to look at themselves and their own racial patterns.[20] I was co-leading an anti-racist workshop with racial justice educator Darlene Flynn. The group of forty participants was racially diverse (approximately half people of color and half white). We were about one-third of the way through an all-day session. I had just finished an in-depth presentation on whiteness that appeared to have gone well; the group listened attentively, and no challenges were raised. Darlene took the floor and began to lead the corollary presentation: the impact of racism on people of color. She prefaced her talk with the statement "I will now be specifically engaging the people of color in the room on the topic of how systematic racism impacts us. This is a very sensitive conversation for us to have in the presence of white people, and I ask the white participants to simply listen."

Yet as she began presenting a list of ways that people of color are impacted by racism, a white woman repeatedly questioned her. Darlene did her best to speak to the woman's questions, but the interruptions continued. Finally, the white woman declared, "I think it's more complex than that." At this point it should be clear why the white woman's engagement was so problematic: white people don't have the experience of internalized racial oppression and were asked to just listen. The white woman was dominating the discussion, her repeated interruptions were derailing Darlene's ability to give her presentation, and she was undermining the leadership of a Black woman and positioning herself as more knowledgeable on issues of internalized racial oppression, while implying that Darlene's analysis was intellectually limited.

Darlene was clearly frustrated but finding it difficult to disengage. I leaned in and quietly asked her if she would like me to intervene. She said yes, and I spoke up. As diplomatically as possible, I attempted to point out to this participant what was racially problematic about her behavior. The woman was shocked and began crying, expressing outrage at the "accusation" that her actions could have a racist impact. The room erupted in a heated argument, dividing along the lines of whether the woman had been "mistreated" or not, with many people speaking at once and others nervously withdrawing. This was classic white fragility, complete with white women's tears, and all further progress was halted.

While this woman was manifesting racial superiority in ways that resulted in harm, her behavior could also be thought of as patterns that have developed as a result of her socialization into the racial hierarchy. While these patterns are not a measure of a person's morality or inherent goodness, they do need to be interrupted and changed. And that can't happen if all challenges are perceived as unfair accusations rather than opportunities for growth.

EXPLAINING AWAY/JUSTIFYING/ MINIMIZING/COMFORTING/CO-OPTING

I believe that very few white people want to deliberately hurt someone based solely on their race. In my experience, when we realize that we *have* hurt people of color—when we can let our defenses down enough to take this in—we are truly remorseful and want to remedy the harm. It is also difficult for us to hear about how another white person hurt a person of color through their unaware racism, and it is common to want to support and comfort the person who was hurt. Unfortunately, in our attempts to do so, we often end up minimizing or invalidating the harm. I have been in countless cross-racial discussions in which a person of color shares an experience of white racism, and a white person then tries to explain to them that it wasn't really racism because the person didn't mean it that way or that the person of color misunderstood the situation. While these responses may come from a desire to minimize the harm—in other words, "if you just understood that they didn't mean that, it wouldn't hurt you so much"—they only make the situation worse. The underlying message to BIPOC people is that we understand racism better than they do and they are overreacting. Of course without ongoing study, accountability, and practice—and even then—white people actually *do not* know more about the reality of racism than BIPOC people. This is a significant reason why many BIPOC people often avoid talking to white people about racism. As British journalist Reni Eddo-Lodge, the author of *Why I'm No Longer Talking to White People About Race*, says:

> I just can't engage with the bewilderment and defensiveness as they try to grapple with the fact that not everyone experiences the world in the way that they do. They have never had to think about, in power terms, what it means to be white, so any time they are vaguely reminded of this fact, they interpret it as an affront. Their eyes glaze over in boredom or widen in indignation. . . . Their throats open up as they try to interrupt, itching to talk over you but not really listen, because they need to let you know that you've got it wrong. I cannot continue to emotionally exhaust myself trying to get this message across, while also toeing a very precarious line that tries not to implicate any one white person in their role in perpetuating structural racism, lest they character assassinate me. So I'm no longer talking to white people about race.[21]

We need to develop the humility to *not know*. We do not have to fully understand a racialized person's experience before it can be validated. We also need to build the capacity to just sit with the discomfort and heartbreak of bearing witness to expressions of pain about racism rather than try to block them, explain them away, or co-opt them with expressions of our own pain.

I witnessed a perhaps more subtle version of white progressive lack of racial humility several years ago during a workshop on racism. A Black woman shared powerfully about how terrifying it was to have Black sons and the daily fear that they would be beaten or killed by the police. She told us about the day she had to "break their hearts" by letting them know that although she saw them as beautiful and good, society at large did not. She had to prepare them for the inevitable interactions they would have with the police and how to be safe when pulled over, to keep both hands visible at all times and to make eye contact. She began to weep, and her grief spread around the room as the other Black mothers broke down in recognition of her story.

The Black women's expressions of grief were intense, and as I sat among them I had the powerful realization that *I had no idea* how all-encompassing racism was for Black people. As a white mother, I did not have a history of police brutality toward my family. I was not able to see the countless unarmed young Black people killed by police and vigilantes as potentially my own children. That I could not identify with these mothers was my first realization. But then as I watched the room, I had a second realization as many of the white women turned to comfort the Black women, crying along with them, trying to hold them and tell them it would be OK. Although motivated by compassion, this seemed deeply inappropriate to me. How could I, as a white mother who did not know and did not *have to know* this pain, tell them it was going to be OK, rub their backs, or give them a hug? Of course I know what it is like to fear for my child, but *not based on their race*. And beyond not knowing these mothers' particular pain, it was *my* son, *my* brother, *my* husband they needed to warn their sons about. I remember when Trayvon Martin was killed, some white people wore T-shirts that said "I am Trayvon." But of course, we are *not* Trayvon.

I do not know how the Black women felt about the offers of support from some of the white women, and I imagine there was a range of reactions. But for me, it was their moment to connect and express their grief with one another and my moment to bear witness.

So what might it look like for a white woman to attempt to connect to a Black woman in this context with love and humility? The reality of racism *should* break our hearts. Sitting there in stoic silence, willing ourselves not to move or cry, would very likely come off as cold and uncaring. There is no single correct answer. In these moments, I strive to remain open and present but not assume what a person of color wants or needs. While there is a natural draw to comfort someone in pain, holding awareness of our racial position is imperative in this situation.

Holding awareness means not being driven by the relief and comfort *we* need. To that end, we must not assume what the person wants but to check with them, to ask for consent, and to do so in a way that takes up as little space as possible. A short simple question such as "May I put my hand on your back?" for example, may be enough. If the person declines the offer, then we accept their response. Unfortunately, the many recent critiques of white women's tears—including my own critique—and all the ways that white women take up space, make ourselves the victims, and co-opt resources has been interpreted to mean that we must never cry in front of Black people. But the point of these critiques is not to avoid expressing grief in the face of racism but to be mindful of our racial positions as we do so. When we cry, what are we crying about? How much space do we take up when expressing our grief? All have an impact on those around us. I was moved to tears that day at the workshop, but I expressed them quietly and would have politely declined an offer of comfort.

Bearing witness includes managing one's own anxiety, grief, and despair. If we have done some of our own racial work, we are more able to hold space for others and engage in mindful listening. The challenge of racial humility is staying connected while also decentering ourselves as white people.

EXPECTING BIPOC PEOPLE TO TEACH US ABOUT RACISM

Another pattern connected to our ignorance coupled with arrogance is that of interrogating BIPOC people about their racial experiences to further our learning. This reinforces several problematic dimensions of racism. First, the idea that racism is something that happens to BIPOC people but doesn't have anything to do with *us*, and thus we cannot be expected to have any knowledge of it, denies that racism is a *relationship* in which both groups are involved.

Second, this request requires nothing of us and reinforces unequal power relations by asking BIPOC people to do our work. There is plenty of material written and produced on the subject by BIPOC people who *are* willing to share the information—and generally *get paid to do so*.

Why haven't we sought it out prior to this conversation? Expecting to be handed the fruits of their labor with no risk or investment on our part is a form of neocolonialism.

Third, this request implies that we have no knowledge about how white racism works, thereby reinforcing the concept of white racial innocence. But of course white people are not innocent about racism. We have been deeply socialized into this construct. We need to be working to uncover and challenge this socialization. There are many workbooks and resources that can guide us. Layla F. Saad's *Me and White Supremacy* workbook is an excellent start, as is Dr. Eddie Moore's 21-Day Racial Equity Habit Building Challenge and resources from Racial Equity Tools.

Fourth, this request does not recognize the history we bring into the room with us and how often BIPOC people have tried to educate us and how often—as Eddo-Lodge describes—we have minimized or dismissed them (often demanding more data or "proof"). To ask BIPOC people to tell us how they experience racism without first building a trusting relationship is a red flag indicating that we are not skilled in anti-racist practice. These discussions also subject racialized people to having to bear witness to white people's confessions. Writer Kelsey Blackwell is clear on this point:

> Expecting people of color to be in the room to help white people learn about race is yet another example of privilege. Being in a space where white people are starting to wake up to their white cultural conditioning is heartbreaking for me. It is a pain that is felt deeply. . . . While there are some people of color who are up for being in conversations with white people about race, this is a gift offered in the service of collective liberation, and it requires tremendous energy, patience, bravery, and effort. It is not every person of color's work to do. . . . Please don't expect it. I believe that in most circumstances, doing race work in an integrated setting is harmful. I open myself up to stories about racist family members, or admissions from former white supremacists. Why do I need to hear this? The fact that racism exists is not a surprise to me. I do not need to hear more stories about it.[22]

In organizations, racialized people are oftentimes assumed to have the skill and interest to do race-related work, just because "they have race." While racialized people are much more likely to have a deeper understanding of systemic racism, they may not have any interest in leading this work given the degree of resistance and white fragility they encounter. A little research can go a long way toward finding interested and experienced racial equity leaders of color. But first we need to recognize racial equity as a field requiring a high level of skill and expertise that should be compensated, and which is not automatically and freely given *just because* someone is racialized.

So how do we gain this information if we don't ask racialized people to give it to us? We can get it in several interconnected ways. We can seek out the information from books, websites, films, and other available sources. There are, of course, many racialized people who are committed to teaching white people about racism (on their own terms and with compensation) and have been offering this information to us for decades, if not centuries. It is our own lack of interest and apathy that has prevented us from receiving it.

Let's break with the apathy of whiteness and *look it up*. A simple Google search of "What white people can do about racism" will return countless resources, including a list on Medium that is constantly updated by Corinne Shutack. At the time of this writing, the list had 103 entries. There are Crystal Marie Fleming's book *How to Be Less Stupid About Race*, Ijeoma Oluo's *So You Want to Talk About Race*, and Glen Singleton's *Courageous Conversations About Race*, among many others. We can also demand that we be given this information in schools and universities, and that we not be required to take special, elective courses in order to receive the information. We can get involved with organizations working for racial justice. And we can build authentic cross-racial relationships and be willing to watch, listen, and learn (which will likely require us to get out of our white comfort zones).

Sometimes, within the context of these relationships, we can ask direct questions and ask for explicit information, but this is not always necessary. Simply by virtue of living an integrated life and paying attention, we will learn much of what we need to know.

MAKING SURE EVERYONE KNOWS YOU ARE MARRIED TO A BLACK MAN (OR OTHER RACIALIZED PERSON, OR HAVE ADOPTED RACIALIZED CHILDREN, OR HAVE RACIALIZED GRANDCHILDREN)

Being a white woman married to a Black man potentially offers deep insights into cross-racial dynamics to bring to the conversation. Sadly, many white women don't demonstrate that their cross-racial relationships have provided a deeper understanding. All too often, these relationships are announced to establish a complete *lack* of racism. Instead, they demonstrate a lack of sensitivity, self-awareness, critical race consciousness, and historical knowledge. Our families are a significant part of our lives, and I am not saying we cannot or should not talk about a cross-racial relationship in a discussion of race. But *how, when, and why* white women bring this up is worthy of exploration.

There is a long and painful history surrounding white women in relationship to Black men. One aspect of this history is how often the violence toward Black men was predicated on claims that they had flirted with or otherwise threatened or caused discomfort to a white woman. The lynching of Emmett Till is perhaps the most famous example. In 1955, Carolyn Bryant, a white woman, claimed that Emmett, a fourteen-year-old Black boy, had offended her in her family's grocery store in Mississippi in 1955. Bryant's husband, Roy, and his half-brother J. W. Milam abducted Emmett, beat and mutilated him, shot him to death, and sunk him in the Tallahatchie River. Roy Bryant and Milam were both acquitted.

Till's murder was not an isolated incident. Between 1882 and 1968, the NAACP reports that at least 3,446 Black people were lynched, most often men (not all lynchings were recorded, and many were predicated on some perceived threat to white women).[23] While many white women do not know this history, most Black women are well aware of it, and it is invoked when white women cavalierly announce their relationships with Black men. Yet again, Black women are reminded of how much white people don't (and don't *have* to) know about our racial history, even when we are in intimate relationships across race.

Of course being in a relationship with a Black man does not free white women from the inevitable anti-Blackness we internalize. White women can and do perpetuate racism in these relations. British writer

Courttia Newland shared in *The Guardian* an incident in which he was fired by his white female boss. This woman had been making inappropriate comments about his attractiveness, and one day she called him and told him she had hurt her leg and insisted he come to her home for their meeting. Feeling very uncomfortable—and likely aware of who would be believed if she were to accuse him of inappropriate behavior—he refused and lost his job. Newland explains, "It's clear to me that this incident is an example of white female privilege being used to dominate a young black man. I was perceived to have no recourse, no agency. I had to submit to being exoticised in accordance with the hypersexualised stereotype that black men are often framed by. When I refused to reciprocate, I was punished."[24]

Newland goes on to acknowledge the need to address the rampant misogyny in a patriarchal society, yet wonders if it's possible to explore the role white women play in the "continual oppression of black men; to speak about this in a historical context, tracing the direct line from enslavement and colonisation to the present day. To have an honest discussion about the fact that white women, who obviously face a cis, white patriarchal system of oppression, also use that patriarchal system to oppress those perceived as lower on the racial and social hierarchy?"

While Newland was not in a committed long-term relationship such as marriage with his white employer, he cites the specter of anti-Blackness surfacing in intimate relationships with white women: "The danger of loving someone who might possibly racially abuse you in the furious heat of a domestic argument. The confusing seesaw desire of wanting to be an ally for someone's struggle while not having your struggle recognized in return."[25] In addition to white women's deep internalization of anti-Blackness that can surface during conflicts when inhibitions are low, Newland names the reality that white women have in no way consistently been advocates for Black liberation, as evidenced by our involvement in enslavement, our active resistance to including Black women in the suffrage movement of the early 1900s, our approval of Jim Crow policies, our embrace of white feminism, and our support of Donald Trump.

White supremacy permeates every aspect of our culture, including standards of beauty. The ideal woman is consistently depicted as
a white woman. In 2015, a link advertised on a CNN page was titled
"The 10 Hottest Women from Around the World." Of these ten, two
were women of color: Rihanna, who is Bajan, and Sofía Vergara, who
is Colombian. None were Asian, although Asian women are literally the
majority of all women in the world. Representing South Africa, a country that is 92 percent Black, was Charlize Theron. Choosing Theron to
represent South Africa is a particularly vivid example of how we are
constantly reinforced to see whiteness—and narrow representations of
white women—as the ideal.

Many Black women share the pain of seeing themselves as inherently outside the standards of beauty that consist of silky (and most often blond) hair, narrow noses, blue eyes, slim hips, and so on. In 2013,
teen filmmaker Kiri Davis made a film titled *A Girl Like Me*, in which
she recreated the famous "doll experiments" of psychologists Kenneth
and Mamie Clark.[26]

The Clarks were interested in the self-esteem of Black children. They
conducted their studies by asking participating children to choose which
doll they preferred, a white doll or a Black doll, in answer to a series of
questions that included "Give me the doll that you like to play with,"
"Give me the doll that is a nice doll," "Give me the doll that looks
bad," and "Give me the doll that is a nice color." The majority of the
children preferred the white doll to the Black. This preference was sta-
ble regardless of whether the children lived in the north or south United
States, although northern children had a more definite preference for
white skin. When asked why the Black doll looked bad, the children
consistently attributed it to the doll's Blackness. The Clarks found that
by age three, Black children had begun to internalize a sense that they
were inferior to whites. By age seven, this sense was firmly in place.

The 1954 *Brown v. Board of Education* Supreme Court decision,
which overturned "separate but equal" laws by arguing that separate
was inherently unequal, was influenced by the Clarks' research, which
led Chief Justice Earl Warren to write in the opinion, "To separate [chil-
dren] from others of similar age and qualifications solely because of

their race generates a feeling of inferiority as to their status in the community that may affect their hearts and minds in a way unlikely to ever be undone."[27] Also note that Chief Justice Warren acknowledges here that the effects of racism do not end when an act of racism ends. Those effects are ongoing and shape generations.

In Kiri Davis's film, the young Black women she interviewed spoke poignantly about the impact of white beauty standards:

STEPHANIE: You have to have permed hair, relaxed hair . . .

WAHIDAH: You know, straight hair, or like blonde hair. You know, long waves or something.

STEPHANIE: And if it's natural, that's even, that's good hair. Like bad hair is hair you have to relax, because it's kinky. . . . I remember when I first started wearing my hair natural, at first my mom was okay with it, and she, she thought it looked nice. And then after like the second day, she was like, "Oh, stop that." She was like, "You're starting to look African." I was like, "Well, I *am* African," and that really pissed me off.

JENNIFER: I guess I sort of felt, like I, there was not any attention towards me because of maybe my skin color, or because my hair was kinky, or, you know, just basically that. Or even . . . when I was younger, like, say there was . . . a doll. I used to have a lot of dolls, but most of them were just white dolls with long, straight hair that I would comb. And I would be like, "Oh, I wish I was just like this Barbie doll."

GLENDA: There are standards that are imposed upon us, like, um . . . You know, you're pretty [but] you're *prettier* if you're light skinned.

JENNIFER: Since I was younger, I also considered being lighter as a form of beauty or, you know . . . more . . . beautiful than being dark skinned, so I used to think of myself as being ugly 'cause I was dark skinned.[28]

Everyone is impacted by the standards of white supremacy that circulate in the culture at large, albeit with different outcomes based on our proximity to them. This, of course, includes Black men, who are not outside of culture or unaffected by representations of ideal beauty. When white women insensitively flaunt their relationships with Black men in front of Black women, the heteronormative message of white women as most desirable may be painfully reinscribed, as well as serving as a reminder of how oblivious white people can remain to white supremacy, even when in intimate cross-racial relationships.

White women who use their cross-racial marriages as evidence that they are free of racism are relying on the form of credentialing I have discussed as *proximity*. This is the notion that a racist could not tolerate being physically near a Black person. Unfortunately, proximity is not a convincing argument for a lack of racism—it only conveys a lack of critical consciousness about white supremacy and how it functions. A white woman who makes this claim to establish a lack of racism is likely not one who will be open to any suggestion to the contrary.

I want to be clear that I am not saying we cannot or should not tell anyone we are married across race. Sharing our racial insights is important, and relationships can be a rich source of insight. I am also not saying that all Black women feel similarly about white women sharing these relationships. But in recognition of a range of possible impacts, white women should share this information with a sense of timing, awareness, and sensitivity.

SEEKING ABSOLUTION

The need to be racially forgiven is perhaps a more subtle form of white fragility and stems from what I term the "good/bad binary." If we define racists as individuals who consciously and intentionally want to hurt people across race, then only some people are racist, and they are bad. Other people are not racist, and they are good. Needing to be on the "good" side of this formula, white progressives in particular can become subservient when given specific feedback about how our racist conditioning is showing up ("I'll do anything you ask to make up for how terrible I am.") ("Do you still like me?"). Or we can beg for absolution ("I am so sorry. I didn't mean to do that; please tell me everything's OK and you're not mad at me."). We may not be in denial that we exhibit racist patterns, but we still find them unbearable to face directly. The binary makes complicity with racism and being a good person mutually exclusive.

Seeking forgiveness directly from the injured party puts an unfair pressure on them to take care of our feelings in addition to dealing with the impact of our actions. Asking for absolution puts the focus back on ourselves and demands more time and attention from those we have harmed. In so doing we recenter ourselves, siphoning off more energy than it took to give us the feedback in the first place. Giving feedback to white people on racism is very risky for people of color, because we are so often defensive and unreceptive. When we are looking to be forgiven, we are not generally defensive, but we are being needy, which is still a burden for those we have hurt.

Sometimes we know enough not to seek absolution from the injured party, but we may try another trick to ease our discomfort. I have been given feedback by one Black friend and then found myself wanting to call another Black friend, slyly hoping for reassurance that I did nothing wrong. When we seek absolution from a third party, we not only undermine the person we injured; we are triangulating across race, pressuring one Black person to align with us and undermine another. A white person engaging in this behavior is not only avoiding responsibility and repair but is also driving wedges between Black people and indirectly pressuring them to go against others or risk their relationships with us.

Instead, we can appreciate the risk taken in providing the feedback, sit with our feelings, and give the other person some space for theirs. Processing those feelings with another white person who can listen with compassion while still holding us accountable for our actions is a much healthier choice. We might also attend a white affinity group and work through our distress there. At the minimum, feeling overwhelmed with guilt and regret should serve as a red flag that we are not ready to make amends and that it would be better for us to take some time to reflect before seeking to resolve the situation. Then, when we are ready, we need to do what is necessary to repair and move forward.

DISMISSING THE ANALYSIS BECAUSE IT
COMES FROM THE US AND YOUR COUNTRY IS DIFFERENT

As we witnessed following the murder of George Floyd, people all over the world came out in support of the Black Lives Matter movement, and protests took place in many countries. These protests were in solidarity with Black people in the US, but they were also an acknowledgment of white supremacy outside the US. My work on white fragility has been circulating outside the US for several years now, and I have been invited to present in South Africa, Canada, Germany, France, Portugal, Australia, Brazil, England, and New Zealand. Each time I present internationally, white people pull me aside to tell me that "things are different here." Sometimes they are willing to acknowledge that racism exists in their country but contend that it is too different from that of the US for my work to be relevant to them. Sometimes they actually claim that there is no racism at all in their country and that racism is "an American problem." And yet, just like in the US, in every country I have visited, racialized people take me aside to tell me the opposite. In fact, most often it is racialized people who have asked me to come, writing to tell me that I have accurately described the dynamics they experience and asking me to help the white people in their country. While the specific histories may be different and the forms of white credentialing may vary slightly from country to country, the outcomes are the same: white supremacy, racial inequality, white denial, and the eruption of white fragility when any of this is challenged.

In addition to claims that are familiar to US readers, I have heard when speaking in Europe: "There is no racism here because there are no Black people here—this is a homogeneous culture" and "I am not racist because I never saw a Black person growing up" (these last two are especially popular in Germany). In South Africa I heard: "I built housing in the townships"; "My children play on a diverse sports team"; "Black people control the politics, so if anything it's reverse racism"; and "It's different here because Black people are the majority." In Canada: "We are a multicultural society;" "We pay respect to Indigenous people"; and "Canada never had slavery." In Australia: "We have Aboriginal people in our family" and "We don't talk about racism; it's not an issue." In New Zealand: "Our culture is different because we have infused the Maori way into how we communicate" and "We did things differently and more equitably than Australia did." Yet in every one of these contexts not only are racialized people challenging these narratives, but racial inequality and white advantage are consistently reproduced.

I have also been in discussions in the US in which a white person who emigrated from Europe insists that because they did not grow up here, racism doesn't apply to them. They base this primarily on the claim that they grew up in a context in which racism did not exist. Of course that is a nonsensical claim on its face. But when I ask them how long they have lived in the US, where they live, and if they have any Black friends, their claim falls apart. Most often, they have lived in the US for decades, live in a white segregated neighborhood, and have no Black friends. Yet like so many white Americans, they see white segregation as racially neutral and believe themselves to be untouched by the forces of the culture that surrounds them.

I can acknowledge that the nuances of racism vary across the world and that the US context is indeed different in some foundational ways. And I understand the resentment some feel about a US-centric focus. But that doesn't mean there is no racism in other cultures, especially those with a history of white settler colonialism,[29] and that the analysis can be dismissed out of hand. It is on white people in these contexts to put in some effort and make the translations needed; the basics are the same. Further, the conversation about race in the US has been going on for a long time—a lot longer than in many other countries. People from the US with experience in these conversations have something to offer, and there is a reason we have been invited to your country. Of course we need to proceed with some humility as guests in your culture, but dismissing the content based on resentment of US dominance only functions to protect your racist status quo. Certainly, white people outside the US are capable of making the necessary adjustments.

FOCUSING ON DELIVERY

When I am asked to mediate a cross-racial conflict, I sometimes encounter a white person who is willing to acknowledge that they said or did something racially problematic. The sticking point, however, is *the way they received the feedback*. Focusing on delivery is a form of tone policing: using the inferred emotions behind a message to dismiss the message itself. "Why did the person have to be so angry? I didn't mean to hurt them, so why can't they recognize my good intentions?" Until the deliverer of the feedback acknowledges the hurt *they* caused through their tone or approach, the white person cannot or will not move on.

During an interview on my book *White Fragility*, I was asked a question that began "Some white people have said they couldn't finish your book because 'they felt screamed at.'" I couldn't help but laugh out loud at this perfect example of white fragility. (Look, I'm not saying that someone who doesn't finish my book is automatically demonstrating white fragility, but if feeling *screamed at* is the reason, I stand by the assessment.)

In the case of a person of color giving feedback or explaining how racism impacts them, to use delivery as the reason for dismissal is particularly oppressive. Writer Tess Martin shares this composite example of an experience she has had many times:

WHITE person: Wow, you are surprisingly well spoken!

PERSON of color: For a black person, you mean? That's really insensitive and I can't believe you thought you had the right to say that to me.

WP: Why are you so upset? I just gave you a compliment.

POC: Do you not even realize what you said and how racist it is for white folks to pat black folks on the head for "speaking so well"? Seriously, think before you say things to people.

WP: You need to calm down. No one is going to listen to what you have to say if you're this angry about it. There's no reason to attack me over nothing. Have you considered the fact that you could be overreacting to this?[30]

There are several key understandings and corresponding skills that a white person is missing in these cases:

- We bring our structural positions with us—this communication is not occurring solely between two different individuals, but also across two different positions of *social and institutional power.*
- It entails great risk for a racialized person to give feedback to a white person on racism, especially when the white person does not acknowledge the differential in racial power. This degree of risk understandably may generate emotions that will inform how the feedback is given.
- While we may see our behavior as minor or isolated, for a racialized person it is not minor or isolated—it represents the relentlessness of whiteness. Our one act may just be the prover- bial straw (and of course, it may *not* be one isolated act at all but rather a consistent pattern we are unaware of).
- Given the risk it takes to give us feedback, many racialized people let a great deal of white racism go unchecked and only bother challenging us when a line is crossed or they are at the end of their patience. Insisting that they deliver this feedback to us calmly is profoundly controlling on our part and functions to prioritize *our* feelings over theirs.
- We need to ask ourselves what we believe to be the "rules" for how a racialized person should give us feedback on racism, how we came to have these rules, and how they function in practice. While certain guidelines may be the norm in some areas of com- munication, if they don't take into account power dynamics, they won't translate to cross-racial contexts.

Having been involved in anti-racist education on cross-racial teams for the past twenty-five years, I have had countless racialized people express their frustration with me over the inevitable surfacing of my racist conditioning. As I receive this feedback, I try to keep in mind that on the one hand I have indeed done something problematic and need to take responsibility for repair. On the other hand, I remember that when emotions are high, they are likely not all about me but also about what I represent. This helps me take the upset less personally and makes it easier to receive the feedback, learn what I can from it, and move forward.

A colleague offered this example of the importance of not taking feedback too personally. During a white affinity-group meeting, a woman shared her confusion about two cross-racial experiences and asked for feedback from the group. These experiences took place years apart, yet each had the same outcome. In both cases, she asked acquaintances of color a question about racism. Each of them responded by asking her, "Do you really want to know?" The white woman wondered what she might have done to inspire this response. She was concerned that somehow she had given the impression that she wasn't genuinely interested. Her fellow group members offered her a series of questions for deeper reflection:

- Remove yourself from the equation and imagine that they would have responded this way to any white person who asked them your question. Why might they respond this way regardless of who asked?
- What was at risk for your friends if they answered your question honestly?
- What does the consistency in their responses tell you about the predictability of these dynamics?
- How might our tendency to make it about ourselves make it more difficult for racialized people to be honest with us?

Writer Ijeoma Oluo speaks to the risk of being honest with white people, writing, "I spend a lot of my day navigating the white people in my life that I love. I try to figure out when to offer comfort, encouragement, hard truths, or humor. I agonize over . . . when to give up, when to take the risk and challenge someone I love who is hurting me."[31]

Oluo shares the advice she offers a young woman of color who is struggling in her relationship with a white friend, telling her: "You will have to decide who is worth the risk. Because it will hurt you almost every time. It will almost never have a happy ending. So if you say something, say it because you love that person enough to risk . . . the pain of realizing that they do not see you and will not risk the discomfort of seeing you. Do it for people who are worth the one in 10 chance that they will respond with the love you need."

Note that Oluo is talking about white people she *knows and loves*. This powerfully illustrates why proximity to—or even close relationships with—Black people does not ensure a lack of racism for white people. Because we tend to see ourselves as individuals, rather than as *white individuals*, we proceed as if power dynamics are not at play in our cross-racial interactions. We don't understand that we bring our histories with us into these interactions, and they are histories of harm. We represent not only ourselves but all the other white people who have hurt their friends of color. If we want to be the one in ten Oluo holds hope for, we will need to earn that trust, not expect it.

CAREFULNESS

Racism is a complex, multilevel system. There are no easy and concise answers or solutions to end it. While we need to develop strategies, no single approach will work in every situation, and some strategies shouldn't be taken to the extreme. For example, *thoughtfulness* is an important strategy. Thoughtfulness can include being cognizant of the history we bring to racial encounters, being considerate about the language we use, being sensitive to group dynamics, and being attentive to our patterns and limited understanding. But thoughtfulness taken to an extreme can become *carefulness*, in which we are so cautious about making a mistake or offending that we end up engaging disingenuously. Psychologist Beverly Daniel Tatum speaks to this when she notes, "Most Americans have internalized the espoused cultural values of fairness and justice for all at the same time that they have been breathing the smog of racial biases and stereotypes pervading popular culture. . . . [It leaves] many Whites feeling uneasy, uncomfortable, and even perhaps fearful in the presence of Black people, often without their conscious awareness of these feelings."[32] This unease is at the root of a concern commonly voiced by white progressives: "I am afraid that I will say the wrong thing."

The problem with carefulness was made clear to me when I expressed my fear about saying the wrong thing to a friend of mine who is Black. I was worried about being too relaxed and then something awful slipping out. I had asked her, "Isn't it important for white people to be careful when interacting across race?" She replied, "Robin . . . *do you think we can't tell when you are being careful*?" She paused and then added, "How do you think white people look when they are being careful across race?"

I suddenly felt *uncovered* as a white person. I realized that I had expected my friend to see me as I saw myself—as just her friend—not as her *white* friend. I suddenly realized what we must look like for Black people when we are being careful around them: stiff, uncomfortable, uptight, reserved. As I pictured myself being careful around Black people in this way, I also saw why they experienced white carefulness as racism. I certainly wasn't warm, relaxed, sincere, or open when I was being overly careful.

This explained why Black people so often shared that white people were cold around them and how awful that felt. My friend's question caused me to realize that while I needed to be *thoughtful* about how I interacted, *carefulness* was not useful. I have come to realize that Black people expect us to manifest our racist conditioning at times and are less concerned about that than about how we respond when this is pointed out, what we are willing to do to repair, and what we learn and will do differently in the future.

SILENCE

Silence is carefulness in the extreme. I have written extensively on white silence in discussions on racism because it is such a ubiquitous, maddening, and problematic pattern. Consider this recent example. I volunteered to give a ninety-minute presentation followed by a Q&A for a friend of mine who runs an internship program for women working on their master's degrees in the counseling field. My friend's program has a focus on anti-racism, and the interns had been reading and discussing these issues for several months. The group consisted of about fifteen people, approximately four of whom were people of color. After some brief remarks on white socialization, I opened the floor to questions. I soon noticed a pattern in which the same few people were speaking, but the majority of the group—and the white people in particular—remained silent. I named this pattern and invited the white people to show themselves. After a few moments of uncomfortable silence, a woman of color who had been sharing previously began to speak again. I asked her to hold back and let the white people feel the pressure and struggle through their silence. This prompted a white woman to voice a concern that I had just silenced the woman of color. She was confused about why I would do this, given that the focus of my talk was on anti-racism. I explained that while I recognized that I had risked the woman of color feeling silenced, my strategy was to interrupt the power dynamics by pressing the white people to take the same risks of vulnerability that the people of color in the conversation were taking. I acknowledged that it might not have been the best decision, but I did not make it unaware. I then checked in with the woman of color about the impact of my asking her to hold her comment. She said that she felt relieved and energized by the shift in pressure onto white people and the exposure of the racism inherent in white silence. It was the first time for her that white people's patterns in these discussions were named and white people were being called in. She shared that in her academic program she dreaded these conversations because of the exact dynamics that were happening here, wherein people of color were expected to be vulnerable and expose themselves—to do all the "race work"—while white people sat back and observed, taking no risks themselves. None of her white professors had the skills to interrupt these patterns. Another person of color agreed that she also found my move empowering.

With some relief that the risk I took was helpful, and that she and another woman of color had not felt silenced, I returned to my pressure on the white participants. I explained how silence from a position of power is a power move. I urged them as white people to take risks and make mistakes in the service of learning and growth. I explained that we needed to show vulnerability and humility in order to build trust across race. I pointed out that BIPOC people in the group had just shared how unsettling it was for them not to know where white people were coming from, and that regardless of our intentions, the impact was a climate that could feel hostile. Still, not one white person who had not already spoken stepped up. I was quite simply stunned that they could remain silent when the hurtful racial impact had been clearly laid out for them by their guest speaker—a white person with years of experience facilitating these dialogues—and several people of color. Stonewalled by the lack of participation, I ended the meeting after seventy-five minutes.

In processing the experience later with the friend who had invited me, she told me that after I left they discussed what had happened. All but one of the white participants said they did not like my "approach." Keep in mind that the people of color had shared openly that they felt a rare sense of being supported by my approach. Still, in the face of that testimony, the white people held to their claim that the problem was mine. This raises the question of what approach would have worked for them? And what were the odds that whatever that approach was, it would have felt supportive to the BIPOC people in the room?

The white people in this group were the epitome of progressives. The group included nonbinary white people, Jewish white people, and white people with disabilities. Most were under thirty. They were interning in a program that centered an anti-oppression framework in counseling, which recognizes that inequality is structured into society and manifests in a range of forms, including classism, sexism, racism, ableism, hetero-sexism, transphobia, ageism, and anti-Semitism. A basic tenet of an anti-oppression framework is that if we are not actively challenging those structures, we are supporting them. They had been reading and study-ing this framework for months. Given that in the case of racism, the worst fear of most white progressives is that they be perceived as racist, and both myself and the BIPOC people in the room gave them direct feedback that the effect of their silence was racism, how could they con-tinue to hold back? What was going on?

In cross-racial discussions it is easy to be distracted by white participants who dominate; indeed, facilitators spend a lot of energy strategizing about how to rein in these participants. We need to also consider the oft-neglected other end of the continuum: white silence. When white normative taboos against talking directly about race are broken, especially within the context of explicitly challenging racial inequality, it is uncomfortable and destabilizing for many white people. Seeking to regain our comfort and sense of racial stability is a predictable yet problematic response, for any white moves that are intended to maintain racial comfort necessarily work to maintain traditional race relations. When white people employ silence to maintain a degree of comfort, that silence functions as a means to maintain control.

In addition to maintaining control, I submit that the issue taken with my approach that day was one of unfulfilled expectations. As white progressives, the participants expected to be validated in their wokeness, not called in and exposed. Their need to maintain face was so powerful as to allow them to continue maintaining silence, even when those they were ostensibly worried about hurting were telling them it was hurtful. This is the heartbreaking power of the white need for racial control. The great irony of silence as a means to save face is that it doesn't convince anyone that we are not racist; it actually conveys the opposite.

Over the years of facilitating discussions with white people on racism, I have heard many rationales for white silence:

- "It's just my personality; I rarely talk in groups."
- "Everyone has already said what I was thinking" or "I don't have much to add."
- "I am trying to be careful not to dominate the discussion."
- "I feel intimidated by people in this group who have power over me."
- "I don't know much about race, so I will just listen."
- "I already know all this."
- "I need time to process."
- "I don't want to be misunderstood."
- "I don't feel safe."

- "I don't want to be judged/attacked."
- "I'm afraid I'll lose my job."
- "I don't want to say the wrong thing and offend anybody."[33]

Every one of these rationales can and should be challenged from an anti-racist framework. From that framework, any default or patterned behavior we engage in as white people is problematic because it is not strategic. There are certainly times when the best strategy is to just listen. But there are also times when the best strategy is to come forward and engage. I may not get that strategy right by everyone—indeed it is unlikely that I will—but I still need to be thinking critically about the choices I make. Defaulting to whatever engagement feels most comfortable is not guided by critical thinking and is not anti-racist.

Readers may be asking, "What about the silence of BIPOC people in cross-racial dialogues?" There are many reasons why BIPOC people might at times choose silence in a cross-racial discussion: as a response to resistance or hostility from white participants; a lack of trust based on well-founded experience of being penalized for challenging white people; a sense of hopelessness in the face of white solidarity; having taken a risk and shown vulnerability only to be met with invalidation; being outnumbered by white people and assessing that there are no allies present; and choosing not to "throw their pearls" to white people who sit back and take but do not give in return. The driving forces behind their silence are not the same.

No matter how progressive the white people in the group might see themselves, no matter how much they might blame me for the cause of their silence, no matter how ineffectively I may have facilitated, in the end they did not show up. They did not demonstrate progressiveness in any identifiable way. And their BIPOC coworkers noticed.

MARVELING AT HOW INTERESTING LEARNING ABOUT RACISM IS!

I often receive emails from white people who read a book or took a workshop and found it so interesting they now want to become racial justice educators. "Is there a program I can take to get certification?"

they ask. I am seldom asked how the person can continue to uncover their own complicity before moving on to teaching others how to uncover theirs. Social justice researcher Angela Park names the impact of this approach directly. "One of the most annoying things I hear from white people is, 'It's just so interesting, these topics.' The way in which white people intellectualize racism . . . is just horrifying," Park says.[34] "I want them to authentically connect to the ways in which racism has deeply shaped who they are and what they see, what they think about, how they show up in the world."

Marveling over how interesting learning about racism is does not indicate that we have connected to our own role, much less the suffering we cause others. This is especially insensitive when we intellectualize in front of BIPOC people.

We could begin to move from our heads and connect to our feelings by asking ourselves why our hearts are not breaking every day. How have we managed not to see? How many videos did we have to watch before we believed? Why did George Floyd's brutalization have to be so clear before we granted that he did not "do something" to bring on his own murder? What inconvenience are we willing to endure in order to build humanizing relationships across race?

Yes, the degree of learning, growth, and insight available to white people willing to engage in anti-racist work is unparalleled. The relationships we could have, the sense of integrity we could know, are invaluable. For me, this journey has been exhilarating and fascinating and inspiring. It has also been heartbreaking and frustrating and discouraging. But if it is *only* painful, or *only* exciting, something essential is missing.

As white people, we have been conditioned not to feel loss in living segregated lives. We have been conditioned into not only an acceptance of, but an *investment in*, systemic racism. We didn't choose this conditioning. But it is deep, and it is not rendered inoperative as soon as we recognize the system for what it is. Countering a lifetime of racist socialization is ongoing, and racist ideology is always circulating and being reinforced. People will be at different stages in the process of coming to racial consciousness, and of course it is wonderful when the learning is new and powerful and we are inspired to get involved. We need that energy to sustain commitment. Even so, we also need to have some sensitivity about how we are conveying our enthusiasm. Engaging at a purely intellectual level can be a hurtful reminder of how disconnected we are.

We so often ask what we should do about racism. Park has a clear directive: "I need you to know all the ways in which you inflict racism on others in this world, on your friends, on people in your family, on your colleagues in organizations, how you perpetuate politically and structurally. Every white person who hasn't interrogated racism deeply is putting their knees on the necks of people of color every day." Yes, she is talking about the knees of nice progressive white people who "believe in justice" and therefore see no need for further examination.

White progressives are not white nationalists. But that does not mean we don't play a role in perpetuating systemic racism. Could we marvel at how interesting learning about racism is if we recognized our *own knees* on the necks of people of color? Again, it is on us to uncover *how* we enact racism as white progressives, but not *if*.

CHAPTER 6

SPIRITUAL, NOT RELIGIOUS

There is a particular strain of white progressive and corresponding set of racial patterns that I want to address in this chapter. These white progressives don't typically identify as religious or with traditional religions such as Christianity or Judaism. In fact, they tend to put a strong emphasis on the point that they are not religious but rather that they are *spiritual*. While this strain of spiritual white progressives (also known as "New Agers") might say they don't believe in God per se (and certainly not a strictly male God), they do believe there is intentionality in the universe—a kind of disembodied consciousness that is aware of, interested in, and can affect our lives and whose intervention can be influenced by the way we think or ask—what we "put out there." Outcomes that are "meant to be" point to this intentional universe.

Many believe that consciousness continues after death in some form, perhaps via reincarnation, and that certain people are in tune with the spirit world and can commune with the dead. Those considered spiritual teachers often include those who serve as conduits and can receive insights from this noncorporeal world ("channels") and those who can feel and take on the emotions of the people around them ("empaths") and/or can predict the future via intuition, psychic ability, or the reading of cards or numbers (e.g., tarot or numerology).

The website for the Global Spiritual Awakening Conference of 2019 illustrates the belief in and reverence for extrasensory abilities and mystical experience, as well as the unexamined whiteness of the spiritual thought leaders. While racial identity can sometimes be ambiguous, of the eighteen featured "world class" speakers, every single one appears to be white. Of the fifteen sets of various musicians pictured, all but one appear to be white. The range of skills and presentations listed for the speakers include tarot readings, the practices of the Druids, alchemy, magic, channeling archangels and other entities, soul readings, palmistry, iris analysis, connecting with the fairies, and reincarnation. As an astounding example of white supremacy, the announcement proposes that these eighteen white speakers, along with what can only be assumed to be an overwhelmingly white crowd of attendees, are likely to change the thinking of the entire world.

The website announces, "The collective energy generated by this group of the world's leading spiritual teachers, combined with the many hundreds or thousands of attendees, will be unsurpassed and is sure to shift the consciousness of humanity." This is the hubris of what sociologist Joe Feagin terms the *white racial frame*: the deeply internalized structure through which whites make racial meaning. This framework includes images, interpretations, perceptions, evaluations, emotions, and actions that position whites as superior and are passed down and reinforced throughout society.[1] Seeing ourselves as unlimited by any particular position or perspective, we can represent all of humanity. And we alone can guide all of humanity into its most evolved state (often based on our interpretations of Black, Indigenous, Asian, and other racialized people's wisdom). Perhaps this is why so much of the teaching of spiritual white progressives is focused on how to transcend the body. This functions as a new-age version of color blindness, wherein one homogeneous group of bodies, primarily living separately from all other types (except when travelling to their communities to collect and study), and at the top of a racist hierarchy, insists that the body doesn't matter.

In her study for the book *White Utopias: The Religious Exoticism of Transformational Festivals*, religious scholar Amanda Lucia attended twenty-three different "transformational festivals"—large-scale gatherings of people attempting to create utopian spaces and gain enlightenment. Lucia observed that the adoption of nonwhite religious and cultural identities reveals a sense of entitlement, a tendency to rely on "racialized others as unsullied, exotic, premodern subjects whose cultural products supply practical, therapeutic tools."[2] She argues that this religious exoticism erases the actual representatives of marginalized spiritual traditions and wonders what makes these festivals such "safe spaces of white ethnic homogeneity." Lucia contends that while participants create temporary utopias at these festivals, they also participate in religious exoticism by co-opting Indigenous and Indic spiritualities, ultimately rendering them *white* utopias. She asks if true transformation can occur if participants are not confronting their own whiteness. Notably, while Lucia did not hide her role as a researcher, when she solicited feedback from the individuals she quoted in her analysis of whiteness that many had "vitriolic reactions" (including those who bill themselves as spiritual gurus). They vehemently objected to the naming of white privilege and the acknowledgment that these festivals occurred within the context of structural white supremacy. (I have to point out how quickly white fragility erupts and how "not nice" white progressives can be when challenged on racism.)

In general, any religion, culture, practice, or form of medicine deemed "old," "pre-industrial," or "non-Western" is preferred by spiritual white progressives; the term "ancient" appears over and over again in online searches of book titles and workshop descriptions. Because so many valued symbols and practices are associated with Indigenous people, there is a particular idealization of all things deemed Indigenous: sustainability, non-capitalistic gift economies, intuition over science. People who are perceived as living closer to the land and the spirit world are more "natural" and, thus, better, and romanticized Indigenous people engaging in traditional practices represent the ultimate in "natural living." Yet, as Lucia notes, this focus on the perceived purity, timelessness, and authenticity of the "other" necessarily severs it from the communities whose practices are emulated. (For a classic confluence of these tropes, see the film *Avatar*.)

In many spiritual white progressive communities, eco-villages, anti-oppression workshops, self-care retreats, peace circles, and other similar gatherings, rituals that are perceived to be associated with Indigenous people are featured, whether or not Indigenous people are actually present, as are practices such as placing tokens on altars; calling spirits into the room; referring to oneself as a warrior and to the group as a tribe; smudging; reverence for self-proclaimed "shamans"; going on "walkabouts" in order to "find oneself"; and the use of psychotropic plants, bells, and prayer bowls. Practices perceived as Indigenous are often merged with those associated with the East, such as reincarnation, astrology, and meditation. I recently asked a white person who enjoys these rituals why—if the group had no Indigenous people in it—they were engaging in them, and she replied that there were likely Indigenous people *in the area*. This response raises a few questions: Which Indigenous groups are in the area? Are these the specific rituals of the specific Indigenous groups in the area? Would the groups in the area feel honored by an overwhelmingly white group enacting rituals associated with their culture? And how would the white people in the group know the answer to these questions?

Annually, millions of white Westerners engage in ethno-tourism in Mexico, Central America, and South America. Ethno-tourism puts economic pressure on Indigenous peoples to pose for photos and otherwise perform in ways that please tourists. The Indigenous person and their environment become exotic resources, there to meet white Western desires for enlightenment and self-fulfillment. Using "primitive" peoples to serve Westerners' interests in this way is a more modern manifestation of a long colonialist history. In Ecuador and Peru, an entire industry has developed for tourists who want to experience "authentic" pre-Columbian practices, going into the rain forest to be guided by shamans in the use of hallucinogenic plants in order to connect to ancient spirits and guides. The irony is that the visitations of white Westerners paying to experience traditional practices fundamentally alters those practices, and in ways that uphold the very power structures that tourists seeking enlightenment profess they want to transcend.

Let's take the current popularity of ayahuasca retreats in South America as an example of this romanticization. Ayahuasca is a psychoactive brew popular among spiritual white progressives seeking enlightenment. According to the online website Healthline, "This drink was used for spiritual and religious purposes by ancient Amazonian tribes and is still used as a sacred beverage by some religious communities in

Brazil and North America, including the Santo Daime."[3] Extractive industries and cultural appropriation have decimated traditional villages in parts of the world like the Amazon. In Peru, where taking ayahuasca is legal, there are up to a hundred retreats in the Iquitos region alone. While most are led by Indigenous people, there are also non-Indigenous white Westerners who lead and profit from these tours. Are the white people flocking by the thousands to the Amazon also involved in efforts to preserve it? Do they engage in ongoing relationships with the local population or is this purely transactional? What impact are they making on the natural environments they claim to value? Do they engage in any critical thinking about the colonialist dynamics embedded in this industry? Do they make the connection to Indigenous struggles in their own backyards?

The federal government recognizes 570 tribes in the US, and many tribes remain unrecognized, such as the Duwamish—whose ancestral lands I live on—in what is now called Seattle. Worldwide, there are estimated to be approximately 370 million Indigenous people belonging to 5,000 different groups, in 90 countries. There is vast diversity among Indigenous groups. A specific nation's values or practices are likely to be unclear to outsiders. Further, all practices associated with Indigenous people may not be worthy of emulation. Many Indigenous Mesoamerican cultures practiced human sacrifice. Some nations were continually at war with other nations. Yet the term "Indigenous" has become a signifier to spiritual white progressives for all things untainted by industrialization; a talisman that confers authenticity and deflects critique. When we idealize a group of people, we make them monolithic. Indigenous cultures are varied, and they change and evolve over time as all cultures do, but romanticizing a fixed and limited idea of who they are essentializes and denies agency. Another example is Buddhism, a particularly favored religion for white progressives. Buddhism is fundamentally patriarchal, and nationalist Buddhist monks in Myanmar have fomented violence against Muslims, but it is sacrilege to raise these points.

Perhaps when white people see how we have historically oppressed others and are close to destroying all life on earth, we want to disassociate ourselves from our whiteness. One way we do this is by romanticizing and emulating Indigenous people. But does this romanticization include the Indigenous life expectancy (in 2017, seventy-five years for Indigenous women compared to eighty-one years for white women)?[4] Or the Indigenous poverty rate (in 2019, 23 percent compared to 7.3 percent for white people)? Within the US and Canada, there is an epidemic of murdered and missing Indigenous women, who are killed at ten times the rate of other women of color. Murder is the third-highest cause of their deaths, according to the Centers for Disease Control. As of 2016 there were 5,712 known cases of murdered or missing Indigenous women reported to the National Crime Information Center.[5] These women are most likely to be killed by non-Indigenous people, on Indigenous-owned lands. There is a growing movement to raise awareness of this genocide, and many opportunities for white people to get involved, rather than simply partaking of idealized consumer versions of Indigenous life in another country. We need to ask ourselves—even if we grant the best of intentions—how consuming Indigenous traditions in small, controlled, and purchased doses for "the experience" actually changes one's life, interrupts racism, or indicates that we are not racist.

There is a taken-for-granted assumption by those who engage in rituals such as putting objects on altars and calling in spirits that everyone is spiritual. If that is based on the suppositions that there are dimensions beyond the one that we can see, that consciousness continues on in some form after death, and that there is intentionality in the universe, then we are *not*, in fact, all spiritual. Not everyone shares these beliefs, and they should not be assumed and imposed in forums in which people are seeking to understand and challenge racism.

To be clear, I am not critiquing the traditional practices of any group of people. Nor am I critiquing a respect for sustainable, pre-industrial, pre-capitalist societies and economies, or how people relate to and engage in practices rooted in their own heritages. And I am certainly not advocating for the other side of that coin—that industrialized capitalist European cultures are superior. I also understand that many Black, Indigenous, Asian, Latinx, and peoples of color identify as spiritual and enjoy these practices. I am critiquing the particular romanticized consumption of traditional practices *by white consumers in ways that essentialize Indigenous people and are not accountable to the impact of their consumption.*

While anti-Blackness drives white people to fear and avoid African Americans in a way that we don't fear (although we certainly avoid) Indigenous people, there are still aspects associated with Black people that spiritual white progressives also idealize and elevate. Because African Americans are associated with Africa, and Africa is seen as undeveloped, African Americans are also objectified. Associations include seeing Black people (especially those with African accents) as spiritual; as shamans, oracles, and healers; engaging in voodoo; and as simultaneously innocent and all-knowing. African Americans are often seen as being more in touch with their essential natures, as mystical or "soulful," and as holding secret knowledge. This knowledge is seen as intuitive rather than academic or intellectual, reinforcing several racist stereotypes.

"Magical Negro" is a term coined by film director Spike Lee. The Magical Negro trope—think Morgan Freeman as God in several films, The Oracle in *The Matrix*, or the supernatural inmate in *The Green Mile*—certainly appeals to white progressives. The Magical Negro is a supporting stock character, most often created by white writers, who comes to the aid of a white protagonist in a film or book. Magical Negro characters possess special insight or mystical powers. The character is often a prisoner, or a janitor or otherwise engaged in menial work, and is constrained or has been maimed by racial prejudice. The character typically simply appears one day to help the white protagonist and will do almost anything, including sacrificing themselves, to provide this help. The character is patient and dispenses words of wisdom, and the wisdom that is dispensed is powerful precisely because it is so simple or "pure." In this way, like Indigenous people, the Magical Negro is closer to the earth, which is always better in the eyes of the spiritual white progressive.

Yet none of this romanticization includes equal relationships. Building authentic cross-racial relationships is essential to challenging white socialization and segregation, but that is not the same as romanticizing and consuming other cultures. Further, elevating Black and Indigenous people because they are seen as closer to the natural world—or to put it bluntly, more primitive—simultaneously elevates white culture as more sophisticated. Romanticizing BIPOC people does not interrupt systemic racism, as Lee notes in a critique of the film *The Legend of Bagger Vance*. In this film, the ghost of Vance, a Black man, serves as a caddie to a broken-down former golf champion played by Matt Damon and teaches him how to come to terms with his personal demons and play golf again. The story takes place in Georgia in 1931. Lee says, "In real life, Black men were being castrated and lynched left and right. With all that going on, why are you fucking trying to teach Matt Damon a golf swing?"[6]

When spiritual white progressives refuse to acknowledge racism and white supremacy in the here and now by continually moving the conversation to an enlightened level we have not yet achieved and a realm we do not occupy, they engage in denial. While we may all be one on another plane we have not yet seen, we are certainly not all one on the physical plane where we actually reside. Not only does this romanticization exempt white people from any analysis of our actual racial reality; it also silences people who want to challenge that reality. This silencing is often done by suggesting that the person challenging racism is the one causing divisiveness. In conservative Christian communities, people who challenge authority are often told to pray harder. People in nontraditional spiritual communities are told to release their negative energy, perhaps through more meditation, yoga, mindfulness, or positive thinking.

Imagine trying to express how you are experiencing racism in a retreat, led by a white person, that has been described as where you will learn to "uncover the ground of your being as the luminous transparency of fundamental consciousness, pervading your body and environment as a unity"[7] and "experience ourselves and everything around us as made of empty, radiant, unified consciousness."[8] (Yes, those are direct quotes that have been checked for typos.) I am reminded of a *New Yorker* cartoon featuring two ducks floating together. One looks depressed. The other one is offering a helpful suggestion: "Maybe you should ask yourself why you're inviting all this duck hunting into your life right now."[9]

As an ultimate example of spiritual white progressiveness, consider an email I received from a white man. He let me know that although he was white in *this* life, he had lived countless previous lives of various races and therefore he *understood the Black experience*. He assured me that people from all over the world came to study in his meditation retreat center and that there was absolutely no racism in his community. I cringe to consider how his claim to understand the Black experience through reincarnation would land on a Black person. And how open is he likely to be to receiving feedback from a Black person who *has* experienced racism in his community? His absolute certainty that there was no racism in his environment—coupled with his definitive claim that he understood the racialized experience—tells me that he would *not* be receptive. Thus, contrary to his claim, we can assume his community to be a hostile place for a Black person seeking to raise race concerns.

Spiritual white progressives who co-opt Indigenous and other groups' rituals and signifiers may be seeking something that white supremacy has robbed us of: a sense of community with those deemed "Other." Unfortunately, seeking community without a structural analysis of racism creates separation, not connection.

CHAPTER 7

LET'S TALK ABOUT SHAME

In my efforts to identify how well-meaning white progressives uphold racism, I have found it useful to consider which narratives we use with ease and which we avoid when engaging in race talk. Why are we more comfortable saying, "I don't know what to do; I feel so much shame about being white," than we are saying, "I don't want to feel bad about racism"? Given that racial inequality is so enduring—despite so many white progressives insisting they do not want to participate in it—how might the claims we make to position ourselves in these conversations about racism be functioning to actually protect racism?

In addition to understanding the sociopolitical nature of language, discourse analysis can help us understand the sociopolitical nature of emotions. We tend to see emotions as natural, emerging unbidden from some internal and private place. And because we see emotions as innate, we tend to take them at face value. Even so, not all emotions are sanctioned; the legitimacy they are granted varies based on why, when, and how they are expressed and who is expressing them. For example, white men can express anger and be seen as powerful leaders, while Black men expressing anger are seen as threatening. White women expressing anger are seen as shrill, while Black women are seen as aggressive and out of control. Even how long we feel particular emotions is shaped by the culture in which they are expressed. In Western cultures, grief is expected when a partner dies, but not too much grief and not for too long or we become concerned about the person's mental health. In other words, we are conditioned to express and interpret emotions in particular ways that have social consequences—they are not purely natural.

In thinking about white emotionality regarding racism, there are two elements to consider. One is the feeling itself, and the other is the expression of that feeling. There are feelings we will easily express and others we will not. When working with white progressives on racism, shame and guilt will inevitably come up in the discussion. Guilt is generally understood as based on something bad we have actually done and for which we are responsible—and shame refers to something we believe we inherently *are* and cannot change. Put simply, guilt is a feeling we have about *doing* bad, and shame is a feeling we have about *being* bad. I have observed that white progressives will readily express feeling shame about racism but hesitate to express guilt. And we will express shame more often than feelings that are likely much more common, such as apathy, defensiveness, and resentment. Why is shame so comfortable for us to acknowledge, when many other thoughts and feelings regarding racism are not? I propose that shame both excuses and legitimizes our racism. (To clarify, I am not referring here to the impact of public call-outs on social media, which are different in that they are *meant* to shame. I am referring to claims that shame is blocking personal progress within the context of *learning about* racism).

In opening the shame narrative to examination, I ask white people in my workshops to turn to one another and share—as honestly as possible—their reflection on the following question: "On a weekly basis, during what percentage of your day do you feel racial shame?" In answering this question myself, if I am being honest, I can say that whole days can pass without feeling racial shame. When I do feel racial shame, it takes up maybe 1 to 2 percent of my day, and that is usually only when I have direct cross-racial contact—either through an interaction or reading something racially challenging. Perhaps on my way into Whole Foods I must walk past an Indigenous man who appears homeless lying on the sidewalk. I see him from down the block and in that moment I become hyper-conscious of our racial positions. My whiteness suddenly feels very "loud," and I "know" that he knows that

I am an imposter and a hypocrite, that my privilege and comfort, my access to resources, are dependent on his position in relation to mine, dependent on his oppression. I feel anxious about having to walk past him, dreading the encounter. For the duration of the approximately two minutes that it takes for me to traverse that sidewalk, I feel racial shame. The shame is heightened as I pass him, smiling to show that I am a nice person and *not racist*, while also avoiding any prolonged eye contact that might allow an opening for him to put me on the spot, asking something from me that I don't want to give. But as soon as I am in the store, my attention is diverted to all the delicious food for sale and I don't give him another thought.

I don't think I am an exception in how infrequently I feel racial shame, and most participants in my sessions report similar low percentages. Whiteness provides a protective barrier against unpleasant racial feelings. I am rarely required to go outside of my racial comfort zone, and when I do, it is often for brief moments such as the trip to Whole Foods described above. Any more sustained cross-racial engagement I can easily avoid and have been warned my entire life *to* avoid. These warnings are implicit in the way we talk about white segregated schools and neighborhoods as "safe" places and ones to be desired, and Black neighborhoods as "sketchy" places to be avoided. Yet curiously, in my workshops, shame is overwhelmingly cited by white progressives as a legitimate stumbling block to their ability to move forward. Given how seldom racial shame surfaces in daily white life, how easy it is to avoid or ignore, and how fleeting and impotent it is, it is notable how quickly we claim to feel shame when addressing racism.

I think shame provides social capital to white people in a few key ways. First, it garners sympathy. In the era of self-care, shame is something we believe we shouldn't feel. If shame says "*I* am bad" rather than "what I *did* was bad," then, in a self-care/self-help framework, no one should feel shame because we are all inherently good. The "I am inherently good" mantra is amplified for white people because our goodness is systematically reinforced across society: "good" neighborhoods and schools being stand-ins for white, and white as a stand-in for ideal human. When that taken-for-granted yet unacknowledged sense of racial goodness is challenged, we feel attacked at our very core. Whiteness studies scholar Michelle Fine speaks to this moral insulation when she says: "Whiteness accrues privilege and status, gets itself surrounded by protective pillows of resources and/or benefits of the doubt; how Whiteness repels gossip and voyeurism and instead demands dignity."[1] White people seldom find ourselves without these "protective pillows," and when we do, it is typically because we have chosen to temporarily step outside our comfort zones. Within our insulated racial environment we come to not only expect racial comfort but to also be less tolerant of racial stress. Expressing shame elicits comfort and relief as we turn to others seeking reassurance, in essence asking to be reminded of our goodness.

For white progressives, shame is seen as socially legitimate (or we wouldn't express it), a sign that we care and that we feel empathy. This may be why we express shame so much more readily than guilt. Guilt means we are responsible for something; shame relieves us of responsibility. If I focus on what I *did*, I must take responsibility for repair. If I focus on what I *am*, it is impossible to change and I am relieved of responsibility.

In distinguishing shame from guilt, psychologist Joseph Burgo explains,

> Although many people use the two words 'guilt' and 'shame' interchangeably, from a psychological perspective, they actually refer to different experiences. Guilt and shame sometimes go hand in hand; the same action may give rise to feelings of both shame and guilt, where the former reflects how we feel about *ourselves* and the latter involves an awareness that our actions have injured *someone else*. In other words, shame relates to self; guilt to others.[2]

If guilt relates to external actions and shame to an internal or private state, we can begin to see why shame is the preferred narrative: it protects our positions within the status quo by making it difficult for anyone outside ourselves to address. (The "personal experience" narrative functions the same way; as soon as I invoke that what I am claiming is "just my personal experience," it becomes private—something internal to myself that only I can know or understand and that therefore cannot be challenged by others.)

Second, it is hard to move forward when we feel shame, as shame tends to be paralyzing; shame actually excuses us from moving forward. What can we do when we feel so bad? We can't act until we work through this feeling, and that will take time and resources. Of course, given the requirement of time and resources, most of us won't work through our feelings at all.

Indulging in racial shame whenever we feel exposed (but only when we feel exposed) puts our focus on ourselves and away from those we may have harmed. In this way, shame functions to deny our power and excuse our paralysis, allowing us to indulge in a sense of our own victimization. Both bell hooks and Audre Lorde have noted that feeling bad about racism or white privilege can function as a form of self-centeredness in which white progressives turn the focus back onto themselves.[3] Hooks considered shame to be the *performance* of whiteness and not an indicator that whiteness was being interrupted.

Feminist writer and independent scholar Sara Ahmed explains, "The shameful white subject expresses shame about its racism, and in expressing its shame, it 'shows' that it is not racist: if we are shamed, we mean well. The white subject that is shamed by whiteness is also a white subject that is proud *about* its shame. The very claim to feel bad (about this or that) also involves a self-perception of 'being good.'"[4] In other words, if I feel bad enough, I both demonstrate and retain my morality. Ahmed raises the question of whether anti-racism is really about "making people feel better: safer, happier, more hopeful, less depressed, and so on." There is certainly much concern within anti-racist education about white people not feeling "too" bad lest they withdraw from engagement, and much time and attention is given to keeping white people in the conversation. This concern is heightened when the shame narrative emerges; we now must tread very carefully so as not to cause the person to disengage. The consequences of being seen as pushing too hard will be especially serious for racialized people. In this way, shame expressed in a public meeting or workshop may function as a means of social control, as facilitators scramble to reassure participants and pull back from directly challenging whiteness.

Another aspect of white racial shame is the shame of being *seen* racially. As white people, we are not used to having our race named or having people proceed as if our race held meaning. To be seen by others as a racial being is to acknowledge that we are not objective, nor do we represent a universal human perspective; we have a specific and necessarily limited perspective. If I accept that my race has meaning, and especially so in a racially unfair society, I also must accept that I did not earn everything I have from simple hard work and exceptionality, that, in fact, I may be a fraud. Imagine how many people I never had to compete with. In these ways, being racially seen undermines ideologies such as individualism and meritocracy. Challenging individualism means I am not as special and different as I want to think I am. Nor have I been exempt from the forces of the culture in which I am embedded and the racist ideologies that circulate there. Challenging meritocracy means accepting that my resources and achievements have not come as a result of my hard work alone but have been enhanced by a system that grants me the benefit of the doubt and rewards my work differently than if I was not white. Facing these realities calls into question key elements of my identity. And not only do I have to face these hard truths within myself, but I also have to face that others have seen this all along. When we realize that racialized people see us in ways that we don't want to be seen, we feel exposed, and shame is a predictable response.

When we understand that we are implicated in racial harm, it is normal to feel some shame, and shame is a very difficult feeling to tolerate. Beverly Daniel Tatum describes white racial guilt and shame as "part of the hidden costs of racism."[5] But as with all feelings regarding race, the key is what we do with those feelings. Do we use them as opportunities for deeper self-awareness or as excuses to disengage? Do we use them as motivators to work through the issue or to lash out at others in our embarrassment? We don't need to be rescued from shame; we need to build our tolerance so we don't fall apart whenever our self-image is challenged. Retreating from feelings of shame keeps us from moving through them. We are not entitled to only feel comfortable feelings in order to face racism.

Jay Smooth, offering more constructive ways to help people see that what they are saying or doing is racially harmful, says, "Distinguish between the 'what they did' conversation and the 'what they are' conversation."[6] In other words: don't get lost in what Jay calls the "rhetorical Bermuda Triangle." That's where what starts off as a "what you said" conversation turns into a "what you are" conversation. The "what you are" (a racist) conversation virtually guarantees shame, defensiveness, and denial. Instead, focus solely on holding that person accountable for his or her racist *deed*. "I don't care what you are," Jay concludes. "I care about what you did." Since shame is a "what *I am*" response, shifting to focusing on what *I did* or am doing can help us move through shame to reparative action.

When we feel shame, we are hooked into the good/bad binary: I am racist and bad; therefore, I feel ashamed. Systemic racism in all its manifestations is of course bad, but we could not have avoided absorbing the racist messages of our culture. It is much more useful to focus on how to take responsibility for the *outcome* of that socialization, rather than collapse in the face of its ugly manifestations. To this end we can ask: How is my socialization into systemic racism expressing itself in my daily life, and what can I do to interrupt it in myself, in those around me, and in our institutions?

ANOTHER CLOSING NOTE ABOUT GUILT

Guilt . . . if it leads to change then it can be useful, since it is then no longer guilt but the beginning of knowledge. Yet all too often, guilt is just another name for impotence, for defensiveness destructive of communication; it becomes a device to protect ignorance and the continuation of things the way they are, the ultimate protection for changelessness.

—AUDRE LORDE[7]

While my focus in this chapter is on shame, the concern about not "making" white people feel guilty continues to come up in discussions on racism, and although I have been clear about where I stand on the issue in my talks and writing, I feel the need to address it, yet again. For example, professor of English and linguistics John McWhorter decried my work as making white people feel guilty during an eight-minute debate on *White Fragility* with Michael Eric Dyson.[8] Choice quotes from McWhorter include the claim that my book conveys "the idea that as many white people as possible need to take themselves into a closet and flagellate themselves daily about their complicitness in whiteness before we can forge social change." He claims I am telling people that "change can't happen until all white people feel so guilty that they don't want to get out of bed." He then closes with a return to flagellation and closets, charging that I would have white people "in closets whipping themselves every morning." In his critique that ran in *The Atlantic*, McWhorter laments the authority that I have been granted "over the way innocent readers think" (just what is an *innocent* reader?).[9] My work "has white Americans muzzled, straitjacketed, tied down, and chloroformed for good measure." Goodness! And this from a linguist. This is a hyperbolic and disingenuous reading of my work, and a non-issue. Seeking to raise awareness about the realities of systemic racism and our role within that system is not some terrible thing that is "done" to innocent white people.

While John McWhorter is not white or a progressive, he is not alone in his concern about invoking white guilt (although his concern seems particularly extreme). Many others have cautioned activists and educators not to use strategies that make white people feel guilty. For example, Kenan Malik, an opinion writer for *The Guardian*, speaking of the global BLM moment of 2020, admonishes, "This is a transformational moment. Let's use it to challenge structural injustice, not to elicit or wallow in guilt. Inequalities cannot be challenged . . . by eliciting guilt."[10] The use of the verb "eliciting" is notable because it takes the emphasis off those who feel guilt and places it onto those who *make them* feel it.

In his important book *Merge Left*, Ian Haney López shares research showing that white people are much more responsive to messages of coalition and shared interests rather than those that name white people as the problem. And I am sure they are, given how much more comfortable a message that is. In an interview with BLM cofounder Alicia Garza, Haney López cautions us, "If you talk about racism as a white problem, you will not be surprised to learn you alienate lots of white folks. If you have tried saying, 'Dear white friend, we're gonna talk about white privilege and why you oughta feel guilty,' it doesn't go so well. . . . We can't build the coalitions we need."[11] I appreciate and respect Haney López's work, but I do not approach white people with the message that they *need to* feel guilty; quite the opposite. And I am unaware of anyone in the field of racial justice education whose strategic approach is guilt elicitation. White people may of course feel guilty when directly confronted with the reality of our role and responsibility in racism and close themselves off to any further engagement. Strategic messaging—which is Haney López's point—is always wise. Be that as it may, I have very little patience for cautions about invoking white guilt. I'd prefer to help those of us who are white to look directly and honestly at how we uphold a system we claim to abhor rather than tie myself into knots navigating the possibility that some of us may feel moments of guilt. Imagine trying to get men to see and take responsibility for the system of patriarchy and all of the ways it harms women—from daily minimizations to *sexual assault and femicide*—and being told not to be so direct about men's role because it makes men *feel bad*. Imagine being told that a better approach is to help men see their shared interests with women. My response to the former goes without saying. As for the latter, I don't think men will get to a place of seeing shared interests with women if they are not *also* addressing the patterns of dominance that result from internalizing the messages of patriarchal superiority. They will be expressing those patterns as they work side by side with women. Ask women what happens when men join their movements. It would be revolutionary for white people to recognize our shared interests with BIPOC people, but we would still be left with the need to address our habits of internalized superiority. Personal work and coalition work need to be done simultaneously.

The white anti-racist movement has exploded in recent times, so clearly many white people are able to withstand and move through any feelings of guilt they may have initially felt. When it is brought to our attention, guilt is a normal and healthy response to reckoning with harm we have caused, however unintentional that harm may have been. I have said over and over in my writing and my talks that while guilt is a normal response for many white people, it must either be temporary or used to motivate action. Otherwise, guilt merely functions to excuse and protect complicity.

Most people do not want to feel unpleasant feelings. Even so, is it really so terrible that white people *might* feel some guilt? And can racism be addressed without some emotional discomfort on the part of white people who perpetuate and benefit from it? Do we really want to compare the devastation of systemic racism on racialized people to the discomfort of white guilt, and posit that discomfort as a legitimate reason why it's just too hard and too high an expectation to be direct about white racism? When we understand white supremacy as a system we didn't have a choice about being socialized into, guilt becomes moot. It is on us to buck up and move through it.

CHAPTER 8

WHAT ABOUT MY TRAUMA?

In many of the courses, affinity groups, and community workshops I have facilitated or participated in, a common white progressive refrain inevitably surfaces, some version of "My trauma has come up and I can't continue to engage." Trauma is generally understood as serious mental and physical distress resulting from a terrible or endangering event. These events are so upsetting that they have long-lasting effects including shock, anxiety, anger, sadness, physical pain, sleep disturbances, and an inability to concentrate. Some traumas are so severe that these responses resurface again and again throughout one's life, often when a person is reminded in some way of the initial event. "Trauma" is a very strong word that speaks to deep distress, and it's an especially strong word for white people to invoke in the context of workshops, courses, and discussions about race.

It is worthy of note that I rarely hear this claim in workplace sessions, perhaps because there are serious consequences in terms of perceptions of one's fitness for duty. This indicates that, in most cases, the person is able to manage their emotions when their livelihoods are at stake. Yet it is a dependable white progressive narrative in sessions voluntarily attended by "the choir." Trauma that may surface for Black and Indigenous people in these settings is a very different issue, which I will raise later in this section.

In my experience, claims of trauma are especially predictable among social workers and social work students in classes and other forums that directly address racism. I have co-taught anti-racism courses in various schools of social work, and in these courses, white students would often protest that the class was "traumatizing" them. We continually had to reiterate that while they may be reminded of past trauma in some way, in the present moment they were safe; nothing dangerous was happening physically or psychologically in learning about and discussing racism. It was normal, however, for these discussions to make them *uncomfortable*. We would explain that as future social workers and therapists, in order to competently treat their clients, they would need to be able to discern the differences between the past and the present, between learning of other people's trauma and their own, and between safety and comfort. This discernment and boundary building is a critical task for mental health professionals, who witness many deeply upsetting situations in the course of their work.

While my training is not in social work, I have taught in schools of social work for an illustrative reason: their primarily white, full-time, and often tenured faculty did not have the qualifications to teach these courses themselves. Thus, the courses that I would argue were the most essential for social workers to take and the most challenging to teach—given the relationship between systemic racism and the mental health system—were most often taught by low-paid adjuncts without benefits who could be dismissed at will. That speaks volumes about the professed anti-racist values of many of these programs. So while I am not a mental health professional and can't provide a psychological, psychiatric, or therapeutic analysis of what is happening when claims of trauma arise in the context of challenging racism, I can offer a brief sociological one. Let's consider an email I received from a white affinity group facilitator:

> Some folks in the group have shared that they struggle with mental health problems stemming from traumatic experiences that sometimes prevent them from being able to speak out against instances of racism on campus. Or that may prevent them from speaking out in group settings, particularly during intense or emotional discussions. I have been looking for resources that speak about not letting past traumas become an explanation for total lack of action.

Two things stood out to me in this email. One was how predictable it is that when white people come together to work on racism, the focus is on how to enlighten other white people who are not in the room, a phenomenon I wrote about earlier. I assume that when they talk about "instances of racism on campus," they are referring to very explicit and obvious examples, such as white people putting a noose in someone's locker, calling the police on BIPOC people napping in a common area, or making physical attacks on BIPOC students. But there are countless microaggressions going on all the time, and we can assume that we perpetuate them too. Silence following racist remarks made in classroom discussions is particularly common.

A Canadian colleague shared with me an incident that occurred in a class of thirty that had only two Indigenous students. They were discussing the history of residential boarding schools for Indigenous children in Canada. These were government-sponsored religious schools that were established to assimilate Indigenous children into Euro-Canadian culture. Their stated mission was to "kill the Indian in the child" and enact cultural genocide.[1] These children were forcibly removed from their families and communities. Their braids were cut; they were forbidden to speak their native languages; and torture, rape, and abuse was rampant. As many as six thousand Indigenous children died in residential institutions, which ran from 1876 to 1996, although the number is likely higher as the government stopped keeping statistics of children's deaths in these schools after 1920. During the class discussion, a white student suggested that maybe the white Canadians had good intentions—after all, boarding schools are very prestigious in England. This was a deeply hurtful and disingenuous suggestion, but no one responded to counter the remark, including the professor. It was left to the Indigenous students to speak up, one of whom did, reminding the class that the stated mission of these schools was to "kill the Indian" and that the torture and abuse that occurred in them was well documented (as they had been studying). There was no need to hypothesize about whether the perpetrators of this national shame had good intentions, and certainly no validity in putting these schools on the same level as prestigious British boarding schools for children of the owning class. While the silence of the other white students and the white professors may not have been as directly hurtful as what was explicitly said, it certainly colluded with the statement and made clear to the Indigenous students that there were no allies in the room. Silence is not empty; it communicates volumes.

The type of racial harm that occurred in that college classroom is much more common than a noose in a locker. While twenty-seven non-Indigenous students made no insensitive remarks that day, twenty-seven non-Indigenous students supported the remark that was made with their silence. Still, returning to the email, the main concern of the members of the white affinity group was how to interrupt *other people's* collusion, rather than their own.

The other familiar pattern that stood out in the email was what prevented the students and professor from intervening: their own trauma. It is beyond question that systemic racism and white supremacy is traumatic for Black, Indigenous, Latinx, Asian American, and other people of color. And, as I argued in *White Fragility*, there is a kind of collective *moral* trauma for white people in what we have done to racialized people and continue to do and have not yet faced. But I do not believe that learning about, discussing, or challenging racism is in itself traumatic for white people, or that doing so triggers old traumas for us that are so debilitating as to be immobilizing. So why is this claim so common?

I consulted with therapist Resmaa Menakem, a racial trauma specialist and author of *My Grandmother's Hands: Racialized Trauma and the Pathways to Mending Our Hearts and Bodies*. Resmaa is a Black man. His revolutionary work on how white supremacy is stored in the body has had a profound influence on me and many others. He agreed that it was common for white people, when hearing or learning about the trauma of Black and Indigenous peoples, to bring their own forms of trauma into the discussion. We spent some time discussing this pattern from our different perspectives.[2]

Resmaa focused his comments on Black and Indigenous peoples, given their relationship to the creation of white supremacy and the racial hierarchy that has flowed from it (there was no concept of distinct racial groups before the genocide of Indigenous people and the theft of their land and the kidnapping and enslavement of Africans in the

Americas). In *My Grandmother's Hands*, he outlined four key dimensions of racial trauma for Black and Indigenous peoples, which he distinguishes as Historical, Institutional, Intergenerational, and Personal (HIIP).[3] The historical dimension speaks to the hundreds of years over which white supremacy has been developed, honed, adapted, and disseminated. The institutional dimension refers to the infusion of white supremacy across all institutions, including the military, medicine, media, criminal justice, policing, finance, industry, education, government, religion, and science. These institutions are interconnected and function together to uphold white supremacy across the whole of society. While some institutions may not be overwhelmingly white at the ground level, they most certainly are at the top level (e.g., while more than 40 percent of active duty personnel in the US military are BIPOC people, seven of the eight Joint Chiefs of Staff are white[4]). The intergenerational dimension refers to how the trauma of white supremacy accumulates over centuries and is passed down and stored in the bodies of Black and Indigenous peoples across generations. The personal dimension speaks to the impact of each individual's specific experiences, responses, and coping mechanisms within the context of white supremacy. These levels of trauma are intertwined and continuously at play. It is not my place as a white person to speak to their impact on Black and Indigenous peoples. I outline them, however, to offer a contrast when reflecting on white claims of racial trauma and how these claims may function.

There are, of course, forms of oppression white people experience to which the HIIP model can be applied. For example, patriarchy also functions at these four levels, and as a woman I am impacted by patriarchy in each dimension (albeit differently than if I were not cis and/or white). Domestic violence, sexual assault, abuse, and violence against trans women are among the deeply traumatic experiences tied to patriarchy that function at the HIIP levels. There are also isolated experiences that cause individual trauma for white people, such as a car accident, plane crash, the unexpected death of a parent or sibling, witnessing or being the recipient of violence, religious shunning, and so forth. Trauma is real, many people experience it, and various stimuli can bring it up. But white people do not experience direct *racial* trauma, and not continuously at the four levels of HIIP. Had the Indigenous student in the classroom felt traumatized, we could clearly connect her distress to all four HIIP levels. If the white student who made the remark claimed to be traumatized by her challenging response, we could not.

As I write that white people don't experience direct racial trauma, I can imagine someone objecting by saying that they were the only white kid in their school and were picked on daily by the Black kids. I have heard that objection more than once, and I grant that it could be traumatic. But it is also the *exception*. Everything outside that school or neighborhood is sending the message of white superiority, and that message is also operating *inside* the school through the implicit biases of the teachers, curriculum, administration, the school funding, where it is located, how it is perceived because it is predominantly Black, and so forth. There is also the difference that this is a temporary, ahistorical situation and one that can be easily avoided once you are grown and have the agency to live and go to school where you choose (and every time I have heard this example, it has been from a white person who *no longer* is one of a few white people in their environment). Yet white supremacy is operating continually for racialized people—and Black and Indigenous people in particular—at the multiple HIIP levels. Resmaa was clear that we cannot and should not use our own trauma to avoid confronting white supremacy. Doing so recenters ourselves and functions as an escape from personal and collective responsibility.

Resmaa stressed that the healing path of white people is not about liberating Black and Indigenous people. It is about what we are going to hand down to our children and our children's children to make sure that white supremacy dies in the next few generations. That is a different healing path than that of a Black or Indigenous person who, Resmaa explained, has to "uncover and excavate the ways in which the standard of white body supremacy has been ingested in our own minds and thwarted our full expression and capacity . . . so that white body supremacy and anti-Blackness dies and does not get passed down to our children."[5] These are two different healing paths, which he refers to as "somatic abolitionism." White body supremacy and somatic abolitionism are terms Resmaa coined to make the point that the trauma of racism is based on our bodies and stored in our bodies. Racism is a somatic experience and must be rooted out at the somatic level. He argues that we cannot address racism intellectually.

Resmaa sees white people who bring up trauma they have experienced (most often at the hands of other white people) when challenged on white supremacy as centering themselves and attempting to make their trauma parallel to his. But white people are in a different racial position and have different work to do in uncovering and challenging our conditioning into white supremacy; white supremacy does not impact us in the same ways, and our struggles cannot be compared to that of Black, Indigenous, and other people of color. He observes, "White people are real slick about recentering themselves. One way they do this is seeing these dynamics as equal. If Resmaa can talk about his trauma, then why can't I talk about mine?" But in doing so, white people recenter ourselves and co-opt his struggle. Resmaa also noted that when white people bring up trauma, it is always at the individual level. We don't often talk about collective trauma.

In thinking about trauma in this context as discourse, I have noticed that in racial discussions, white people often revert to their individual experiences in ways that inoculate their claims from further challenge or critique. Since I do not and cannot know your experience—in this case, your trauma experience—I am now shut out; you have retreated to an interior place only accessible to you. In this way, trauma discourse can function as a kind of protective wall, warding off outsiders. This exempts us from accountability and responsibility in at least two ways:

1. I have trauma so I am also a victim and therefore I cannot be a victimizer.
2. I have trauma so I understand your experience of victimization. Because I understand your victimization, I am aligned with you and cannot be a victimizer.

This move is based in the ideology of individualism that characterizes Western notions of self. When one's language, ideas, feelings, and experiences are seen as existing "inside" a discrete self, then the self becomes non-social, private, and inaccessible to anyone outside the person, rather than as social or inter-relational. Experience becomes depoliticized. Since no one else has access to my interior world, my personal experience is incontestable. But concepts of the self are not outside the sociopolitical forces that render their meaning. Nor is experience, language, or emotion. Whiteness is a *collective* experience. I am white because I have been conditioned into and am responded to by others as a member of the socially assigned group termed "white." Whiteness is a shared experience, and it can only exist in relationship to who is *not white*. Resmaa cautions that if white people are going to be engaged in this work, it must be done with other white people as a collective experience. This means that we need to organize and build anti-racist community with other white people.

For white people to focus on the collective work of anti-racism, we must learn to compartmentalize our own forms of trauma. Compartmentalizing does not mean suppressing or denying. Certainly, someone who has very present or unresolved trauma can find it stimulated in an emotionally intense racial discussion. If someone feels they may have a breakdown, they should leave and seek professional support. And all of us should be attending to any distress in our lives that gets in the way of anti-racist struggle. If not, we likely won't show up as effectively in collective and cross-racial work. But similar to the critique of white women's tears, *how, when, and where* we bring up and express our distress is critical, for our actions impact others. Clearly, many of us are capable of attending to these questions. When it doesn't serve us to make our traumas visible, we don't. Again, I am not talking about someone who is so debilitated by their trauma that they are unable to function. I'm referring to white progressives who conflate strong and uncomfortable emotions with trauma. Is being confronted with the reality of systemic racism startling, upsetting, even shocking? Yes. Traumatizing? No.

If we as white progressives are afraid to engage in this work for whatever reason, then we need to find ways to move through our fear. A white affinity group is a great place to begin that practice. Avoidance holds in place the issues that prevent us from constructive engagement. Yes, it is hard, but there is healing in the struggle.

Resmaa's distinction between "clean pain" and "dirty pain" may be useful in clarifying the confusion between the difficult feelings that anti-racist work often brings up for white people and the idea that the feelings in and of themselves indicate real and present trauma: "*Clean pain* is the pain that mends and can build your capacity for growth. . . . *Dirty pain* is the pain of avoidance, blame, and denial. When people respond from their most wounded parts, become cruel or violent, or physically or emotionally run away, they experience dirty pain. They also create more of it for themselves and others."

There comes a time when we should be able to say our efforts have resulted in the basic skills and emotional stamina to engage. Otherwise the familiar refrain "I'm working on this" becomes an excuse. We are all in process in the sense that this work is never done, but if our process never results in change and no one would know we are engaged in a process at all, then the subtext of "I'm working on this" is "I am not going to change."

Claims of trauma may be thought of as one of the "softer" forms of white fragility. We may not be lashing out in defensiveness and anger, but we are still blocking the engagement that can lead to growth via sympathy-generating claims of our own victimization. This form of white fragility is often expressed in the expectation that white people should be made to feel comfortable in anti-racist endeavors, cloaked in the call to create a "safe" space. This normalizes the myth that racial dialogues are somehow dangerous for white people and our safety must be ensured before we can proceed. In turn, the true direction of racial harm is perverted. Facing the reality of systemic racism and our role in it is upsetting, as it should be. But let's not lose sight of who bears the burden of racist abuse and co-opt that burden with our own pain.

CHAPTER 9

WE AREN'T ACTUALLY THAT NICE

I have consistently found that if you just scratch lightly on the surface of white progressive niceness, some not-so-nice resentment and contempt burst through. We see this with the rash of recorded 911 calls and videos of white people exploding in racist rants in public places, and I have certainly been ranted at by white progressives for the smallest of challenges to their racial positions. For example, on a book tour in London I got into a cab and was chatting amicably with the white male driver. We had much in common and were making many connections until he asked me what I was doing in London. I told him that I had written a book and was being interviewed by the BBC and doing several university presentations. He asked me the name of the book. With an internal sigh (here we go!), I replied, *"White Fragility: Why It's So Hard for White People to Talk About Racism."* That was the extent of my reply—I simply said the title of my book. "I am so tired of being told I am racist!" he exploded in outrage. He then went on a long diatribe about how no one could say anything anymore, about political correctness, special rights, and so on.

When he finally took a breath, I calmly asked him, "Are you often told you are racist?" That seemed to give him pause. "Well . . . no," he replied and settled down a little. He then went on to express resentment about a group of Black men who stood on the corner near his home and made him afraid to walk by lest he be "knifed." And there it was! White fragility erupting based on the *title* of my book, a long-winded rant of resentment and a closing shot of racist discourse. This is the all-too-familiar move of "How dare you suggest I am racist! In my defense, I am going to express racism to show that my racism is justified!" Also worthy of note was his typical white lack of racial curiosity or humility about the limits of his knowledge; he had the author of a *New York Times* best-selling book who was in town to do interviews for the BBC in his cab, and he did not ask a single question about my thoughts on the matter.

While I certainly receive emails from trolls who insult me in nonsensical, threatening, and misogynist ways, I also receive dismissive emails from white progressives. For example, I received an email from an NPR listener after I did a brief interview with Scott Simon of *Weekend Edition* about Joe Biden's comments, discussed in chapter 5, praising the civility of white segregationists in Congress in the 1970s.[1] The day the three-minute interview aired, I received this email:

> In your interview with Scott Simon on WESAT [Weekend Edition Saturday] this morning, you said:
>
> > "If you are white, you necessarily have blind spots."
>
> and
>
> > "If you are in your seventies, as Joe Biden is, you have a world view that unfortunately seems to have remained in place."
>
> What these statements illustrate is not anything about white people or the elderly. What they illustrate is YOUR narrow minded prejudice.
>
> As a 75 year old white man, I take personal offense at your silly comments. As soon as I learned of the existence of racism (at about age 12 in my sheltered environment), I started to fight it actively and I have never stopped. As I have aged, my world view has not remained in place. I have moved further and continue to move further left.
>
> It is especially offensive to be lumped together in a category with Joe Biden, who exemplifies everything I despise.
>
> I suggest that you rethink your views and watch your language.

This email perfectly and succinctly captures so much of what can be problematic about white progressives, for it could just as easily have been written by a white conservative. In addition, given that the writer is a white man chastising a white woman with more knowledge of the matter than he has, it also nicely illustrates the intersection of white and male arrogance: both whitesplaining and mansplaining. We can deduce several unspoken white racial "rules" from this email.

The email starts with the writer's umbrage at my generalizations. The first statement he takes offense to is my claim that if you are white you necessarily have blind spots on race. It remains difficult for me to imagine the lack of humility it takes for a white person to claim that they have no blind spots whatsoever on the topic of race, even though I am faced with that lack of humility every day. Yet the point I was making was simple: by virtue of your position as a white person, there will be some aspects of racial life that you can see and understand, and other aspects that you necessarily cannot. African Americans—for example—have a racial experience that is different than that of white Americans. I cannot fully know what it is to experience my life as an African American. Nor can African Americans know what it is to be white (although they may have more insight than many white people, given that they swim against the racial current while white people swim with it). There is copious empirical research demonstrating racial bias infused in all aspects of society; we do indeed have different experiences based on race. My first point—that if you are white you necessarily have blind spots—was simply one of perspective and humility.

In the same vein, the writer takes offense at my statement "If you are in your seventies, as Joe Biden is, you have a worldview that unfortunately seems to have remained in place."[2] While I wish I had been a bit clearer, my use of "seems" was meant to convey that not all white people in their seventies have a worldview that has stayed in place, but that Joe Biden certainly demonstrated that he did. He did so by his defensiveness, his refusal to engage with the feedback he was given, and the tired and nonsensical claim that he didn't "have a racist bone in his body." (To his credit, Biden has recently demonstrated the capacity for significant growth in anti-racism awareness and skill.) Nonetheless, the essential issue for the writer is that I generalized about older white people, and that makes me the racist (or in this case, narrow-minded and prejudiced).

Rule 1: Do not generalize about the patterns of white people; doing so makes you the racist.

The writer's next move is to insult my intelligence and minimize my expertise. National Public Radio wasn't doing a "person on the street" opinion piece; I was invited to comment because I have internationally recognized academic and practical expertise in these dynamics and have written about them extensively. But like many white people, he loses his humility when the topic is race and feels free to dismiss any expertise I might have—and in a most simplistic and condescending way—by calling them "silly."

Let's use the analogy of my opinion on the sky to illustrate the difference between an opinion on a topic that anyone can, and likely does have, and an informed opinion on that topic. I have looked up at the sky virtually every day of my life and have of course a basic understanding of what's up there. I like it best at dusk when the stars start to show, I can sometimes predict the weather based on its color, and I can point out the North Star and the Big and Little Dippers. I was introduced to astronomy in school, have read a few articles since, and have watched Carl Sagan's series *Cosmos* (and the recent reboot). I once met a cosmologist at a party and we had a fascinating chat. Just by living my life I have accumulated some very basic knowledge and have developed an *opinion* on the sky, like anyone else who is aware of its existence. Still, I recognize that my understanding of the sky is limited. So if Neil deGrasse Tyson shows up to provide an accessible astronomy lecture, I am going to listen with curiosity and intellectual humility. I recognize that the field of astrophysics is ever-evolving and that there are disagreements among scientists. Still, while I may ask Dr. Tyson questions, I certainly wouldn't put my opinion on par with his. If he gives me an answer that I don't understand, my assumption will be that *I* am lacking knowledge, not Dr. Tyson. (I am not comparing myself to

Dr. Tyson or claiming to have anywhere near the expertise in my field as he has in his; I am just using a clear example to illustrate the difference between popular and informed opinions.) Unfortunately, racism is not typically viewed as a deeply complex issue that mainstream culture does not prepare white people to engage critically with and thus requires ongoing study and engagement by white people to gain some measure of expertise. When it comes to racism, white people tend to hold up all opinions as equally valid.

Critical thinking goes beyond simply having a different opinion; critical thinking is the result of gaining a more informed perspective by engaging with evidence, study, practice, and multiple layers of complexity. Having an opinion is not predicated on any of this; we are not required to have an actual understanding of an issue before forming an opinion. That does not mean that superficial opinions do not have strong emotions associated with them; indeed many are held and expressed quite passionately. Unfortunately, this passion often grants uninformed opinions more legitimacy by those who are also uninformed on the issue, and cows those who are informed into silence, wanting to avoid conflict and endless debate.

Rule 2: My opinion on racism is equal to anyone's.

The writer then goes on to establish his non-racist credentials, stating that he has actively been fighting racism since he was twelve and first realized racism existed. How he fights it he does not say, but presumably the racism he has been fighting does not reside within himself or I would expect to see more humility. I have been fighting racism for two decades now, but that does not mean I am free of it myself or never perpetrate it, even if unintentionally. Like many, he has an idea of a racist as a fixed either/or: you are either racist or you are not.

Further, what we understand about racism is constantly evolving. For example, when this writer was twelve, we did not know that race wasn't biological. We didn't even use the term "people of color," much less "BIPOC people," or have a common understanding of the term "white privilege." This was in part my point about Joe Biden—that he needed to continually be growing in his understanding of what is arguably the most complex, nuanced, politically charged social dilemma of the last several hundred years. Nonsensical phrases like "I don't have a racist bone in my body" don't indicate that he is engaged in that growth, nor did this man's email. Yet this writer claims to have been certified as not-racist decades ago.

Rule 3: Being against racism makes one free of racism.

Next, he expresses his offense at being lumped in with the likes of Joe Biden, whom he despises. In this way, he distances himself from other white people he sees as less progressive. Identifying racism in others does not necessitate cutting them off. As discussed in chapter 2, this distancing makes collective actions difficult. But if Joe Biden is the one who doesn't "get it," then I have no responsibility or requirement to help him move forward. If he hurts people racially, that is on him, not me. In fact, the more clueless another white person is, the more they demonstrate how aware *I* am. The underlying framework of this logic is the good/bad binary.

Rule 4: Some white people are racist; some are not. I am not; therefore, it's not my problem.

Now let's look at the emailer's condescending dismissal of my thinking. In his opening, he calls my comments "silly." In his closing, he says: "I suggest that you rethink your views"—along with a warning to watch my language. He may as well have added "young lady!" It's hard to imagine a white male who has expertise on a topic being told his comments are "silly." Regardless, the impact of the emailer's condescension toward me was in the form of scolding, an example of mansplaining, wherein men explain a topic to a woman who actually has more knowledge of the topic than he does. Author Rebecca Solnit ascribes the phenomenon to a combination of "overconfidence and cluelessness."[3] Several rules surface here:

Rule 5: I know all I need to know.

Rule 6: My opinion is not only equal to but in fact superior to that of people with expertise in the field.

Rule 7: People I don't agree with are worthy of my contempt.

Rule 8: I do not have to consider my social position and how it informs my responses and the impact of my behavior on others.

The writer's hostility and condescension also illustrate white fragility—the mere suggestion that being white has any kind of shared meaning triggers umbrage, argumentation, and dismissal. While white fragility is triggered by a challenge to the white worldview, it is born of feelings of superiority and entitlement. White fragility is a powerful means of white racial control. Just as Joe Biden did, this writer angrily refuses to consider the limits of his racial understanding.

Rule 9: I am the victim here, and you are the aggressor.

Rule 10: I don't actually have to be nice at all.

There is deep racial resentment roiling just under the surface for many white people (and barely concealed resentment toward women under the surface for many men). Therein lies a confusing mix of guilt and shame, superiority and contempt. We clearly see a large-scale eruption of racial resentment leading up to and beyond the 2016 presidential election. And while this racial resentment is associated with those whom we don't see as progressive, we certainly are not free of these feelings ourselves. As white progressives we may be more able to admit to guilt and shame, but we still cannot or will not admit to superiority and contempt. As a white person, I have been conditioned by a culture that relentlessly telegraphs white superiority. At the same time, my culture tells me that it is bad to feel superior. Thus, we express superiority in coded and indirect ways, making us much more passive-aggressive in our racism, while the outcomes remain the same.

CHAPTER 10

HOW WHITE PEOPLE WHO EXPERIENCE OTHER OPPRESSIONS CAN STILL BE RACIST, OR "BUT I'M A MINORITY MYSELF!"

The true focus of revolutionary change is never merely the oppressive situations which we seek to escape, but that piece of the oppressor which is planted deep within each of us, and which knows only the oppressors' tactics, the oppressors' relationships.

—Audre Lorde[1]

White progressives may be more able to acknowledge the reality of structural inequality because they tend to be people who experience other forms of oppression or have marginalized people close in their lives. People on the left side of the political spectrum are more likely to be racialized, queer, nonbinary, and sometimes working class. Black, Latinx, and Asian American voters are overwhelmingly Democrats: 84 percent of African American voters, 65 percent of Asian American voters, and 63 percent of Latinx voters.[2] Ideally, we would use our own experiences with oppression and the experiences of our loved ones as a way in to an understanding of racism, but all too often white progressives use the forms of oppression we experience as a way out. I have found that white people with marginalized identities can be the most defensive and resistant when challenged on racism.

For example, I identify as a feminist and have been aware of the injustice of patriarchy and sexism for most of my life. I could describe in great and passionate detail (and often have) the destructive toxicity of patriarchy and misogyny. But I was in my thirties and a college-educated parent before I ever thought about how I was complicit in and benefited from someone else's oppression. I had never considered how being white shaped my identity as a woman and mitigated my experience of sexism. I also grew up in poverty, and it wasn't until I graduated from college, at age thirty-four as a single mother, that I began to make a living wage that no longer required me to rent and live with roommates. I could easily talk about the unfairness of classism. But I had never considered how being white not only shaped my experience of poverty but also how I left it.

I was born to working-class parents; my father was a construction worker, and my mother held various menial jobs. When I was two, my parents divorced, and my mother began to raise my sisters and me on her own. As a single mother in the late 1950s and early 1960s, she had virtually no safety net. I have never understood people who say, "We were poor but we didn't know it because we had lots of love." The pain and humiliation of poverty are visceral. Poverty isn't romantic or some form of "simple living." The lack of medical and dental care, the hunger, and the ostracization are concrete. The stress of poverty made my household much more chaotic than loving.

We were evicted frequently and moved four to five times a year. There were periods when oatmeal was the only food in our house. I had no health or dental care during my childhood. If we got sick, my mother would scream that we could not get sick because she could not afford to take us to the doctor. We occasionally had to live in our car, and during one period I was left with relatives whom I did not know in another state, separated from my mother and sisters for months while my mother tried to secure housing. My teacher once held my hands up to my fourth-grade class as an example of poor hygiene, and with the class as her audience, told me to go home and tell my mother to wash me. I was indeed dirty, and I am sure that I smelled from going unbathed and living in our car for extended periods of time. In addition, my mother was struggling with leukemia, and over the last five years of her life she became progressively more ill; she simply could not hold a job and did not have the energy to properly care for us.

I used to stare at the other girls in my classes and ache to be like them, to have many dresses that were not torn, to go to camp, to take lessons, to attend slumber parties. I wanted to sit with those clean and pretty girls, but I knew that I couldn't because I was not like them. We were poor and I wasn't clean, and that meant I couldn't join them in school or go to their houses or have the same things they had. But the moment the real meaning of poverty crystallized for me came one day when I was seven and my mother took us to visit another family. My sisters and I played with their children while the adults visited, and as we were leaving I was the last one out the door. As I passed through I heard one of the children ask her mother, "What's wrong with them?" This was literally her question: *"What's wrong with them?"* I stopped, riveted. What would be her mother's answer? What *was* wrong with us? The mother held her finger to her lips and whispered, "Shhh, they're poor."

This was a revelatory moment for me. The shock came not just in the knowledge that we were poor, but that it was exposed. There was something wrong with us, indeed, and it was something that was obvious to others and that we couldn't hide, something shameful that could be plainly seen but never named. It took me many years to gain a structural analysis of class that would help me challenge the shame I internalized through these experiences. My mother, Marianne DiAngelo, died in 1967 at the age of thirty-seven. I was eleven.

I share my class background because it deeply informs my understanding of race. From an early age I had the sense of being an outsider; I was acutely aware that I was poor, that I was dirty, that I was not "normal," and that there was something "wrong" with me. But I also knew that I was *not Black*. We were at the lower rungs of society, but there was always someone on the ladder, just below us. I knew that "colored" meant Black people and that Black people should be avoided. I can remember many occasions when I reached for candy or uneaten food lying out in public and was admonished by my grandmother not to touch it because a "colored person" may have touched it. I was told not to sit in certain places lest a "colored" person had sat there. The message was clear: if a Black person touched something, it became dirty. The irony here is that the marks of poverty were clearly visible on me: poor hygiene, torn clothes, homelessness, rotten teeth, hunger. Yet through comments such as my grandmother's, a racial Other was formed in my consciousness, an Other through whom I became clean.

I left home as a teenager and struggled to survive. As I looked at what lay ahead, I could see no path out of poverty other than education. The decision to take that path was frightening for me; I had never gotten the message that I was smart, and academia was a completely foreign social context. But once I was in academia, I understood that a college degree is not conferred upon those who are smarter or who try harder than others. Going to college is not a result of the "cream rising." The opportunity to go to college comes through a complex web of intersecting systems of privilege that include internal expectations as well as external resources. In academia, racism—a system from which I benefited—helped to mediate my class-based disadvantages. While I was not raised with resources or high expectations and graduated with my BA at age thirty-four as a "nontraditional" student, being white not only helped me fit in at college but buoyed me, as virtually all my professors, all my classmates, and the entire curriculum represented and included me racially.

As I reflect on the early messages I received about being poor and being white, I now realize that my grandmother and I needed Black people to project our class shame onto, to cleanse and realign us with the dominant white culture that our poverty separated us from. I now ask myself how the classist messages I internalized growing up led me to collude in racism. For example, as a child who grew up in poverty, I received constant reminders that I was stupid, lazy, dirty, and a drain on the resources of hardworking people. I internalized these messages and they often silenced me; I still struggle against them now. Unless I work to uproot them, I am less likely to trust my own perceptions or feel like I have a "right" to speak up. I may fail to interrupt racism because the social context in which it is occurring intimidates me. My silence on

these occasions may be coming from a place of internalized class inferiority, but *in practice* my silence colludes with racism and ultimately
benefits me by maintaining racial solidarity with other white people.
This solidarity connects and realigns me with white people across other
lines of difference, such as the very class locations that have silenced me
in the first place. So regardless of what is informing my silence—even if
it is a sense of inferiority—it still functions to maintain white solidarity
and uphold racism.

Many of us who grew up poor or working class have a hard time
owning racial privilege, but while my specific class background mediated the way I learned racism and how I enact it, in the end it still socialized me to collude with the overall structure. Poor and working-class
white people don't necessarily have any less racism than middle or
upper-class white people (nor do we have more); it is just conveyed in
different ways and we enact it from a different social location than the
middle or upper classes.

While I still carry the marks of poverty, those marks are now only
internal. But these marks limit me in more than what I believe I deserve
or where I think I belong. They also interfere with my ability to stand
up against injustice, for as long as I believe that I am not as smart or
as valuable as other white people, I won't have the courage to challenge racism. In order for white people to unravel our internalized racial
dominance, we have two interwoven tasks. One is to work on our own
internalized oppression—the ways in which we impose limitations on
ourselves based on the societal messages we have received about the
inferiority of the lower-status groups to which we may belong.

The other task is to face the internalized superiority that results from
being socialized in a racist society—the ways in which we consciously or
unconsciously believe that we are more important, more valuable, more
intelligent, and more deserving than Black people. We have not missed
that message. I cannot address every complexity of other white people's
social locations. However, after years facilitating dialogues on race with
thousands of white people from a range of class positions (as well as
varied gender identity and expression, sexual orientation, nationalities,
religions, and ability positions), and bearing witness to countless stories

and challenges from Black people about my own racism and that of other white people, I have come to see some very common patterns of internalized superiority. These patterns are shared across other social positions due to the bottom-line nature of racism: regardless of one's other positions, white people know on some level that being white in this society is "better" than being a person of color, and this, along with the very real doors opened by whiteness, serves to mediate the forms of oppression we experience. Reaching for racial humility as a white person, however, is not the same as being mired in class shame.

Of course my class position is only one social location from which I learned to collude with racism. For example, I have also asked myself how I learned to collude with racism as someone raised Catholic and female. How did it shape my sense of racial belonging, of racial correctness, to be presented with depictions of God, the ultimate and universal authority, as white? How did the active erasure of Jesus's race and ethnicity shape my racial consciousness? How did the teaching of Catholicism as the true religion for all people of the world engender racial superiority within me when all the authorities within that religion were white like myself? At the same time, how did my conditioning under Catholicism to not question authority—and in particular not the authority of the white male priests who spoke for a white male God— lead me to silently collude with the racism of other white people?

As a cisgender white woman, how did I internalize racial superiority through the culture's representation of white women as the embodiment of ultimate beauty? What has it meant for me to have a key signifier of female perfection—whiteness—available to me? How has mainstream feminism's articulation of white women's issues as *universal* women's issues shaped what I care about? At the same time, what has it meant to live under patriarchy and to be taught that as a female I am less intelligent, that I should not speak up, that I should defer to men, and that I should at all times be pretty and pleasing? How have these messages ultimately set me up to collude with systemic racism?

By asking questions such as these, I have been able to gain a much deeper and more useful analysis of racism. Rather than finding that centering racism denies my own experience of oppression, I have found that centering racism has been a profound way to address the complexity of all my social locations. I would ask any white person who does not think they have racial privilege or superiority based on their own marginalized identity to ask themselves what racism looks like in their communities. For example, what does anti-Blackness look like among white, queer, cis men? What does anti-Blackness look like among Ashkenazi Jews of European descent? How is navigating the social service system as a person with a disability mitigated by not *also* dealing with racism in the social service system?

In a book challenging white progressives, I would be remiss if I did not make a point of specifically challenging white feminists. So, white feminists: we have to stop the channel-changing from racism to sexism. If we want to talk about our experiences within patriarchy (and we need to), we also need to acknowledge that being white shapes those experiences. A recent example of white women *not* being able to do so occurred in a workshop I led for a Hollywood writers' group. A white woman came up to me afterward and opened with, "Yes but . . .," and then continued on at length about how much sexism there is in Hollywood. Yes, it is clear that there is copious sexism in Hollywood. Copious. It is also clear that the women in Hollywood who do succeed and have succeeded for decades are overwhelmingly white. And white women in Hollywood have historically not been advocates for women of color. Yet after three hours of discussing systemic racism, engaging in reflection exercises, and seeing example after example of racism in film, this white woman did not have one insight to share about her own whiteness. I wonder if she could even take it in, given her resentment about her own disadvantage. This was not an isolated incident; white women have often let me know during or after a session that the real oppression is sexism. I wonder what Asian American, Latinx, Indigenous, and Black women in Hollywood would say about that. Actually, their voices can be heard if one takes the effort to seek them out and listen. We must acknowledge that there is not a universal woman's experience or shared sisterhood between white women and women of color. We may be "all one" out there on the spiritual plane, but we are definitely not all one on the profoundly unequal physical plane on which we actually live. Yes, I have resentment about the deep injustices of patriarchy. But I can suffer under patriarchy and still perpetuate racism.

Erin Trent Johnson, a Black woman and founder of Community Equity Partners, a consulting and coaching practice focused on liberated leadership and anti-racist practices, shares that a room full of white women is a much more dangerous space for her than a room full of white men. "I have no expectations of support from white men because of the history of not being seen or valued by whiteness or patriarchy. I don't expect them to see me as human or as a real woman," she explains. "In the room with white women there is a slight hope for solidarity in womanhood, but to be a woman is to be an unspoken white woman and to have to find ways to make white women comfortable. That room is more threatening because of the way white women passively expect their comfort to be maintained and elevated above mine. There is a tacit understanding that their experiences are more human and require more care. My very body is a threat."[3]

I cannot talk about being a (cis) woman without talking about being a *white woman* any more than I can talk about growing up poor without also acknowledging that I was poor *and white*. And the truth is that white women have not been supportive to women of color in any clear or consistent way, not historically and not currently. Some of the most intense white fragility erupts regularly on progressive Facebook groups such as Pantsuit Nation when white women are challenged racially.

Black feminists in particular have been challenging white women on their racism for decades. Legal scholar Kimberlé Williams Crenshaw co-developed the theory of intersectionality and coined the term in 1989.[4] Intersectionality is the recognition that we occupy multiple social positions within hierarchical societies and these positions interact in complex ways that must be acknowledged and addressed. Her scholarship has been foundational in the development of intersectional feminism. She explains, "Intersectionality is an analytic sensibility, a way of thinking about identity and its relationship to power. Originally articulated on behalf of Black women, the term brought to light the invisibility of many constituents within groups that claim them as members but often fail to represent them."

Alice Walker coined the term "womanist" in 1983 to distinguish between mainstream White feminists and feminist of color and to challenge anti-Blackness within the feminist movement. In the seminal 1977 work by Black feminists, *The Combahee River Collective Statement*, Demita Frazier, Beverly Smith, and Barbara Smith write, "Our situation as Black people necessitates that we have solidarity around the fact of race, which white women of course do not need to have with white men, unless it is their negative solidarity as racial oppressors. We struggle together with Black men against racism, while we also struggle with Black men about sexism."[5] Black women have continually challenged each successive wave of feminism. They gave us the term "white feminism" to mark where our analysis and activism are not intersectional.

White feminists, through our direct experience of marginalization under patriarchy, have a powerful entry point to understand our complicity with racism. But we must use that experience as a way in, not a way out. So how might I use my experience of marginalization as a woman to help me understand and challenge my participation in racism (among other forms of oppression from which I benefit)? When I am challenged by feedback from a person of color and do not understand the feedback or feel defensive about it, I change the roles in my mind. I imagine that I have just challenged a man on sexism and he is saying out loud to me the same things I am thinking about the feedback I just received. Changing the roles usually makes what is off in my thinking obvious.

Here is an example of how changing the roles can reveal underlying dynamics. Imagine a room full of particularly powerful white men seated around a conference table. Perhaps they are the CEOs of large corporations, and they have been pressured to be more representative and include women. I will leave readers to imagine how the CEOs might feel about that pressure and how long it might take them to act on it, but eventually they come to you (a woman) and ask you to join their group. In particular, they want you to help them see their sexism. Now, they likely would not use language that direct—they are more likely to say they need "a woman's perspective" and your help in seeing if there are any gender biases in the policies they write. You agree to join them, although of course they will not be paying you anything extra for your intellectual or emotional labor.

The first time you walk into that room, how might it feel? Would you be acutely aware of yourself as the only woman in the room? Would the embodiment of institutional power backed with legal authority held by those men be almost *palpable* to you? It certainly would to me. If you were keeping a list of all the ways that you experienced sexism in that room over a course of three months, how long do you think your list would be? What reception do you think you would get if you raised your hand and shared that list with them? How much white male fragility would erupt and what would it look like? (If you are having trouble imagining this, just ask yourself how often you have tried to give a man feedback on his sexism and had that go well.)

Imagine that following the meeting and the debate, denial, devil's advocacy, rebuttals, minimizations, gaslighting, hurt feelings, and silence in response to your list (and that is just how they reacted *in front of* you), one of the men—one you thought was a supportive ally but who was silent during the meeting—comes by your office to let you know that he agreed with what you said. You tell him that you appreciate knowing that but add that it would have been so much more powerful for the group and supportive to you if he had expressed that in the room. You ask him why he didn't speak up in the meeting. He replies, "*I didn't feel safe.*"

Imagining that scenario helped me unpack the difference between *safety* and *comfort* across positions of power, and why dominant group demands for a "safe" climate are a dishonest perversion of the true historical direction of collective violence. Seeing the absurdity as well as the insult has enabled me to challenge that narrative with white people who insist that they need to feel safe or that safety must be created in the group before they can *merely engage in a discussion* of racism.

Now imagine a room full of white women sitting around a conference table. They really need a woman of color on their board. Can you imagine how that room might feel to a Black woman? Can you see the same dynamics erupting were she to call in any of the white women on their racist assumptions and interactions? As a white woman, I can be in the room with the male CEOs and experience sexism, and also be in the room of white women perpetuating racism. White women certainly benefit from and collude in racism, and we must stop using sexism to protect our racism. As Crenshaw advises, "The better we understand how identities and power work together from one context to another, the less likely our movements for change are to fracture." I think of this task in terms of saliency. It is on me to continually ask, "Which identity is most salient in this context and how can I use it strategically?"

A CLOSING NOTE ABOUT THE INTERSECTION OF RACE AND CLASS

A common debate among progressives in anti-oppression work is that of the "first" oppression that sets up all others. Some say patriarchy is the foundation, because the moment a baby is born it is placed into one or the other category—"male" or "female"—with their corresponding statuses. Others say the first oppression is adultism because all children are controlled by adults—for example, the bodies of male babies in the US are routinely cut and permanently altered without their consent during circumcision. Others argue that it is all related to economics or class because regardless of what axis we sort people on, that sorting leads to who gets resources and who doesn't. While we do need to recognize all forms of oppression, how they manifest and intersect, and the role we can play to ameliorate them, I'm not sure it is particularly useful to establish which oppression is "first." I do, however, want to make a case for the importance of understanding the specific relationship between racism and classism.

More and more wealth is being concentrated into fewer and fewer hands.[6] The US has the highest level of income inequality among G7 countries. The wealth gap between America's richest and poorest families more than doubled from 1989 to 2016. The percentage of taxes paid by billionaires has fallen 79 percent since 1980. As of March 2020, US billionaires' total wealth increased by $308 billion.[7] Billionaires hold a combined net worth of $3.229 trillion, and their collective wealth rose 1,130 percent between 1990 and 2020. During the height of the COVID-19 pandemic, the wealth of Jeff Bezos, CEO of Amazon, increased by $25 billion. The banks that processed the $349 billion loan program charged up to 5 percent in fees, earning $10 billion, even though they took on little or no risk, as the loans were guaranteed by the Small Business Administration.

But where do our leaders direct our attention? To the racial "Other." To this end, Trump's insistence on calling COVID-19 the "China virus" was strategic. Class warfare uses racism to divert our attention away from the top and toward the bottom; dog-whistle racism—the use of coded or suggestive language to signal a racist message while still offering plausible deniability—is a tool of class warfare.[8]

Kimberlé Crenshaw uses the term "disaster white supremacy" to capture the ways in which elites use natural crises to expedite the racist project.[9] Disaster white supremacy accomplishes two objectives: the continued suppression of Black people and the concentration of wealth, the former as the tool of the latter. We have seen this most recently during the COVID-19 crisis. The pandemic has provided cover for the acceleration of extreme anti-immigration laws, voter suppression, and ever more tax cuts and bailouts to wealthy corporations, while requiring "essential workers"—most of whom are poor BIPOC people already at risk due to racial weathering from centuries of discrimination—to work in unsafe conditions, often without healthcare or a living wage.

From its inception, racism has been used as a class project to obscure the concentration of wealth into the hands of an elite few. Invoking racial resentment among the white masses is effective to this end. Psychiatrist Jonathan Metzl, in his book *Dying of Whiteness: How the Politics of Racial Resentment Is Killing America's Heartland*, examines how racial resentment has fueled pro-gun laws in Missouri, obstruction of the Affordable Care Act in Tennessee, and cuts to schools and social services in Kansas. The result is increased deaths by gun suicide, lowered life expectancies, and rising dropout rates. Metzl tells the story of "Trevor," a white Tennessean dying of liver disease. Had Trevor lived one state over, he would have been eligible for treatment that could have saved his life via the ACA. But Tennessee had blocked these healthcare reforms. Still, Trevor says, "Ain't no way I would ever support Obamacare or sign up for it. I would rather die. . . . No way I want my tax dollars paying for Mexicans or welfare queens."[10] Trevor's story shows how effective dog-whistle racism can be. It also shows us that what is really in white Americans' best interests is the refusal of white supremacist propaganda.

I am not making the case that we should focus on classism and in so doing, we will simultaneously be addressing racism. As Metzl argues, racial resentment sets up poor whites to accept and endure class oppression; we can't address the one without also addressing the other. Similarly, in *Dog Whistle Politics: How Coded Racial Appeals Have Reinvented Racism and Wrecked the Middle Class*, Haney López argues that class grievance has been and continues to be channeled into racial animus by political elites, who succeed over and over in persuading poor and working-class whites to support regressive policies that are profitable for corporations but harmful to themselves.[11] While the impact is far greater on Black and Brown people, this business model hurts all but those elites. We won't eradicate economic injustice as long as we leave racism unaddressed and remain susceptible to racist manipulation.

Civil rights scholar john a. powell's concept of "targeted universalism" illustrates the case for centering racism.[12] Targeted universalism is the idea that focusing on specific goals will address universal goals, but focusing on universal goals will not address specific goals. Take for example what is often termed "the achievement gap." Imagine that a hundred students—both white and of color—are not achieving in school based on a list of barriers. If we address the set of barriers that both the white kids and the kids of color are facing—the universal barriers—we will be helping the white kids but only partially helping the kids of color. This is because the kids of color will have an additional set of barriers not faced by the white kids, barriers that are the result of structural racism. If we center the kids of color and address the barriers they face, we will simultaneously be addressing those faced by the white kids. In centering race in our analysis, we interrupt problematic dynamics such as dog-whistle manipulation and white feminism.

CHAPTER 11

HOW DO YOU MAKE A WHITE PROGRESSIVE A BETTER RACIST?

We know, in the case of the person, that whoever cannot tell himself the truth about his past is trapped in it, is immobilized in the prison of his discovered self. We know how a person, in such paralysis, is unable to assess either his weaknesses or his strengths and how frequently indeed he mistakes one for the other.

—James Baldwin[1]

Given the system of white supremacy in which we are embedded, can anything ever be outside of it? How can white progressives strive for accountability from within this system? Here I want to talk about the pitfall of actually becoming *more effective* in reproducing racial inequality using the tools of anti-racism, rather than less. In other words, can anti-racist education make white people more efficient racists? This is especially crucial to consider given the surge of white interest in anti-racism following the lynching of George Floyd and the subsequent worldwide protests against racial injustice. This interest is heartening but also lets loose thousands of white people feeling the urgency to "fix" racism, but with only a superficial and tenuous understanding of its systemic nature and our own complicity. That urgency leads to an expectation for quick fixes and easy answers. I have lost count of the organizations that have never addressed racism before but want a forty-five-minute presentation that offers "solutions" and "best practices." There is no simple solution or imagined finish line.

(SLIGHTLY MORE) SAVVY RACISM. Sociologist Ellen Berrey, in her study of workplace diversity programs, argues that diversity is a form of symbolic politics that emerged to reconcile a contradiction: it is undesirable for liberal institutions to be portrayed as "racist," but at the same time institutional elites have no desire to change existing racist power structures. While these programs affirm the importance of diversity, they steadfastly resist meaningful cultural and programmatic change.[2] More companies are now offering racial equity training and can tick off that box, but this training must be supported and sustained to have any meaningful impact. When it is not followed with ongoing education and resources, attendees may feel momentarily inspired to get involved, but the pressure to not name racism—and the rewards that go with that pressure—is powerful. While the goal of anti-racist education is to enable white people to see (or admit to) problematic racial dynamics and stop engaging in them, this requires continual self-reflection, education, relationship building, and practice. Just enough awareness can inspire white people to run out to save the world, but without any strategy or skill.

Because racism is institutionalized in our society, an organization's so-called "race neutral" policies will still result in racial inequity. Such policies include requiring that everyone have the same college degree, dress codes, mandatory drug testing, and criminal background checks, and not collecting data based on race. Further, these "race neutral" policies do not account for implicit bias in assessment and implementation. For example, a 2018 survey showed that African Americans are much more likely to face repercussions for failing a drug test than white people; 9.2 percent of Blacks reported being reprimanded or even fired for failing a drug test, more than double that of the 4.4 percent reported by whites.[3] The list of industries that most frequently drug-test their employees overwhelmingly represent the labor of BIPOC people. While 12.3 percent of the US population is Black and 12.5 percent is Hispanic, Black and Hispanic Americans make up nearly 30 percent of the military, 39 percent of transportation and warehouse workers, and 30 percent of healthcare workers.

When organizations have covered themselves with equity committees and sporadic training, the rationales to justify their outcomes may be more sophisticated, but the outcomes remain the same. For example, how often have we heard that the lack of racial diversity at the top of organizations is a "pipeline" issue? The pipeline rationale posits that given all the institutional racism and educational inequality, "they just aren't coming down the pipeline." In other words, we can't find any strong candidates because they aren't out there. So what can we do? Similarly, I have often heard, "Well, when you do have that rare talented and educated person of color, everyone wants them, so they just don't stay." Or, "Why would the ones with choices go into fields that don't pay well, like education?" These narratives appear to acknowledge structural inequality but are actually based on inaccurate stereotypes and are profoundly insulting to BIPOC people. Further, it is simply not true—the data is clear that it is not a pipeline issue; it is a bias issue.

OVERCONFIDENCE. Many workplaces now have committees titled with some combination of the words "equity," "diversity," and "inclusion," with acronyms like D.E I. or E & I. The specific terms and their order can vary, as long as the title is indirect and includes every possible group so as not to highlight race and cause white people to feel threatened. In other words, as long as they don't mention racial equity, racial justice, systemic racism, or whiteness in the title or description. Members are tasked with getting all forms of oppression on the table in a way that is sure to push racism off the table or at least make it difficult to address in any depth. Typically, employees of color are randomly assigned to head these groups, regardless of whether they have any interest or skill in doing so. The underlying assumption is that "race work" is for racialized people, while white people can cover everything else. People of color must jump through endless hoops based on the implicit assumption that they are inherently unqualified to sit at tables other than those few reserved for diversity work. I once applied for the job of director of equity for a city government. I was one of the final two candidates, the other being a Black man. When I got the call telling me they had chosen the other candidate, they explained that they thought it was important for a Black person to have the diversity position, but that the position of executive director of the entire office was opening up soon, and they really hoped I would apply. They needed a Black man for the diversity department and apparently saw his qualifications as not reaching beyond that position. But they saw me as qualified for leading *all* departments, even though I had never held an executive director position! Again, racial or multicultural issues are seen as the domain of racialized people, but "normal" issues are the domain of white people.

Conversely, the white people who are assigned or volunteer to join diversity committees may have a background in an anti-racist framework but often don't; they are simply interested. Regardless, our interest gets us a seat at the diversity table, as well as all of the other tables. I am all for organizations having equity committees, and certainly there are strong advocates and effective committees. At the same time, some of the most obstructionist and gate-keeping white people I have encountered are involved in equity work. Because they are involved in this work, they can be the most defensive about suggestions of racism. The more our identities are attached to the idea that we are among the "woke ones," the more resistant we can be to owning our own patterns of collusion. When called in on those patterns, we make the move of credentialing, citing our committee involvement as evidence to rebut the charge. Do we actually "get it" if we think anything could or does certify us as unable to cause racial harm?

Involvement in anti-racism efforts can become "stylish" for white people, something cool that provides intense feelings and entertaining insights to be consumed in manageable doses. People become conversant with the terminology, but in practice the terms are almost meaningless. I have heard many white people glibly say, "I know I have white privilege," but that is as far as they go; nothing in their behavior actually changes. For example, I have been in cross-racial discussions in which a white person will be doing most of the talking. At some point, when it becomes very obvious that they are taking all the air out of the room, they will exclaim, "I know I am dominating the conversation!" followed by a laugh . . . and on they continue dominating the conversation. I call this the "I'm Covered" move. Apparently, naming bad behavior excuses one from it. But if you can recognize that what you are doing is problematic, why not take the next step and *just stop doing it*?

Journalist Erin Aubry Kaplan reminds us that white America's a-ha moment following George Floyd's murder is a beginning, not an end. Whether that beginning will be sustained in continued engagement will tell how meaningful that a-ha was. She writes, "Racism is a form of convenience, in the sense that it's designed to make life easier for its beneficiaries . . . the phenomenon of not having to think about the costs of oppression, or about Black people at all. Antiracism requires the opposite: engagement. Being truly antiracist will require white people to be inconvenienced by new policies and practices, legal and social, that affect everything in everyone's daily lives."[4] White people have not demonstrated yet—across the centuries—that we will align our professed values with our actions. In her post "Dear White People: Antiracism Is Not a Trend," blogger Rashida Campbell-Allen observes, "The death of George Floyd is not a wake-up call. In fact, the same alarm has been echoing since 1619, but ignorance and privilege have hit the snooze button time and time again."[5] Campbell-Allen cautions that anti-racism is a "lifelong commitment to self-reflection, action, education, awareness and listening to constructive criticism. . . . Your shock is not enough. In this case, actions need to speak louder than words." The adage to show rather than tell is relevant here, as it is to many other aspects of white anti-racist practice.

DEFERRING. One of the most predictable questions I get from white people following a presentation or workshop is "But what if a person of color is wrong and it isn't really racism?" Let's take a moment to notice the stunning self-centeredness and denial in this question. When they have just been presented with information that includes the stark reality that whether we will survive our birth and how long we will live can be predicted based on our racial categorization, the immediate concern from a white person is whether something a person of color says is racism *may not really be*. After hours of evidence illustrating the enduring tragedy of systemic racism and anti-Blackness over the last four hundred years, beginning with genocide toward Indigenous people and three hundred years of kidnapping, enslavement, torture, rape, and brutality toward African Americans, up through the present day with mass incarceration and police executions, with an epidemic in missing and murdered Indigenous women and white nationalism on the rise, with children separated from parents and incarcerated at the Mexico border, and the consistent outcomes of profound racial inequality at every measure, why is "But what if it isn't really racism?" the first place so many white people go? That so many do powerfully illustrates how myopic, disconnected, and—might I say—racist we are.

First, you cannot sort out race from a cross-racial interaction any more than you can sort out gender from a cross-gender interaction. I may not be consciously thinking of race or gender in every moment, but I am always implicitly aware, and that awareness has an impact on everything that happens in that interaction. While this seems like common sense if one has any understanding of socialization, decades of research on implicit bias certainly backs up the statement. For example, if I am in an argument with someone and they raise their voice at me, it will have a different impact based on factors that include my stereotypes about the person's social group and whether there is a history of harm between our groups. A man raising his voice will feel more threatening than a woman raising hers. But a Black woman raising her voice will feel threatening in a way that a white woman raising hers does not. Even what I talk about and how I talk about it are shaped by my awareness of who I am talking to and their structural position in relation to mine. As one example, I generally don't talk about the challenges of menstruation with men I am not intimate with, but I easily bring this subject up with women, even if we are only acquaintances. These dynamics make it impossible to say that race or gender had absolutely nothing to do with how I perceive a given interaction.

Second, my not seeing or not understanding how something is racist is not the most reliable criteria, given my socialization not to see or understand racism; racism comes *from* me, not *at* me. Inevitably, there will be aspects of it that I am not ever going to fully understand given my position within a racist society. Of course, I certainly understand vastly more than I used to, and I can and should continually try to further my understanding. But there is a point at which I need to simply accept the feedback I am given and focus on repair.

This brings us to the dilemma of deferring. Yes, even after accounting for all of the dynamics discussed above, it is possible that a person of color may simply be exaggerating, excusing bad behavior, or just plain wrong. Maybe they really did misunderstand me. Maybe they really are not fulfilling the requirements of their job. Maybe it would be more strategic to focus on the forest for now and not the trees. In some cases, such as job performance, there is a bottom line, and one may need to hold firm. But in most cases, if you can just defer, why not do so? Given the centuries in which BIPOC people have been trying to get white people to stop denying racism, given how many millions of times they have *not* been wrong but we have refused to own up, why focus on a theoretical exception to the rule? It is a healthy interruption to white superiority and racial arrogance to defer to BIPOC people in these infrequent cases. Often, all that is at risk is our pride.

Some critics of my work have misunderstood my guidance to defer to racialized people's judgment on what constitutes racism. Some have taken this to mean that I believe that racialized people are never and can never be wrong. Given the diversity in perspective among racialized people, it would be absurd for me to think that. Do I think all feedback I am given from BIPOC people is 100 percent correct and should be followed? How could I? On a daily basis I receive conflicting feedback from BIPOC people and would be immobilized if I tried to follow all of it. Some BIPOC people undoubtedly have opinions I see as fundamentally wrong, and they can have personal issues and dysfunctions in the same ways that white people do. Of course I must make a determination on what to take in and how to respond. My guidance to defer is within the context of Anti-Racism 101, where I am working with white people who have never before reflected on what it means to be white, who cannot begin to answer the question of how race shapes their lives, who do not have any (or have very few) cross-racial relationships and virtually no education on systemic racism (the majority of white people on all counts). A white person with no racial self-awareness—especially one who defines racism as intentional acts of meanness—is in no position to determine whether a person of color's perspective is legitimate or not.

When a deeper analysis is gained and more skill is developed, then my guidance is to reflect on the feedback, take what is useful, and leave the rest. Even with experience, making this determination can be difficult. At these times, I consult with white colleagues who have education and experience and colleagues of color who have agreed to coach me on these matters. I advise other white people to do the same. In the final analysis, of course, we do have to reflect on the value of the feedback and decide what to take and what to leave. Complete deference merely functions as a kind of soft racism in which BIPOC people are set up to fail and our relationships are inauthentic.

LAPSES IN HUMILITY. Those of us who are actively engaged in racial justice work have many opportunities to cause racial harm and to inflict that harm more efficiently. On a daily basis, we walk into rooms of strangers and talk openly about racism, most often in mixed-race or multiracial groups. As white facilitators, we bring into those rooms the same patterns as other white people. Hopefully, we have done more personal work and cause less harm less often. But this cannot be assumed, because we are not free of our own racist conditioning. We have to be clear and confident when we are facilitating a session, but that clarity and confidence can also set us up to stop listening, to ignore the expertise already in the room. When we become complacent, our conditioning surfaces with ease.

Consider a recent example of my own lapse in humility. I was asked to be a guest speaker and give a presentation on white fragility for a group composed mostly of BIPOC people, with a leadership team composed of Black women. I met with the leadership beforehand, and they shared with me that the members had wide and deep experience in racial equity leadership in a range of fields. This group had been meeting regularly and had built a deep sense of community. It was a rare and precious space for them in which white people did not set the agenda, and they did not feel colonized by the culture of whiteness.

The session took place in a smaller, more intimate setting than the venues in which I typically present. While I was aware that the group was about 90 percent BIPOC people, I set my sights on the few white members. The leaders—who had years of experience leading racial justice work with a wide range of groups and skill levels—had told me that this group was special, but—confident that I knew "my people" best—I didn't really believe that the white people would be any more advanced than most. I decided to give my usual presentation, directed toward that small group of white participants. Proceeding with an unchecked assumption that the BIPOC people would appreciate seeing the approach I take with white people, I explained what I would be covering and how, and I gave a brief overview of the terms I would be using. Feeling that my opening adequately provided the rationale for my approach, I gave my presentation on white fragility.

Early on, a participant of color had a question, but I asked him to hold it until I was finished. This is a request I typically make when presenting to majority-white groups, in order to help white participants develop the capacity to lean into discomfort and ambiguity and also allow me to get through sensitive content so I have a framework to draw from when responding. Of course this was not a majority-white group. Although I sensed that he felt silenced, and I was aware that this was a questionable move on my part, I tucked this feeling away. Time was limited, I had an agenda, and I carried on. When I finished, I opened the floor to questions but at that point there were none. They gave me a lukewarm round of applause, and we broke for lunch.

When we returned from our break, we met in affinity groups and then came back together for a closing circle. I had an hour before I needed to go to the airport, and my host from the leadership team and I went for a walk to debrief. My host and I were friends; we had an ongoing relationship and had worked together for several years, and she had some feedback to share with me. She told me that I had deeply offended the BIPOC people and broke it down for me in detail. I was surprised but initially calm and open; I could see truth in the feedback, but I also believed I had delivered what I had been asked to deliver, so it wasn't really my fault that it wasn't well received.

As I drove to the airport and had time to reflect on the feedback, however, my missteps became clearer. By the time I got to the airport, I had gone from calm to mortified. I realized that I had not in fact delivered what I had been asked to deliver; I had delivered what *I wanted to deliver*, as a white person to a room full of BIPOC people! I felt like a fraud, exposed and chagrined at how disrespectfully I had treated the group and the leaders. A few hours later, I was immobilized with shame, wanting to go home and never talk about race again. But hiding in my house and remaining silent about racism for the rest of my life was not an option. Pushing through the powerful pull to avoid the discomfort of facing my host, I scheduled a call with her to seek some closure and repair. In the meantime, I worked on my feelings with supportive and experienced white colleagues. We identified my missteps at each point and talked through strategies for better decisions in the future.

In my follow-up call with the host, I listened as openly as possible as she gave me more detailed feedback. I reflected on what I understood her to be saying, and we talked through what I could have done differently. I apologized and committed to do better. I took notes on the feedback to bring to my support circle and guide my continuing work. I was able to reach out to the participant whose question I had shut down, and he graciously granted me the opportunity to have a conversation to acknowledge and repair. Over time, I came to terms with my behavior, took the lessons learned, and moved forward. Still, I regret that the lessons came at such a cost to BIPOC people. I cannot say there was a tidy ending and that everyone felt resolved. My impact did not end when I left.

Looking back, I can clearly see that the many differences between this group and those I typically work with should have been a signal to me to take a different approach. Unfortunately, I did not pay attention. Nor did I listen to or believe the leadership team when they told me that the group had their own expertise on the topic. As a white outsider to a group composed primarily of BIPOC people and led by Black women, I felt confident to decide for myself what they wanted and needed. I stood in front of them and arrogantly lectured for two hours on whiteness (oh the irony!). I did not ask them what they wanted to hear from me, much less consider what I could learn from them. I did not adapt to the norms of the culture I was in or learn their language and terms; I told them what my language and terms would be. I did not open the floor to questions or comments until the end, even though I was aware that someone had a question well before that. I was inflexible and did not make pedagogical decisions strategically based on an awareness of my racial position in relation to others. I did not check in and listen when I felt something was off cross-racially. I did not include my host, a Black woman with whom I had experience co-facilitating and who had an invaluable perspective to share. I silenced their questions, I insulted their expertise, and I subjected them to white domination—in this rare and precious space where up until my visit they had been able to enjoy some reprieve from white control. This was poor pedagogy in any context, but in this particular context the impact was profound—the impact was racism.

I also put my host—a Black woman—in the very difficult position of having to give this feedback to a white person. We were (and remain) friends, but we had not yet faced my patterns of white domination to this degree. There is a deep history of harm between Black and white people, and she had no guarantee that I would not argue, minimize, retaliate, pressure her to absolve me, make her the aggressor and demand more resources to cope with her "mistreatment" of me, or withdraw from the relationship altogether. Having literally written the book on white fragility did not mean I was free of it, only that I understood it in part because I recognized it within myself. As white people, we tend to focus on the personal impact of receiving feedback on our racism without acknowledging the cost to BIPOC people for *giving us* this feedback. In large part, white fragility functions to police BIPOC people into *not* giving us this feedback, lest they risk invalidation and abandonment. She had to push through her own history of punishments—both large and small—from white people for daring to speak her truth. In this way, the repercussions continued long after the workshop was over. Each follow-up conversation seeking repair came at the continual price of her emotional, intellectual, and psychic labor.

If I could go back and do that day over, there are so many things I would change. First, I would slow down and listen to the leaders, integrating their guidance into my presentation. I would center the needs and interests of the BIPOC people who were the majority of participants, knowing that there would be an opportunity to work directly with the white people in an affinity space later. Given how intimate and connected the group was, I would sit with them rather than stand in front of them. I would ask for clarification on their language and terms, rather than tell them what I would be using. Knowing that as BIPOC people they were all too familiar with white fragility and had an understanding of it that I didn't—being on the receiving end of it all their lives—I would ask what they wanted to hear from me on the topic, rather than assume. I would acknowledge and respect their expertise and ask about their experiences, examples, and insights. I would be flexible, welcome questions, and let their interests shape the direction of the session. When I sensed that a move I made was racially problematic, I would listen to that sense and check in, rather than compartmentalize and push forward. I would model cross-racial alliance and humility by sharing the floor with my host. I would name the honor I felt to be in this rare and precious space they had designed as a reprieve from the racially hostile outside world. I would tread lightly as a guest in that space.

I have found again and again that the moment I am complacent and stop paying attention, I inevitably step back into white habits and do racial harm. These habits include not asking BIPOC people what is needed and not listening to and believing what they say when they tell me, inflexibly imposing our own agenda, putting our thinking above theirs without curiosity about or consideration of the expertise they bring into the room, patronizing, silencing, and controlling.

Paying attention is not the same as walking on eggshells. I did not need to walk on eggshells that day, but I definitely needed to respect my audience and engage with a sense of mutuality and racial humility. I am a nice white progressive with years of experience who knows better, and I caused this harm in two short hours. Imagine what we do every day in our workplaces and committees. Such is the power of whiteness and the vigilance required to keep it in check.

CHAPTER 12

NICENESS IS NOT COURAGEOUS

*How to Align Your Professed Values
with Your Actual Practice*

*We are so past white people telling us what they think and
what they feel. We don't really care about that anymore. We
want to see what you do. What life are you living? What's
different? You have a sign on your lawn or a flag up, but
who's in your house? Who's not in your house? Is your skin
in the game? I feel like I wasted my time, frankly, because
I put everything out there for you to pick through and you
haven't done anything with it. So I'm done.*

—Anika Nailah[1]

Niceness is pleasant. Niceness is comfortable. Niceness is generally appreciated. But niceness alone is not anti-racism. Niceness does not absolve white people from racism. Nor does niceness prove that someone is not racist (much less anti-racist). And a culture of niceness is not an indication that the culture is free of racism. Anti-racism takes courage, commitment, and accountability; niceness does not.

COURAGE

Anyone notice how explosively defensive white people are about racism? I have termed this explosiveness "white fragility," but white fragility is not defensiveness alone, which can be a natural part of a process. White fragility is refusal. It is white people digging their heels in deeper and protecting their worldview, blocking any further engagement that could expand that worldview. White fragility functions to deter any additional challenge and bully people into backing off. It functions as a protective force field preventing growth.

I don't think there is any one single cause for white fragility, but rather multiple causes coming together. One such cause, which I explored in chapter 2, is the ideology of individualism, which allows white people to exempt themselves from the cultural water in which we swim and to claim ourselves as unique exceptions to all sociopolitical patterns. At the same time that we are claiming to be unique individuals, we are also claiming to be objective representations of humanity, capable of speaking for everyone and determining the validity of their claims. Certainly, guilt about the centuries of discrimination is a factor, coupled with resentment that white advantage puts the lie to the precious myth of meritocracy. Taboos against talking openly about race make us hesitant and fearful when the topic comes up, especially in racially mixed company. The idea that only bad people can be racist is certainly a key pillar of white fragility. Add ignorance about systemic racism coupled with arrogance about the value of our uninformed opinions. And all of this rests on a foundation of white supremacy, which we begin to internalize from childhood: the belief that we are better people and deserve what we have (but can never admit to that directly). The convergence of these dynamics in the white psyche produces irrationality, but how we protect our positions doesn't have to be rational; it just has to work, and it does.

White supremacy is so ubiquitous it is mostly invisible to us. And yet we know, on a fundamental level, that it is better in US and other Western-oriented societies to be white. And except perhaps for those who fetishize racialized people, virtually all white people come to feel superior to racialized people. I would not be involved in efforts to challenge this belief if I didn't think it could be changed, but it is absolutely the starting premise. If "superior" is too strong a word for you, reflect on white comfort with segregation, the white lack of interest in developing relationships across race, and the arrogance of seeing ourselves as the objective arbiters of whether racialized people's experiences are legitimate. Think about the patronizing benevolence in our "charity" and missionary work. About how much—or how little—racial diversity we can tolerate in our movies, magazines, models, employees, leaders, schools, neighborhoods, and so on. Think about the assumptions behind the claim "I am all for equal rights but not special rights." Reflect on the images of Africa you've consumed over your life, the images of Black criminality. And if you are the exception—a white person who hasn't and doesn't live in segregation, who has a wide variety of authentic relationships across race and sincerely cannot find the mark of white superiority within you—reflect on how a lifetime of institutional white advantage, cultural representation, control, and benefiting from policies that have excluded others within a culture of white supremacy has shaped you.

White supremacy provides very real material and psychological benefits for white people. The investments are deep, and so are the forces protecting those investments. It is exceedingly difficult to challenge within ourselves, much less in others. Thus, anti-racism takes both personal and public courage to stand firm in the face of the inevitable pushback, retaliation, and seductive rewards for silence and complicity. Niceness is not courageous and will not sustain us in the face of resistance.

LIFELONG COMMITMENT

As I have argued throughout, we must not ever consider our work toward racial justice to be finished. No one arrives at a racism-free state, and even if we personally could find a way to live a fully integrated life, free from the forces of white supremacy, in which we never thought, said, or did anything racially problematic, society would still be projecting whiteness onto us. We would still be moving through the world as a white person, responded to as white, and receiving the benefits of whiteness within a white supremacist society. Given our own implicit investments and the resistance we meet when we challenge the investments of others, we must be strategic in setting up systems of support. Ideally, this support will be on multiple levels.

CONTINUAL EDUCATION. We must continuously educate ourselves through books, films, discussions, conferences, community groups, workbooks, and activism. In an era of social media and the internet, we have access to more excellent educational resources than ever before. There simply is no excuse not to break with the apathy of whiteness and delve into these resources!

Because race is a sociopolitical construct, it is ever-changing. Systems of power are not fixed and eternal; they are constantly being challenged and adapting to those challenges. Language is also sociopolitical and constantly evolving. The language we employ conveys ideas and images that shape how we see and respond to others, and as our awareness becomes sharper, so does our language. As marginalized groups gain visibility, they determine for themselves how they identify and how others should identify them. When I was growing up, it was acceptable in the white mainstream to use terms such as "Negro" and "Oriental." Today these terms are understood by most people to be offensive. Binary categories such as male and female have been deconstructed, and pronouns should no longer be assumed. As culture shifts and orthodoxy is challenged in an ongoing process, we must make an effort to keep up. It should not be on those who are marginalized to adapt to language we find more familiar and comfortable—it is on us to evolve.

White people are not outside of race. Our voices and perspectives on racism and anti-racism are critical. All too often, we have been a missing piece of the puzzle. Only engaging with racialized people's perspectives reinforces the idea that racism is not a white problem, which is problematic for all the reasons already discussed. But the foundation of our education must be rooted in their voices and perspectives. We will never understand racism in isolation.

BUILDING AUTHENTIC RELATIONSHIPS. One of the most important ways I have worked to challenge my socialization has been to build relationships across race. Nothing in the trajectory of my life would have ensured that I had these relationships. In fact, though I grew up in urban poverty, upward mobility took me further and further away from integrated spaces. Building relationships across race will require most white people to get out of their comfort zones and put themselves in new and unfamiliar environments. This is different from our usual approach in which we invite racialized people to join boards, committees, places of worship—groups white people already control. In this "additive" approach to diversity, we have done no work to expand our own consciousness, and we have developed no skills or strategies for navigating race. In effect, we are inviting BIPOC people into hostile water, and then we are dismayed and confused when they choose to leave.

So what *are* authentic relationships across race? They are not casual acquaintances we meet at work and use to claim diversity cover. They cannot be built with people we employ and whose livelihoods we control. We don't get them by latching on to any person of color in the vicinity; these are forms of objectification. Authentic relationships are those based on mutual interest. They develop over time, and they are sustained, not abandoned when conflict arises.

There are two significant positive outcomes of building authentic relationships across race that I want to highlight. One is how much more we can see and understand about the subtleties (subtle to white people) of racism BIPOC people experience on a daily basis. Paying attention and listening with openness and humility provides an incomparable eye-opening education. We don't need to interrogate or ask to be taught to see racism; when we pay attention, it becomes clear. The other positive outcome is how much more motivated and courageous we are when we feel connected, see the humanity in one another, and bear witness to injustice.

CIRCLES OF SUPPORT. Most of us could quickly and easily find fifty white people who would grant legitimacy to the idea that BIPOC people are somehow wrong about racism: they are overreacting, playing the race card, seeing race everywhere, have more rights than we do now, and so on. These are not the people we should seek out when we are processing new racial insights, struggling to understand, or feeling defensive. We have heard these rebuttals our whole lives and do not need them reinforced. When we are newer to an anti-racist framework, this pushback can undermine our confidence. Not having the skills to counter these narratives, we may give up, thinking that an ability to argue strongly is the same as having a strong argument.

Instead, it is critical that we have a circle of supportive white people who have a strong anti-racist analysis and experience doing their own internal work. Having quick access to fellow white people to struggle through challenges is invaluable. I will never forget asking for a meeting with my friend and colleague Christine Saxman shortly after an encounter with a Black colleague for whom we both had deep respect. I was distraught over how I had inadvertently disrespected this colleague and needed help working through my emotions. Christine was clear that I had a repair to make but also treated me with compassion and understanding. She gave me a supportive place to vent my emotions and then hone my thinking about how racism was at play in the encounter, all while holding me in what Christine calls "loving accountability."[2] Loving accountability in the context of anti-racism means I can show myself and admit to my racial patterns without risking abandonment, while also expecting to be held to the anti-racist standard that our professed values and actual practices must be in alignment.

Having a circle of BIPOC people with whom we are in close relationship and can talk through issues and challenges is also invaluable. Accountability is especially critical here, as it takes even more courage to show ourselves to racialized people. It is also trickier, as we need to not burden them with our internal processes or put them on the spot to absolve us. If we are in authentic relationships, we should be able to talk through these struggles as long as we are thoughtful about the pitfalls. There are also people who provide this service as personal coaches and who are paid for their expertise. I believe that if we do not have professional coaches of color in our circle of support, we should offer to pay our BIPOC friends and colleagues for their time and expertise. I will discuss this in more detail in the accountability section.

AFFINITY GROUPS. In chapter 5, I introduced the technique of affinity groups, wherein people who share the same racial identity meet on a regular basis to address the challenges specific to their group. White affinity groups are an important way for white people to keep racism on the radar and continue to work on our racist socialization. It is important for white people to be able to acknowledge and recognize our collective racial experience, which interrupts the tendency to see ourselves as unique individuals (or "just human") and thus outside the forces of race. Intentionally meeting *specifically as white people* for this purpose is a powerful contradiction.

Many of us who lead anti-racist education and organizing see affinity groups as an invaluable tool for consciousness-raising, healing, and ongoing skill building. There may be white affinity groups already organized in your area, or you can consider starting one. Effective groups are not too large, meet regularly, and have strong facilitation. Joining such a group in order to deepen our anti-racist skills and awareness does not mean white patterns will not be manifesting in the group. These patterns will invariably manifest and typically include distancing ourselves by talking in big generalities such as "Society should . . ."; focusing on other white people's frustrating patterns; domination of the discussion by some and silence by others; hopelessness and discouraging negativity; "out woking" one another; and credentialing. Strong facilitators can name and interrupt these patterns and use them as teachable moments.

ACCOUNTABILITY

Accountability within anti-racist work is the understanding that what I profess to value must be demonstrated in action, and that action must be answerable to BIPOC people. I cannot make a determination of how well I am doing in isolation. This is why I don't call myself an ally; it is for racialized people to decide if—in any given moment—I am *behaving* as an ally. Allyship is not a state of being that, once achieved, is static and unchanging. In this sense, allyship should be thought of as a verb, not a noun. In some moments I behave as an ally, and in others I choose comfort and complicity. I am the least likely to recognize my complicity and the most invested in not recognizing it. This is why there is no allyship without accountability.

Accountability requires trust, transparency, and action. As a white person seeking to be accountable I must continually check my certitude and ask myself, "How do I know how I am doing?" To answer this question, I need to check in and find out. I can do this in several ways, including by directly asking people with whom I have trusting relationships; talking to other white people who have an anti-racist framework; reading the work of BIPOC people who are clear about what they want and need (this work is easy to find, and many racial justice educators have good resource lists on their websites); and engaging in the exercises BIPOC people provide in online classes and workbooks. When I find that I am out of alignment, I need to do what is necessary and to the best of my ability to remedy the situation. And yes, the more experience and practice I have in anti-racist work, the more thoughtfully I will be able to determine what feedback to keep and what to let go.

The following are the basics of how I seek to be accountable. Much on this list has been discussed in more detail in the previous chapters, but I offer them here in what I hope is a concise and useful way. This is in no way an exhaustive list, and there are many good resources focused on accountability in a range of contexts, including schools, neighborhoods, raising children, talking with our families, and working in government, corporations, nonprofits, and communities (look it up!). These are the basics I follow:

1. Donate a percentage of your income to racial justice organizations led by BIPOC people.
2. Get involved in and donate your time and services to BIPOC-led racial justice efforts. Consider yourself a guest in these organizations; listen and follow their leadership. Do not take over or decide for yourself what is needed.
3. When organizing events, make sure they are accessible and that scholarships are available for BIPOC people who may need them. Donate proceeds from events to racial justice organizations led by BIPOC people.
4. Promote the work and services of BIPOC people. Channel work to BIPOC people. Seek out and choose BIPOC-owned businesses and service providers. Co-lead paid work with BIPOC people when possible.
5. Always cite and give credit to the work of BIPOC people who have informed your thinking.

6. Develop accountability partners of color. An accountability partner is someone with whom you have built a trusting relationship and who has agreed to coach you, talk through challenges with you, think with you, and challenge you on issues of racism. An accountability partner may also be a friend or colleague, but an accountability partner is a specific, defined, transparent role. Accountability partners of color should be paid for their time. If they are also personal friends, they may not accept payment, but you should approach the relationship with the expectation that this work should not be unpaid labor. If payment for their services is declined, ask if there are racial justice organizations to which you can donate in lieu of payment. If they don't have a suggestion, do some research and choose one (see #1).

7. Build relationships with white people who have a strong anti-racist analysis and who can serve as white accountability partners. These are people with whom you have personal relationships, who can listen when you need to work through your defensiveness or confusion about racism. They will help you work through your feelings, hold you accountable, and prepare you to make racial repair when needed. I do not offer to pay white friends for this (however, there are white people with strong analysis and deep experience who do offer professional paid coaching).

8. Attend white affinity groups.

9. Never consider your learning finished. Continually participate in every racial justice education forum you can (conferences, workshops, talks). Continually read and learn from the work of BIPOC people. Take online classes taught by BIPOC people.

10. Break white silence on racism. Make sure that anti-racism gets on the table and stays on the table in your workplaces, social circles, places of worship, and other organizations.

11. Ibram X. Kendi defines a racist policy as any policy with a racially inequitable outcome. Look at your organization's policies. If they are producing racially inequitable outcomes, get

them back on the table and keep working. Individual transformation *must* lead to structural change.

12. Join organizations and groups working for racial justice. Organize other white people into the cause. While it is vitally important that each of us does less harm in our daily personal interactions, our eyes should always be on the ultimate prize of changing the structures of systemic racism.

13. Subscribe to online sources that publish lists, guides, and tools for racial justice work.

14. Find your particular strength and apply it to the work of racial justice. We need educators, organizers, policy wonks, support staff, legal experts, teachers, writers, clergy, and so on.

In particular, we need to start seeing the intellectual and emotional labor that racialized people do to navigate and survive in white supremacist societies as labor that needs to be compensated. When we ask racialized people to join our committees, boards, advisory councils, organizations, and other groups in order to have "diversity," we should actually *pay them* for their time and labor. If these positions are already paid positions, we should pay racialized people *more* for them. If we are inviting them because they are offering a perspective that is missing, then they have expertise we don't have. Further, given that sharing their expertise is often fraught with danger, these are high-risk jobs that require a very specialized set of skills. Let's show that we understand the value of what BIPOC people bring by *paying* for what they bring. Even then, we will be up against the implicit bias and internalized superiority that cause us to devalue the perspectives we claim to want. We can never be complacent. The current political climate is sad testimony that progress does not arc toward justice unaided but must be continually fought for. When victories are won, large or small, they will continually be challenged.

How do we live anti-racist lives as white people within a racist society? Again, as Kendi instructs us, "The opposite of 'racist' isn't 'not racist.' The opposite of racist is *antiracist*."[3] "Anti-racist" is active; "not racist" is passive, and passivity in a racist society is racist. For me, living an anti-racist life means integrating an anti-racist lens into how I see the world and the actions I take in the world. Anti-racism is not something I can add on whenever I may find it interesting and convenient to do so. Racism is not an aberration; it is the norm, operating continuously. An anti-racist lens should also be operating continuously, transforming who is in my life, who I connect with, what I see, what I care about, what I talk about, what I read about, what I buy, how I work, what I am willing to feel, what I can bear witness to, what discomfort I can withstand, and what risks I am willing to take.

Ijeoma Oluo offers an important reminder: "The beauty of anti-racism is that you don't have to pretend to be free of racism to be an anti-racist. Anti-racism is the commitment to fight racism wherever you find it, including in yourself. And it's the only way forward."[4] And given that I can fairly easily avoid accountability, anti-racism means I do not rely solely on external pressure. I seek a state in which being "not racist" in a racist society is what actually makes me uncomfortable. Anti-racist action is the answer to "What do I do?" Niceness won't cover it.

STUDY GUIDE

In this section, I offer reflection questions for each chapter. Readers may find journaling their responses useful. For those engaging in discussion with other readers or in study groups, the questions have been designed to avoid a common white pattern, what I call "rehearsing." Rehearsing occurs when we repeat the same opinions, evidence, platitudes, stories, and arguments we always repeat when the topic of racism comes up. Rehearsing functions as a white move in several ways: to provide evidence of how aware we are; as an opportunity to lecture and instruct other white people; as a way to reinforce the opinions we already hold; and to block risk-taking, vulnerability, and openness. The kinds of claims that are offered up in rehearsing tend to be definitive and close-ended, making it difficult for others to provide feedback or challenge. There is no growth for us in rehearsing unless we are applying a *new lens* to our familiar narratives.

Racism is a deeply complex issue that the mainstream does not prepare us to engage in with nuance and skill. We need to move beyond merely sharing our opinions on racism and recognize that our opinions are likely not as informed as we may think. Therefore, the questions here do not ask for readers' opinions or whether readers agree or disagree with the content. Instead, they are designed to help readers go deeper into and *grapple* with the content. The overarching objective is to practice understanding, articulating, and applying the concepts from an anti-racist lens. Understanding is not the same as agreeing and does not require agreement. For example, before I reject the concept of systemic racism, am I able to clearly and coherently explain it? Before I state that I disagree that all white people are racist, can I explain this idea from an anti-racist framework?

Readers in discussion groups will likely notice that grappling with understanding is much more difficult than opining. That difficulty indicates the direction of our growth. This grappling also calls upon us to practice strategic interventions when we notice discussion group members engaging in rehearsing. Discussants can notice what is happening in their bodies as they struggle against the pull to rehearse or intervene on behalf of others, and practice slowing down, breathing, listening, moving through defensiveness, and breaking with white solidarity. We can also pay attention to the group dynamics and how rehearsing impacts those dynamics. All are rich sources of potential insight on how racism works and opportunities to interrupt whiteness. An overarching question that can be applied to every chapter and used as a prompt when needed is, "Was there anything particularly challenging for you in this chapter?" If so, discuss what and why without discussing whether you agree or disagree.

The questions are written for white people. For racialized readers, the book will hopefully validate your lived experience and offer some helpful insight into the challenges of navigating the "nicer" forms of racism. Readers of color who are interested in discussing the book using these reflection questions can replace "we and us" with "white people" where needed.

For some helpful tips on leading group discussions, see the *White Fragility Reading Group Study Guide*, by Özlem Sensoy and Robin DiAngelo, available at https://www.beacon.org/assets/pdfs/whitefragility readingguide.pdf.

QUESTIONS FOR REFLECTION / DISCUSSION ON CHAPTER 1:
WHAT IS A NICE RACIST?

1. What are some examples of racism at each of the four levels on which racism manifests: institutional, cultural, interpersonal, and personal? What connections can you draw between these levels?
2. How does "white emotionality" structure racial outcomes?
3. The author identifies three patterns that emerge when white people reflect on the question "What are some of the ways in which your race(s) has shaped your life?" Discuss these patterns and what they illustrate about whiteness.

4. What patterns did you notice in your own answers to the reflection questions on page 12–13?

5. The author states that common discussion guidelines don't account for power, assume a universal experience, and function to police racialized people into keeping white people comfortable. Discuss each of these points and provide examples.

6. The author quotes Ibram X. Kendi, who says, "The opposite of 'racist' isn't 'not racist.'" What does Kendi mean by this?

7. How does the author challenge the idea that the presence of niceness indicates the absence of racism?

QUESTIONS FOR REFLECTION / DISCUSSION ON CHAPTER 2: WHY IT'S OK TO GENERALIZE ABOUT WHITE PEOPLE

1. What is the ideology of individualism? Share some examples of this ideology in mainstream culture.

2. What is the ideology of universalism? Share some examples of this ideology in mainstream culture.

3. Summarize the author's argument for why it is important to focus on the collective experience of whiteness in the context of challenging racism.

4. What are some examples of whiteness as a shared experience?

5. The author asks, "How does the insistence that we all be seen as unique individuals—specifically in the context of discussions of racism—*function*? What dynamics might the ideology of individualism protect and obscure?" Using her argument, how would you answer that question?

6. Consider some of the common reasons you have heard a white person give for why they are not racist. Apply the question "How does your race shape how you experienced that exception?" to those examples.

7. What are some of the reasons you have given for why you are not racist (or are less racist than other white people)? Apply the same question to your examples.

QUESTIONS FOR REFLECTION / DISCUSSION ON CHAPTER 3:
THERE IS NO CHOIR

1. What definition of racism is the author using?
2. How is it possible that white people who know and love Black and other racialized people can still enact racism? As you answer that question, consider how you are defining racism.
3. The author provides a list of common patterns of racism in the workplace. How have you seen these patterns?
4. On page 41 there is a list of key skills and perspectives that an aware white person should demonstrate. Discuss what items on the list you feel confident that you demonstrate. What items do you struggle with, and why? How might you address these areas?
5. On page 45 there is a list of examples of implicit racism, the type that progressive white people are more likely to demonstrate. How have you seen some of these examples enacted among white progressives? Which behaviors have you enacted? What would it take for you to change that behavior?
6. Why is white people's sense that they are "in the choir" untrustworthy?
7. Why is it important that we do not consider our anti-racist work finished?

QUESTIONS FOR REFLECTION / DISCUSSION ON CHAPTER 4:
WHAT'S WRONG WITH NICENESS?

1. Give some examples of what is problematic about viewing niceness as the indication that racism is not present.
2. Anika Nailah provides examples of the impact of white progressive niceness on her as a Black woman. Without giving your opinion or commenting on their validity, discuss your understanding of these examples. Where have you seen these expectations play out?
3. Was anyone in the group unable to resist giving their opinion on Anika's examples? e.g., which ones they agreed with and which

ones they did not agree with or felt the need to explain that she was misunderstanding? If so, what patterns of whiteness does that demonstrate?

4. If the answer to question 3 was yes, what happened in the group when you honestly identified that pattern? If the answer to question 3 was yes, but no one admitted to that pattern, how did that impact the group?

5. Discuss Resmaa Menakem's quote from the introduction: "The white body is the supreme standard by which all bodies' humanity shall be measured. If the white body is the standard of humanity, then it stands that the black body is inhuman and the antithesis of humanity. Every hue further away from that standard is deemed less human." What are some examples of the white body as the standard of humanity in your daily life? What are some ways in which that standard shapes white identity?

6. Now consider the above quote in the context of "niceness" as the answer to racism. How does the quote challenge the concept of niceness as an indication that racism is absent?

7. In what ways can niceness actually function to protect and uphold racism?

8. Explore the idea that white supremacy may *also be* what is in our "true hearts."

QUESTIONS FOR REFLECTION / DISCUSSION ON CHAPTER 5:
THE MOVES OF WHITE PROGRESSIVES

1. What is discourse analysis?
2. What are "moves" in the context of racism?
3. Discuss the concept of "credentialing." What examples did you recognize? Which ones have you used yourself? Why is credentialing so often unconvincing to those who understand systemic racism?
4. Which moves were the most challenging for you to read?
5. Which moves have you seen other white people make?

6. Which moves have you made?
7. What does the author mean when she says, "Silence from a position of power is a power move"?
8. Why is the impact of certain personality traits different across race?
9. Using the framework of systemic racism and anti-racist practice, what would you say to someone who asked, "So now I have to watch everything I say and do?"

QUESTIONS FOR REFLECTION / DISCUSSION ON CHAPTER 6: SPIRITUAL, NOT RELIGIOUS

1. What are some of the ways in which whiteness manifests in spiritual communities?
2. The author has said that this chapter will likely be the most controversial for white progressives. Why might that be?
3. Why does the author say that the statement she quotes from a website, "The collective energy generated by this group of the world's leading spiritual teachers, combined with the many hundreds or thousands of attendees, will be unsurpassed and is sure to shift the consciousness of humanity" is an example of white supremacy?
4. Discuss the concept of the "white racial frame." What are some examples in mainstream culture?
5. What does it mean to "essentialize" Black and Indigenous peoples? Provide some examples from film and television.
6. How might we respect and honor Indigenous peoples without also essentializing them?
7. What are some examples of the "Magical Negro" trope in film and television?
8. Discuss the author's statement that white people wanting to transcend the body is ". . . a new-age version of color blindness, wherein one homogeneous group of bodies, primarily living separately from all other types (except when travelling to their communities to collect and study), and at the top of a racist hierarchy, insists that the body doesn't matter." What do you understand her to be saying?

QUESTIONS FOR REFLECTION / DISCUSSION ON CHAPTER 7:
LET'S TALK ABOUT SHAME

1. The author suggests that shame is more comfortable for white progressives to express than guilt. Why might that be?
2. Why is racial shame more commonly expressed by white progressives than racial anger, fear, or resentment?
3. What is meant by the term "social capital"?
4. What are some of the forms of social capital that racial shame grants to white people?
5. The author shares an example of walking down the street to enter Whole Foods and feeling shame. Did you recognize yourself in this example?
6. What is the difference between shame and humility?
7. What are some ways white people can move through shame so that it does not become immobilizing?
8. Why is there so much concern about white people feeling guilty? How does that concern, as well as the guilt itself, function in terms of upholding or challenging racism?

QUESTIONS FOR REFLECTION / DISCUSSION ON CHAPTER 8:
WHAT ABOUT MY TRAUMA?

1. What are some ways in which the ideology of individualism is at play when white people center their own trauma in anti-racist endeavors?
2. How can we affirm the reality of a white person's trauma without centering it or placing it on the same level as racialized trauma?
3. How can white trauma function as a form of "softer" white fragility?
4. Discuss this statement: "White people do not experience direct *racial* trauma, and not continuously at the four levels of HIIP."
5. Discuss how reverting to a discourse of individual experience in anti-racist work can inoculate white people's claims from further challenge or critique.
6. What does it mean to say that "experience becomes depoliticized," or, conversely, that experience is political?

QUESTIONS FOR REFLECTION / DISCUSSION ON CHAPTER 9: WE AREN'T ACTUALLY THAT NICE

1. Discuss examples you have seen (or enacted) of white people quickly moving from being nice across race to not being nice when their expectations are challenged.
2. Go through each of the unwritten "rules" and share examples of where and how you have seen these rules informing a white person's responses.
3. Reflect upon the common claim "I don't have a racist bone in my body." How is racism being defined through this claim? What framework of meaning underlies this claim?
4. What are some examples of culture that relentlessly telegraph white superiority?
5. Work through the email the author shares here and identify the underlying assumptions you notice.
6. The author states that there is sexism in the email she received. Discuss where you see sexism at play.

QUESTIONS FOR REFLECTION / DISCUSSION ON CHAPTER 10: HOW WHITE PEOPLE WHO EXPERIENCE OTHER OPPRESSIONS CAN STILL BE RACIST, OR "BUT I'M A MINORITY MYSELF!"

1. Discuss the concept of intersectionality and practice explaining it in your own words.
2. Consider an aspect of your own identity that is salient for you other than race (e.g., age, ability, gender identity):

   · What patterns do I have as a result of my socialization into this identity?
   · How do these patterns set me up to collude with racism?
   · How can working on racism help to interrupt these patterns?

3. Using an anti-racism framework, how might you respond to a white person who said, "I don't have privilege because I grew up/am poor"?
4. Using an anti-racism framework, how might you respond to a white person who said, "I know what it means to experience racism

because I experience _____ (sexism, heterosexism, anti-Semitism, ableism, etc.)?

5. Using an anti-racism framework, how might you respond to a white person who said, "The real oppression is class"?

6. What are some ways in which white people lose in a society based in systemic racism?

QUESTIONS FOR REFLECTION / DISCUSSION ON CHAPTER 11: HOW DO YOU MAKE A WHITE PROGRESSIVE A BETTER RACIST?

1. Discuss each of the ways the author identifies that can make us more effective at perpetuating racial harm. Share examples of where you have seen these dynamics.

2. What is the distinction the author makes between carefulness and thoughtfulness?

3. What structures of support can you put in place to keep yourself from falling into complacency?

4. Discuss Berrey's finding that diversity is a form of symbolic politics that emerged to reconcile a contradiction: it is undesirable for liberal institutions to be portrayed as "racist," but at the same time institutional elites have no desire to change existing racist power structures. While these programs affirm the importance of diversity, they steadfastly resist meaningful cultural and programmatic change. How do these programs accomplish this? What strategies can help prevent this stasis?

5. What is at risk in BIPOC people giving us honest feedback on our behavior? What are some ways we can demonstrate that we can receive this feedback and change our behavior?

6. Why are white people so often concerned that people of color might be wrong in their assessments of racism? How does this concern function? What guidance on deferring does the author offer?

7. Discuss the example the author gives of an enactment of racism she perpetrated on a group of BIPOC people. What were some of her missteps? What could she have done differently at various points?

8. Was there anything particularly challenging for you in this chapter? If so, discuss what and why without discussing whether you agree or disagree.

QUESTIONS FOR REFLECTION / DISCUSSION ON CHAPTER 12:
NICENESS IS NOT COURAGEOUS: HOW TO ALIGN YOUR PROFESSED VALUES WITH YOUR ACTUAL PRACTICE

1. What are some ways that white people can find answers to the question of what to do about racism?
2. What is problematic about focusing on "helping" racialized people? What are some of the underlying assumptions in this focus?
3. How does the conversation and resultant action change when we shift our focus onto our own complicity?
4. Discuss the suggestions for accountability. Which ones—if any— are you already doing? Which ones seem easy for you, and why? Which are more challenging, and why?
5. How might you build authentic relationships without objectifying or tokenizing racialized people? How can you build these relationships when you don't live or work with racialized people?
6. What kinds of support can you set up to help keep you accountable?

ACKNOWLEDGMENTS

My deepest gratitude to all who have supported, guided, and contributed to this work: Anika Nailah, Aisha Hauser, Erin Trent Johnson, Shakti Butler, Heather McGhee, Edwin Cleophas, Resmaa Menakem, Dr. Eddie Moore, Stan Henkeman, Darlene Flynn, Deborah Terry, Victoria Santos, Angela Park, Michael Eric Dyson, Shelly Tochluk, Christine Saxman, Jenna Chandler Ward, Elizabeth Denevi, Dr. Kathy Obear, Jacqueline Battalora, Debby Irving, Carlin Quinn, Amy Burtaine, Colin Beavan, and Jason Toews.

Thank you, Simone, for the hours you spend and emotional labor you give securing the perimeter. I feel your hands bracing my back. Thank you to Edwin Cleophas for his racial justice work in the South African context and his gracious hosting of my visit there.

A very special thank-you to my editor at Beacon Press, Rachael Marks. It is a gift to work with someone I both trust and adore.

And to my publicist at Beacon, Caitlin Meyer. You are always there for me the moment I need you, with wisdom and encouragement. Thank you.

To my exceptionally competent and patient agent, Lauren E. Abramo at Dystel, Goderich & Bourret (thank you, Ijeoma, for the referral).

NOTES

INTRODUCTION

1. Sherene Razack, *Looking White People in the Eye: Gender, Race, and Culture in Courtrooms and Classrooms* (UK: University of Toronto Press, 1998).
2. Audre Lorde, "The Master's Tools Will Never Dismantle the Master's House" (1984), in *Sister Outsider: Essays and Speeches* (Berkeley, CA: Crossing Press, 2007), 110–14.
3. Sandra E. Garcia, "BIPOC: What Does It Mean?," *New York Times*, June 17, 2020, https://www.nytimes.com/article/what-is-bipoc.html.
4. David Bauder, "AP Says It Will Capitalize Black but Not White," AP News, July 20, 2020, https://apnews.com/article/7e36c00c5af0436abc 09e051261fff1f.
5. Nancy Coleman, "Why We're Capitalizing Black," *New York Times*, July 5, 2020, https://www.nytimes.com/2020/07/05/insider/capitalized-black .html.
6. Michel Foucault, *Power/Knowledge: Selected Interviews and Other Writings, 1972–1977*, ed. Colin Gordon (New York: Pantheon, 1980).
7. Resmaa Menakem, *My Grandmother's Hands: Racialized Trauma and the Pathway to Mending Our Hearts and Bodies* (Las Vegas: Central Recovery Press, 2017).

CHAPTER 1: WHAT IS A NICE RACIST?

1. Wendell Berry, *The Hidden Wound* (Boston: Houghton Mifflin, 1970), 7.
2. Martin Luther King Jr., *Letter from the Birmingham Jail* (1963) (San Francisco: Harper San Francisco, 1994).
3. Thaoai Lu, "Michelle Alexander: More Black Men in Prison Than Were Enslaved in 1850," *Colorlines*, March 30, 2011, https://www.colorlines .com/articles/michelle-alexander-more-black-men-prison-were-enslaved -1850.
4. James Baldwin, response to Paul Weiss, *The Dick Cavett Show*, 1965, video available at https://www.youtube.com/watch?v=a6WlM1dca18 &fbclid=IwAR2C04uF76bHk2P49rOxFqWTNZ_BT-PAZeXbVA6vl5Tdu _-D9_lp7mxRxZI.

5. Jay Smooth, "How I Learned to Stop Worrying and Love Discussing Race," TEDxHampshireCollege, 2014, video available at https://www.youtube.com/watch?v=MbdxeFcQtaU&feature=emb_title.

6. Southern Poverty Law Center, "The Year in Hate 2019: White Nationalist Groups Rise for a Second Year in a Row—Up 55% Since 2017," press release, March 18, 2020, https://www.splcenter.org/presscenter/year-hate-2019-white-nationalist-groups-rise-second-year-row-55-2017.

7. Anti-Defamation League, "ADL H.E.A.T. Map," https://www.adl.org/education-and-resources/resource-knowledge-base/adl-heat-map.

8. Anti-Defamation League, *New Hate and Old: The Changing Face of American White Supremacy: A Report from the Center on Extremism*, https://www.adl.org/new-hate-and-old.

9. Michael Edison Hayden, "Neo-Nazi Website Daily Stormer Is 'Designed to Target Children' as Young as 11 for Radicalization, Editor Claims," *Newsweek*, January 16, 2018, https://www.newsweek.com/website-daily-stormer-designed-target-children-editor-claims-782401.

10. Tess Martin, "So You've Been Called Out: A White Person's Guide to Doing Better," *Medium*, March 22, 2020, https://tessmartin.medium.com/so-youve-been-called-out-a-white-person-s-guide-to-doing-better-918493706c49.

11. James Baldwin, *The Fire Next Time* (1963) (New York: Vintage, 1992).

12. KIRO 7 News Staff, "Issaquah School District, Teen in Picture Respond to Racist Photo," KIRO 7 News, updated April 3, 2019, https://www.kiro7.com/news/local/issaquah-school-district-responds-to-racially-insensitive-photo/936127384.

13. Derald Wing Sue, *Microaggressions in Everyday Life: Race, Gender, and Sexual Orientation* (Hoboken, NJ: John Wiley & Sons, 2010); Camille Lloyd, "Black Adults Disproportionately Experience Microaggressions," Gallup, July 15, 2020, https://news.gallup.com/poll/315695/black-adults-disproportionately-experience-microaggressions.aspx.

14. Carol Anderson, *White Rage: The Unspoken Truth of Our Racial Divide* (New York: Bloomsbury, 2016).

15. Melissa Phruksachart, "The Literature of White Liberalism," *Boston Review*, August 21, 2020, http://bostonreview.net/race/melissa-phruksachart-literature-white-liberalism.

16. Heather McGhee, *The Sum of Us: What Racism Costs Everyone and How We Can Prosper Together* (New York: Penguin Random House, 2021).

17. Cited in "Term Limits," BoardSource, https://boardsource.org/resources/term-limits, last updated August 16, 2019.

18. McGhee, *The Sum of Us*.

19. Ibram X. Kendi, *How to Be an Antiracist* (New York: One World, 2019).

CHAPTER 2: WHY IT'S OK TO GENERALIZE ABOUT WHITE PEOPLE

1. Wendy Hollway, "Gender Differences and the Production of Subjectivity," in *Changing the Subject: Psychology, Social Regulation, and Subjectivity*,

ed. J. Henriques, W. Hollway, C. Urwin, C. Venn, and V. Walkerdine (London: Methuen, 1984), 227–63.

2. Jane Flax, *The American Dream in Black and White: The Clarence Thomas Hearings* (Ithaca, NY: Cornell University Press, 1998).

3. This example based in part on Robin J. DiAngelo, "Why Can't We All Just Be Individuals? Countering the Discourse of Individualism in Anti-Racist Education," *InterActions: UCLA Journal of Education and Information Studies* 6, no. 1 (January 2010), retrieved from http://escholarship.org/uc/item/5fm4h8wm.

4. Jennifer Eberhardt, *Biased: Uncovering the Hidden Prejudice That Shapes What We See, Think, and Do* (New York: Viking, 2019).

5. Quoted in Bessel van der Kolk, MD, *The Body Keeps the Score: Brain, Mind, and Body in the Healing of Trauma* (New York: Penguin, 2015).

6. Pablo Mitnik and David Grusky, *Economic Mobility in the United States* (Pew Charitable Trusts/Russell Sage Foundation, July 2015), https://web.stanford.edu/~pmitnik/EconomicMobilityintheUnitedStates.pdf.

7. Nikole Hannah-Jones, "We Are Owed," *New York Times Magazine*, June 30, 2020, https://www.nytimes.com/interactive/2020/06/24/magazine/reparations-slavery.html.

8. Jacqueline Battalora, *Birth of a White Nation: The Invention of White People and Its Relevance Today* (Houston: Strategic Book Publishing and Rights, 2013).

9. Keeanga-Yamahtta Taylor, *Race for Profit: How Banks and the Real Estate Industry Undermined Black Homeownership* (Chapel Hill: University of North Carolina Press, 2019).

10. Taylor, *Race for Profit*.

11. Nikole Hannah-Jones, "How The Systemic Segregation of Schools Is Maintained by 'Individual Choices,'" *Fresh Air*, NPR, January 16, 2017, https://www.npr.org/sections/ed/2017/01/16/509325266/how-the-systemic-segregation-of-schools-is-maintained-by-individual-choices.

12. Neil deGrasse Tyson, Twitter, May 15, 2018, https://twitter.com/neiltyson/status/996488935369916416.

13. Kendi, *How to Be an Antiracist*.

CHAPTER 3: THERE IS NO CHOIR

1. "Ian Haney López and Alicia Garza: How The Left Can Win Again," Commonwealth Club of California, November 14, 2019, YouTube, https://www.youtube.com/watch?v=daHZbDbT12w.

2. Michael W. Kraus, Ivuoma N. Onyeador, Natalie M. Daumeyer, Julian M. Rucker, and Jennifer A. Richeson, "The Misperception of Racial Economic Inequality," *Perspectives on Psychological Science* 14, no. 6 (2019): 899–921, https://journals.sagepub.com/doi/full/10.1177/1745691619863049.

3. John Raible, 1994, http://web.cortland.edu/russellk/courses/hdouts/raible.htm.

4. Kendi, *How to Be an Antiracist.*
5. Beverly Daniel Tatum, *Why Are All the Black Kids Sitting Together? And Other Conversations About Race* (1997) (New York: Basic Books, 2017).
6. Kendi, *How to Be an Antiracist.*
7. "The History and Dictionary Meaning of Racism," Merriam-Webster, https://www.merriam-webster.com/dictionary/racism, accessed January 6, 2021.
8. Annie Reneau, "Using the 'Dictionary Definition of Racism' Defense Is a Sure Sign You Don't Understand Racism," *Upworthy*, July 17, 2019, https://www.upworthy.com/pulling-out-the-dictionary-definition-of -racism-is-a-surefire-sign-that-you-dont-understand-racism.
9. Faima Bakar, "The Way You Define Racism May Stop You from Seeing It—So What Definition Do You Hold?," *Metro UK*, February 28, 2020, https://metro.co.uk/2020/02/28/way-define-racism-may-stop-seeing -definition-hold-12287889/?ito=cbshare?ito=cbshare.
10. Paul Gorski and Noura Erakat, "Racism, Whiteness, and Burnout in Antiracism Movements: How White Racial Justice Activists Elevate Burnout in Racial Justice Activists of Color in the United States," *Ethnicities* 19 (2019): 784–808, https://doi.org/10.1177/1468796819833871.

CHAPTER 4: WHAT'S WRONG WITH NICENESS?

1. Alix E. Harrow, *The Ten Thousand Doors of January* (New York: Redhook, 2019).
2. Janelle Griffith, "Outrage After Idaho Elementary School Staff Dress as Border Wall and 'Mexicans' for Halloween," NBC News, November 2, 2018, https://www.nbcnews.com/news/us-news/outrage-after-idaho -elementary-school-staff-dress-border-wall-mexicans-n930671.
3. Kaitlyn Greenidge, Twitter, November 2, 2018, https://twitter.com/surly bassey/status/1058418530021003264.
4. Debby Irving, *Waking Up White: And Finding Myself in the Story of Race* (Cambridge, MA: Elephant Room Press, 2014).
5. Irving, *Waking Up White.*
6. Angelina E. Castagno, *The Price of Nice: How Good Intentions Maintain Educational Inequity* (Minneapolis: University of Minnesota Press, 2019).
7. Anika Nailah, interview with author via Zoom, October 5, 2020.

CHAPTER 5: THE MOVES OF WHITE PROGRESSIVES

1. "Ian Haney López and Alicia Garza: How The Left Can Win Again," Commonwealth Club of California, November 14, 2019, YouTube, https://www.youtube.com/watch?v=daHZbDbT12w.
2. James Paul Gee, *An Introduction to Discourse Analysis: Theory & Method* (New York: Routledge, 1999), 63.
3. Signithia Fordham and John Ogbu, "Black Students' School Success: Coping with the Burden of 'Acting White,'" *Urban Review* 18 (1986), https:// doi.org/10.1007/BF01112192.

4. Akilah Johnson, Todd Wallack, Nicole Dungca, Liz Kowalczyk, Andrew Ryan, Adrian Walker, and editor Patricia Wen, "Boston. Racism. Image. Reality," *Boston Globe*, December 10, 2017, https://apps.bostonglobe.com /spotlight/boston-racism-image-reality/series/image.

5. Nik DeCosta-Klipa, "SNL Weekend Update Host Says He Loves 'Racist' Boston Like He Loves His Racist Grandma," Boston.com, March 26, 2017, https://www.boston.com/news/tv/2017/03/26/snl-weekend-update -host-says-he-loves-racist-boston-like-he-loves-his-racist-grandma.

6. Johnson et al., "Boston. Racism. Image. Reality."

7. For more information, see Eberhardt, *Biased*.

8. Matthew Choi, "Rashida Tlaib Berates Mark Meadows for Using Black Woman as 'a Prop' at Hearing," Politico.com, February 27, 2019, https:// www.politico.com/story/2019/02/27/rashida-talib-mark-meadows -1193943.

9. Katie Glueck, "Biden, Recalling 'Civility' in Senate, Invokes Two Segrega- tionist Senators," *New York Times*, June 19, 2019, https://www.nytimes .com/2019/06/19/us/politics/biden-segregationists.html.

10. Beverly Daniel Tatum, *Can We Talk About Race? And Other Conversa- tions in an Era of School Resegregation* (Boston: Beacon Press, 2007).

11. Christine Saxman, meeting with author, Kansas City, Kansas, April 10, 2018.

12. Kad Smith, "Race Caucusing in an Organizational Context: A POC's Ex- perience," *Compass Point* (blog), https://www.compasspoint.org/blog /race-caucusing-organizational-context-poc%E2%80%99s-experience, accessed December 16, 2020.

13. Rev. angel Kyodo williams, "Why Your Liberation Is Bound Up With Mine," Podcast 194, Meditation in the City, May 20, 2018, https:// ny.shambhala.org/2018/05/20/rev-angel-kyodo-williams-why-your -liberation-is-bound-up-with-mine-podcast-194.

14. H. B. Johnson and T. M. Shapiro, "Good Neighborhoods, Good Schools: Race and the Good Choices of White Families," in *White Out: The Con- tinued Significance of Racism*, ed. E. Bonilla-Silva and A. W. Doane (New York: Routledge, 2003), 182–83.

15. S. Matlock and R. DiAngelo, "We Put It In Terms of 'Not-Nice': White Anti- Racist Parenting," *Journal of Progressive Human Services* 26, no. 2 (2015).

16. J. Oakes, "Keeping Track: Structuring Equality and Inequality in an Era of Accountability," *Teachers College Record* 110, no. 3 (2008): 700–12.

17. Sarah Amanda Matlock, "White Anti-Racism in the Context of Parent- ing," master's thesis, Smith College, 2011, https://scholarworks.smith.edu /cgi/viewcontent.cgi?article=1635&context=theses.

18. Hannah-Jones, "How the Systemic Segregation of Schools Is Maintained by 'Individual Choices.'"

19. Christopher Ingraham, "Three Quarters of Whites Don't Have Non-White Friends," *Washington Post*, August 24, 2014, https://www.washington post.com/news/wonk/wp/2014/08/25/three-quarters-of-whites-dont-have -any-non-white-friends.

20. Robin DiAngelo and Darlene Flynn, "Showing What We Tell: Facilitating Antiracist Education in Cross-Racial Teams," *Understanding & Dismantling Privilege* 1, no. 1 (2010): 2.

21. Reni Eddo-Lodge, *Why I'm No Longer Talking to White People About Race* (London: Bloomsbury Circus, 2017).

22. Kelsey Blackwell, "Why People of Color Need Spaces Without White People," *The Arrow*, August 9, 2018, https://arrow-journal.org/why -people-of-color-need-spaces-without-white-people.

23. "History of Lynchings," NAACP, https://www.naacp.org/history-of -lynchings.

24. Courttia Newland, "I Had to Submit to Being Exoticised by White Women. If I Didn't, I Was Punished," *Guardian*, February 27, 2019, https://www.theguardian.com/world/2019/feb/27/white-privilege-is -used-by-women-against-black-men-as-a-tool-of-oppression.

25. Newland, "I Had to Submit to Being Exoticised by White Women. If I Didn't, I Was Punished."

26. Kenneth B. Clark and Mamie P. Clark, "The Development of Consciousness of Self and the Emergence of Racial Identification in Negro Preschool Children," *Journal of Social Psychology* 10 (1939).

27. Chief Justice Earl Warren, "Order of Argument in the Case, Brown v. Board of Education," School Segregation Cases—Order of Argument Record Group 267: Records of the Supreme Court, National Archives, https://www.archives.gov/education/lessons/brown-case-order#documents.

28. Kiri Davis, *A Girl Like Me*, Reel Works Teen Filmmaking (USA) (DVD), 7 minutes, June 1, 2005.

29. White settler colonialism is a specific type of colonization that seeks to replace an Indigenous population with white "settlers" through a process of domination and genocide and to enforce a culture of white supremacy.

30. Tess Martin, "Racism 101: Tone Policing," January 12, 2018, https:// tessmartin.medium.com/racism-101-tone-policing-92481c044b6a.

31. Ijeoma Oluo, "White People Will Always Let You Down," Medium, June 12, 2017, https://medium.com/the-establishment/white-people-will-always -let-you-down-c6fb3c03ddb7.

32. Tatum, *Can We Talk About Race?*

33. Robin DiAngelo, "Nothing to Add: The Role of White Silence in Cross-Racial Dialogues," *Understanding & Dismantling Privilege* 2, no. 1 (2012).

34. Angela Park, interview with author via Zoom, November 24, 2020.

CHAPTER 6: SPIRITUAL, NOT RELIGIOUS

1. Joe Feagin, *The White Racial Frame: Centuries of Racial Framing and Counter-Framing* (New York: Routledge, 2009).

2. Amanda Lucia, *White Utopias: The Religious Exoticism of Transformational Festivals* (Oakland: University of California Press, 2020).

3. Jillian Kubala, "What Is Ayahuasca: Experience, Benefits, and Side Effects," Healthline, June 26, 2019, https://www.healthline.com/nutrition /ayahuasca#what-it-is.

4. "Basic Statistics," Talk Poverty, https://talkpoverty.org/basics/, accessed January 25, 2021.

5. Center for Public Integrity, *Murdered and Missing Native American Women Challenge Police and Courts*, August 27, 2018, updated October 29, 2018, https://publicintegrity.org/politics/murdered-and-missing-native-american-women-challenge-police-and-courts.

6. Henry Barnes, "Spike Lee Tipped to Direct Oldboy Remake," *Guardian*, July 6, 2011, https://www.theguardian.com/film/2011/jul/06/spike-lee-oldboy-remake.

7. "Realization Process," Center of the Soul—Soul Work in New Jersey, https://www.journey2cots.com/realization-process, accessed January 25, 2021.

8. "Realization Process," https://realizationprocess.org, accessed January 25, 2021.

9. Cartoon by Bruce Eric Kaplan, *New Yorker*, November 25, 2002.

CHAPTER 7: LET'S TALK ABOUT SHAME

1. Michelle Fine, "Witnessing Whiteness," in *Off White: Readings on Race, Power, and Society*, ed. Michelle Fine, Lois Weis, Linda Powell Pruitt, and April Burns (New York: Routledge, 1997), 57.

2. Joseph Burgo, "The Difference Between Guilt and Shame," *Psychology Today*, May 30, 2013, https://www.psychologytoday.com/us/blog/shame/201305/the-difference-between-guilt-and-shame.

3. bell hooks, *Talking Back: Thinking Feminist, Thinking Black* (Toronto: Between the Lines, 1989); Lorde, *Sister Outsider*.

4. Sara Ahmed, "Declarations of Whiteness: The Non-Performativity of Anti-Racism," *Borderlands* 3, no. 2 (2004).

5. Tatum, *Why Are All the Black Kids Sitting Together in the Cafeteria?*

6. Jay Smooth, "How I Learned to Stop Worrying and Love Discussing Race," TEDxHampshireCollege, 2014, video available at https://www.youtube.com/watch?v=MbdxeFcQtaU&feature=emb_title.

7. Audre Lorde, "The Uses of Anger: Women Responding to Racism," 1981, keynote presentation, National Women's Studies Association Conference, Storrs, CT; available at https://www.blackpast.org/african-american-history/speeches-african-american-history/1981-audre-lorde-uses-anger-women-responding-racism.

8. "Debating 'White Fragility' in America," MSNBC, July 22, 2020, https://www.msn.com/en-us/news/politics/debating-white-fragility-in-america/vi-BB173Don.

9. John McWhorter, "The Dehumanizing Condescension of *White Fragility*," *Atlantic*, July 15, 2020, https://www.theatlantic.com/ideas/archive/2020/07/dehumanizing-condescension-white-fragility/614146.

10. Kenan Malik, "'White Privilege' Is a Distraction, Leaving Racism and Power Untouched," *Guardian*, June 14, 2020, https://www.theguardian.com/commentisfree/2020/jun/14/white-privilege-is-a-lazy-distraction-leaving-racism-and-power-untouched.

11. "Ian Haney López and Alicia Garza: How The Left Can Win Again."

CHAPTER 8: WHAT ABOUT MY TRAUMA?

1. "Honouring the Truth, Reconciling for the Future: Summary of the Final Report of the Truth and Reconciliation Commission of Canada," National Centre for Truth and Reconciliation, Truth and Reconciliation Commission of Canada, May 31, 2015. Archived from the original (PDF) on July 6, 2016.
2. Resmaa Menakem, interview with author via Zoom, October 21, 2020.
3. Menakem, *My Grandmother's Hands*.
4. *Department of Defense Board on Diversity and Inclusion Report: Recommendations to Improve Racial and Ethnic Diversity and Inclusion in the U.S. Military* (2020), https://media.defense.gov/2020/Dec/18/2002554852/-1/-1/0/DOD-DIVERSITY-AND-INCLUSION-FINAL-BOARD-REPORT.PDF.
5. Menakem, interview with author.

CHAPTER 9: WE AREN'T ACTUALLY THAT NICE

1. Robin DiAngelo, interview with Scott Simon, "How White Politicians Can Talk About Race," NPR, June 22, 2019, https://www.npr.org/2019/06/22/735005851/how-white-politicians-can-talk-about-race.
2. DiAngelo, interview with Scott Simon.
3. Rebecca Solnit, "Men Explain Things to Me," *Guernica*, August 12, 2012, https://www.guernicamag.com/rebecca-solnit-men-explain-things-to-me.

CHAPTER 10: HOW WHITE PEOPLE WHO EXPERIENCE OTHER OPPRESSIONS CAN STILL BE RACIST, OR "BUT I'M A MINORITY MYSELF!"

1. In Lorde, *Sister Outsider*.
2. "Trends in Party Affiliation Among Demographic Groups," in *Wide Gender Gap, Growing Educational Divide in Voters' Party Identification* (Washington, DC: Pew Research Center, March 20, 2018), https://www.pewresearch.org/politics/2018/03/20/1-trends-in-party-affiliation-among-demographic-groups.
3. Erin Trent Johnson to author.
4. Kimberlé Crenshaw, "Demarginalizing the Intersection of Race and Sex: A Black Feminist Critique of Antidiscrimination Doctrine, Feminist Theory and Antiracist Politics," *University of Chicago Legal Forum* 1989, no. 1, article 8 (1989): 139–67.
5. *The Combahee River Collective Statement*, 1977, Women's and Gender Studies Web Archive, Library of Congress, https://www.loc.gov/item/lcwaN0028151.
6. Katherine Schaeffer, "6 Facts About Economic Inequality in the U.S.," FactTank, Pew Research Center, February 7, 2020, https://www.pewresearch.org/fact-tank/2020/02/07/6-facts-about-economic-inequality-in-the-u-s.
7. Jack Kelly, "Billionaires Are Getting Richer During the COVID-19 Pandemic While Most Americans Suffer," *Forbes*, April 23, 2020, https://

www.forbes.com/sites/jackkelly/2020/04/27/billionaires-are-getting-richer
-during-the-covid-19-pandemic-while-most-americans-suffer.

8. Kelly, "Billionaires Are Getting Richer During the COVID-19 Pandemic
While Most Americans Suffer."

9. Kimberlé Crenshaw, "Under The Black Light: The Intersectional Failures
That Covid Lays Bare," African American Policy Forum, March 25,
2020, available at https://www.youtube.com/watch?v=OsBstnmBTaI.

10. Jonathan Metzl, *Dying of Whiteness: How the Politics of Racial Resentment Is Killing America's Heartland* (New York: Basic Books, 2019).

11. Ian Haney López, *Dog Whistle Politics: How Coded Racial Appeals Have
Reinvented Racism and Wrecked the Middle Class* (New York: Oxford
University Press, 2015).

12. john a. powell, Stephen Menendian, and Wendy Ake, *Targeted Universalism: Policy & Practice* (Berkeley, CA: Haas Institute, May 2019), https://
escholarship.org/uc/item/9sm8b0q8.

CHAPTER 11: HOW DO YOU MAKE A WHITE PROGRESSIVE A BETTER RACIST?

1. James Baldwin, "The Creative Process," 1962, in *The Price of the Ticket:
Collected Nonfiction, 1948–1985* (New York: St. Martin's, 1985).

2. Ellen Berrey, *The Enigma of Diversity: The Language of Race and the
Limits of Racial Justice* (Chicago: University of Chicago Press, 2015).

3. Liz Posner, "Why Mandatory Drug Tests at Work Are Fundamentally
Racist," *Salon,* March 27, 2018, https://www.salon.com/2018/03/27
/why-mandatory-drug-tests-at-work-are-fundamentally-racist_partner.

4. Erin Aubry Kaplan, "Everyone's an Antiracist. Now What?," *New York
Times,* July 6, 2020, https://www.nytimes.com/2020/07/06/opinion
/antiracism-what-comes-next.html.

5. Rashida Campbell-Allen, "Dear White People: Antiracism Is Not a
Trend," *PGR Sociology @ Newcastle University*, June 22, 2020, https://
blogs.ncl.ac.uk/pgrsociology/2020/06/22/dear-white-people-anti-racism
-is-not-a-trend.

CHAPTER 12: NICENESS IS NOT COURAGEOUS

1. Anika Nailah, interview with author via Zoom, December 22, 2020.

2. Saxman, meeting with author.

3. Kendi, *How to Be an Antiracist.*

4. Ijeoma Oluo, Twitter, July 14, 2019, https://twitter.com/IjeomaOluo
/status/1150565193832943617.